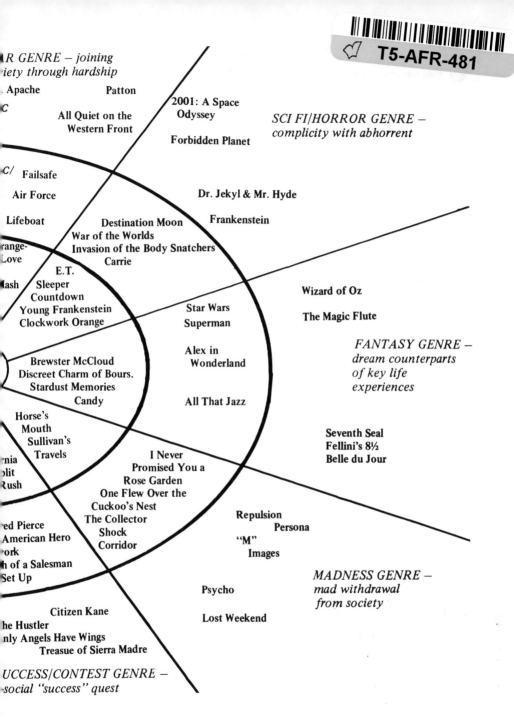

ramatic; comic/ironic), with exemplary films. Acclaimed films often lie near margins e themes. Minor genres (e.g. musical. epic) may be charted as narrow rings about the ques. Note upper curve holds social sublimation genres (e.g., western) and lower curve sy and performance (show business). Last, the chart is not pieshaped but a torus or ones.

AMERICAN SKEPTIC

pierian press 1982

AMERICAN SKEPTIC:
Robert Altman's Genre-Commentary Films

by Norman Kagan

ISBN 0-87650-144-7
LC 82-61033

The Pierian Press
P.O. Box 1808
Ann Arbor, MI 48106

to the memory of
Janis Ann Siegel,
forever in my heart,
and to her parents,
Mike and Bertha

Contents

Illustrations

Foreword

The Man With No Genre

Norman Kagan's study of Robert Altman's films is crucial for understanding not only Altman as *auteur*, but how genres work and what they are. It's equally relevant therefore to a full understanding of the Hollywood system, and to whatever that reveals (and conceals) about America's popular thinking.

"Popular thought" — there's an almost virgin continent of social history. Here high culture disqualifies itself, almost by definition; here the mass media meet (and yet don't meet) oral culture; here the key tests are people's conversations, which vanish as swiftly as ripples in the river of time; and they, too, leave much unspoken, often the most powerful attitudes, lest they provoke shame, disapproval or uneasiness. Often, to see them more clearly, we must turn to the mass media; although they — and so it goes.

What goes on in these silences, those spaces? As that English proverb has it: "A nod is as good as a wink to a blind horse." Often our speech has a forked tongue and a heart of darkness. "Silence," said La Rochefoucauld, "is the tribute which vice pays to virtue." But not only vice. There are also tendernesses and pangs of conscience which we do not speak, subtleties for which we lack the verbal skills, or the time, or the place. Various and devious, they may exert very heavy pressures on our actions, and therefore on the world.

Thus the Great Unspoken is never as impotent, never as marginal, never as unconscious as some theorists of signs suppose. Even Freudians incline to underestimate the vastness of the preconscious (and Altman is very much an explorer of the preconscious, of everything in it which is unknown and strewn with ambushes). Somehow his films upfront the mental reservations, the hypocrisies, the choices and the freedoms which his characters never knew they had, which his films never knew they had, which we never knew we had. His shifting mise-en-scene suggests the stirring and shifting of inchoate freedoms. Each tacit refusal of a genre's gambits is a game played against them by a surly sense of truth. And yet with them.

The "classical" Hollywood genres pertain to a market system which worked to America's vaguest common denominators, and so tended to flatten out local specifics and subcultures into a kind of aggregate. Hollywood itself is one such subculture. No doubt it's a paradoxical one, for, on top of the fact that every subculture is a mosaic of subsubcultures (by sex, by age, by family networking, by everything which sociologists call microsociology), the business of the subculture called Hollywood is to understand that aggregate, and one or two things about each kind of audience. And yet its very professional deformities conspire to keep it aloof from them. Showbiz, like every operating system, has its assumptions, its lazy habits, its fail-safe self-censorship, its rules of thumb, and its theories of what the public wants.

Which often means what the aggregate market "wants." Moreover, the market is defined by the system, as well as vice versa, and the market economy is just as complicated as sociology. For all these cultural matters, the best external paradigm is ecology. The market too has cross-cultural cultures, interface-cultures . . . .

As the ecology of audio-visual culture becomes more complex, with Hollywood's old hegemony undermined by the underground, direct-cinema, TV, videos, and whatever, so the market becomes freer and more confusing, less interested in gross formulae and more alert to fine-tuned detail. Altman's *oeuvre* isn't only a fascinating frieze of diverse lifestyles, some mythical, some real. It's also a fasciating prism for Hollywood's history, as it improvises changing responses to this changing situation.

Changes rarely come singly, and all this coincides with the greening of America, with a new unsureness and curiosity about established categories and assumptions, to which the old genres were geared. One thinks, for example, of the frontier thesis, with its corollary that the closing of the wild frontier would lead to a grey flannel order and the disappearance of violence. Or of a kind of Middle West assumption, that Country-and-Western music echoed a downhome simplicity compared with which Manhattan complexity and California laxity were positively European.

Altman, like Orson Welles, whom he somehow evokes (with his virtuosity, his low budgets, his multi-media skills, his highly controlled casualness, his dialogue overlaps, and his "deep" mise-en-scene), has a more complicated mind. **Citizen Kane** has a "cubist" multiplicity of perspective, through its narrative-line; Altman's movies have a multiplicity of perspective, through their follow-zoom style. (Maybe Welles's tight compositions are claustrophobic whereas Altman's roaming is agorophobic; but that's another book . . . .) And if America is really about moral simplicity, then Altman, like Welles, is vaguely un-American and obstinately ultra-American; as nimble as a gadfly and as conservative as a grizzly bear; as wicked as Robert Aldrich and as puritanical as Joe Losey.

Welles, to be sure, started at the top and worked his way to the bottom. At the time of writing, Altman's Hollywood career has another shape: it's a classical arch, a perfect rise and fall. But just as the "well-constructed" story has gone the way of the classical genres, so the rules of the new games privilege surprises, and tag endings which swell into new Acts, so The Robert Altman Story has a good few reels to run.

Kagan's masterly work concentrates on Act Two, the studio productions with which Altman achieved his spiritual independence, and through which he systematically reopened the questions and the offkey possibilities which genres may tend to close. For let's face it: genres, much as we may love them, are constantly, and by their very nature, ravaged by cliches, formulae, and stereotypes; they risk ruling out of order every basic question, or obstinate contradiction, or intermediate formulation. They're rarely mythlike and usually closer to routine than to ritual. This isn't to dismiss or disqualify them, but simply to defetishise them. Kagan is well equipped to do so, for he knows their subtleties and their virtues very well — as evidenced by his earlier survey of The War Film, and by the work within his chapters here.

As Kagan and John Belton point out, the films of Altman's fuller independence, at Lion's Gate, tend to be one notch remoter from genres and their content. Rather, they split focus with another level, a new awareness of life as performance, or at least appearance, which misleads the performers. The style becomes more philosophical: Pirandello meets cinema-verite. Yet the mask-games which come to loom so large share a living substance with the more intimate subversions of Act II. For what Altman turns "against" the genres isn't some mechanical system of surprises, some systemic exploitation of his (exceptionally astute) sense of how sensitively audiences can spot the possibilities of subtle details (so long as they're interested in them). It's one thing to start from the formula and devise a sequence of twists-on-the-twists. It's quite another thing to achieve such a sequence because one has started from somewhere else. Altman's work is rooted in an appeal to real life, to off-screen life, to how it's always messy, always wrong, other *other*, always faintly ridiculous even when it ends happily (for a little while).

The way **M.A.S.H.** turns war movies downside up and outside in for 100 percent eventual recycling into something which might not even be a genre at all depends on the audience's delight in recognising the mass of frictions and factions, snafus and sidewindings, that almost everything is, when you see it from close to and in the round together. (And don't Altman's very set-ups have that strange combination of up-close and ring-dance, with the hierarchic order of old deep-focus yanked into a mosaic of saccades?) I've seen a London moviehouse audience ripple with excitement from the very first shots of **M.A.S.H.**, as they catch war's weird mixture of the shifting and the relentless, the vivid and the opaque, the atrocious and the irrelevant.

Altman doesn't just *subvert* the genres. It's as true to say that he *fulfills* them. Even when he undermines the very idea of a genre, that too is a fulfillment of the thoughts which genres exist, not just to fixate, but to further. For genres, too, point beyond themselves.

There's a shrewd theory that Hollywood artists make their best films before they're too free from its formulae and constraints, and that European-type art freedom insidiously uproots them. They lose the feedback from what they fight against, and substitute simpler and more earnest states of mind. It's tempting to apply that theory even when the directors, like Altman and Woody Allen, become Europeans at home. But the theory's temptation is to privilege genres and formulae over direct observation, over working from life. Probably it would make good sense to treat **Three Women** as an essay in an Antonionian genre (the study of sensibility with ellipsis of plot); and surely Altman, in preparing it, bore arthouse/middle class markets somewhere in the back of his mind. But it has an American kind of mental space, whereas the characters in **Zabriskie Point** can hardly be said to think at all. Altman declares that the root idea came to him in a dream, and insofar as dreams resemble free associations, they disrespect genres. Similarly, for Altman, the genre is more scaffolding than carapace, more starting-point than game-plan, more set-of-references than obsessions.

It's tempting, too, to attribute the relative unpopularity of Altman's "abstract" period to its distance from familiar genre-content. But I suspect that it comes also from a different kind of distance, an abstraction of familiar involvements. There's some hard-to-analyse conjunction of (a) Altman's delight in subtly revelatory detail, (b) his arthouse material, and (c) his reaching a kind of philosophical altitude, where the air is rarefied, where familiarity is flattened out. Maybe that's a genre too, and Bergman's **Persona** and Tarkovski's **Stalker** belong to it.

At any rate, one might see in Altman, not a dialectic, but a kind of triadic action, between (1) genristics, (2) his style as his mind's-eye-view and (3) the world out there. (Naturally, if we look at the reverse of the tapestry, which is what theory exists to do, we find that all these threads connect, so that these three "levels" are really one. And they are; we have to separate them out before we can talk about a relationship. Ah, the pitfalls of language!) Even here we've been schematic. For example, I suspect that audience expectations are nimbler and freer than the features that link a genre's workaday routines with its apotheosis-by-transcendence; and that's why genres crossbreed so swiftly that we may need a critic like Kagan to point out to us that a film belongs to a genre, or to several genres at once and therefore none. Altman's commentaries on genres are always critical, and the criticism is based on a kind of realism (not on another genre), on the gritty observation with which he loads the gaps and fissures in the formulae. Keats advised Shelley to load every rift with ore. Altman packs every crevice with sweating sticks of dynamite, and the block of ideas floats slowly down to earth, in little particles now freed to recombine or not. This metaphor has a major disadvantage. It shortchanges Altman's gentleness, his careful patience, his respect for the hopes and virtues that get trapped by illusions, or overwhelm them, and enable human life to mean something or other, though who knows what.

Buffalo Bill and the Indians advises against printing the legend. After all, John Ford debunked a legend that hardly any cinema spectator believes in anyway (it's always the other person who believes the Wild West myth). But, and this is much more serious, to dismiss a legend is not to tell the truth. It's the truth that sets you free, where mere scepticism leaves you bewildered and paralytic. It's an extremely effective form of mystification, and mere debunking, like mere deconstruction, leads nowhere else but limbo. **Sitting Bull's History Lesson** (the other half of Altman's title) is as painful as books like *Bury My Heart at Wounded Knee*. There's something so acrid and sidelong about it that it's even more painful than **Soldier Blue**. It's Altman's most depressing movie until **Quintet** (which gets into Tarkovski country just as Woody Allen gets into Bergman country). All the same: Paul Newman isn't "just" a charlatan, the characters hesitate and breathe, they were something once, or they might have been something once, and they're still somehow on some kind of edge even if they can't quite fall . . . .

It may well be that Kagan's formidable catalogue of details and resemblances would reveal "genristics" even in the more abstract films. Certainly Kagan's deft avoidance of the intentional fallacy accommodates the extent to which Altman's films relate to genres by *convergence* rather than *divergence*. If **Buffalo Bill and the Indians** is rather remote from the Western genre on one hand, and from the showbiz genre (if there is one) on the other, it's not only for finding a no-man's land in between, but for referring to ideas basic to both. To be sure, it doesn't closely follow every move in so close a precedent as **The Plainsman** (on the Western side of the Great Divide between the genres). Nor, on the other hand, does it first imitate and then distend its relative musical format (in the style of **Calamity Jane** or **Annie Get Your Gun**). It's remoter from both than

The Long Goodbye is from Raymond Chandler. But the references have a longer fuse, that's all; and the space between the genres allows a third to take part: the historical film (and the history of history).

Similarly, it makes sense to treat **Three Women** as a derivative hybrid from already existing genres, mixing as it does (1) films of feminine neurosis (**Persona, The Red Desert, Jeanne Dielman**, etc.), (2) films of South-Western buddies (it's "California Split-Personality"), and (3) tragi-comedies of alienation ("Three Umarried Women," "Shelley and Sissy and Janice and Robert and Ruth and John"). It's even more like the very new genre about female buddies (**Julia, The Turning Point** — if that's a genre as distinct from a hot topic). It appears in the same year as those films (1977), before the establishment of the theme (of which a subsequent modulation is **Nine to Five**).

Did Altman arrive at the new genre accidentally, as it were, by commenting on the old? Or was his interest participative rather than critical, i.e., had he become interested in problems which they hadn't yet focused on? Or (and this is what would most interest realism theory) did he think out the new film on the basis of what he, like other writers, directors and actors, was noticing in life around, and inside, him, and responding to it directly (from living in the social world) rather than indirectly (from keeping an eye on other movies)?

Here "commentary" reaches a fascinating sense. Altman isn't only commenting on an existing genre; he's constructing a new one. This in no way controverts Kagan's stress on commentary (which in another vocabulary would be self-reflexivity). On the contrary. Surprising as it may seem, comment precedes construction, just as narration precedes narrative. Look at it this way. Before a story can exist, it has to be told. It's extremely rare, and probably impossible, to tell a story without making a selection which amounts to a comment on something connected with the story. That's why we so often ask: "What is the point of the story?" i.e., what comment does this story make, on something which one deduces from the story! (It's tempting to talk of "levels" in the story, but there are no levels in the story; you can't disentangle the narration from the narrative, and if you can't separate them, what's the point of talking about "levels"?) It's tempting to say that commentary and construction are two sides of the same coin, but it's truer to say that they're the same side of the same coin. The *mosaic* nature of commentary and construction is underlined since the new genres are sharply critical (i.e., anxious) about the new mores as well as the old.

A word about Kagan's ingenious genre-chart. Only a three-dimensional structure could more vividly present those links between genres (and themes) which can't be neighbours in two-dimensional space.

Indeed, mental space resembles physical space in that the brain is it-self a three-dimensional structure, with a hugely complex lattice of connections and filaments running in every direction. (Semantic space is another can of worms!) And as for ideas, some principle of association, connection and overlap is of their very essence. Kagan's very elegant torus pushes our thinking clear of the confines of that very inadequate medium for semantic mapping, a sheet of paper.

It's surprisingly difficult to develop a subject like genre pre-cisely, thoroughly and in detail, while leaving open all its connec-tions with non-textual matters like the way we live now. And in do-ing that, about Altman, and the new Hollywood, where it's a major dynamic, Kagan has put us all in his debt.

Raymond Durgnat

Generalized Genre Theory:
An Introduction

" . . . Still, it may be significant that he spent the first quarter century of his career out in the wilderness as a small-time entrepreneur in the entertainment business. By the time he could come out of the cold to express himself personally, he was too old to compromise. There was no more room to maneuver. The best years of his life had been spent in anonymous drudgery and in endless wheeling without dealing. *All that was left was the long twilight of inventive intransigence.*"[0.0] (my italics)

— Andrew Sarris, 1976

Both American film genres and the major American filmmaker Robert Altman have already been the subjects of serious scholarly studies.[0.1],[0.2] It is my intention to demonstrate that the first ten theatrical films of Robert Altman represent a unique set of "commentary counterparts" of significant American film genres and works.

The purpose of this introduction is to set out my scholarly methodology and apparatus, clarify the scope of the task, deal with the conceptual and critical problems which arise, and sketch the value of my contentions.

Firstly, in terms of my scholarly methodology and apparatus, several terms used herein should be understood in the way I will be using them:

> *genre*: a body, group, or category of similar works: this similarity being defined as the sharing of a sufficient number of motifs so that we can identify works which properly fall within a particular kind or style of film

> *theme*: a basic conceptual or intellectual premise underlying a specific work or body of work

motif: a dominant, generally recurring idea or dramatization designed, in most cases, to enhance the theme or themes of the director

archetype: manifestations in image, dialogue, or character recognizable as basic elements of a culture's experience as a whole[0.3]

anti-genre: element of the film which tends to explicitly differ from, and often comment on, the motifs and themes of the film's apparent genre

modernistic: an aspect of the film which calls attention to the film's nature as an artifact, disrupting the viewer's mood of suspended disbelief.

It is understood that these are working definitions, chosen to facilitate critical discussion, and not intended to resolve the many profound film-theoretic questions and problems surrounding the complex concept of film genre.

My analysis proceeds from these concepts to relate two basic types of critical discourse. In the generic/theoretic area, it considers existing genre and critical literature to determine reasonable, applicable genre formulations which apply to Altman's *oeuvre*. In the stylistic/thematic area, Altman's films are considered to trace each one's treatment of these themes, motifs, archetypes, and visual conventions. The goal, as stated, is integration of the first area with the second to demonstrate that Altman's first ten theatrical films represent a unique set of "commentary counterparts" of significant American film genres and works.

The text proceeds film by film, first formulating each genre or classical film analysis in reference to significant genre-critical literature or, where this is inadequate, from significant reviews and my own analysis. The Altman counterpart is then critiqued in terms of its illumination of themes, motifs, archetypes, and stylistic conventions. A concluding chapter systematically classifies and clarifies Altman's artistic/analytic structures and strategies, and discusses their significance and value for the film scholar.

The scope of the project (**Countdown** through **Nashville**, see the Table of Contents) was chosen for several reasons. As the Table of Contents schematizes, each film deals with a distinct, different genre. Moreover, as shown in the Conclusions, they reveal the development of Altman's artistic/analytic strategies of genre commentary.

The decision to stop with **Nashville** follows from my intuition, along with that of several other critics, that with **Buffalo Bill** Altman's interests shift from genre to the illusionary nature of entertainment as a whole. As C.W. Billman notes:

> [In **Buffalo Bill**] the prevailing vision of the show business world and the illusions spun out there to hoodwink its audiences — of which contrived history is but one aspect — are the director's emphases. Altman calls attention to the power of realistic illusions of reality to shape the thinking of audiences until it is they who are clamoring for more. As Buffalo Bill asks while gazing dubiously at a large-as-life painting of himself on his white stallion, "My God . . . ain't he riding that horse right? well, if he ain't . . . how come you all took him for a king?"[0.4]

Richard Combs also sees this much more general focus:

> Too large to be called their theme, too amorphous to be called their subject, Altman's concern with "performance," with what happens to truth when one tries to find it through illusion, explains why these films were made.[0.5]

As Professor John Belton pointed out in conversation, the films after **Nashville** deal with the genres already covered, but from an abstract perspective: **Buffalo Bill** (western as showbusiness), **Three Women** (madness as performance), **A Wedding** (love obsession as showbusiness), **Quintet** (science fiction as performance), **Perfect Couple** (love obsession as showbusiness). Critically, I think of **Countdown** through **Nashville** as Altman's *Ulysses* period (probing genres), and from **Buffalo Bill** on as his *Finnegan's Wake* period (probing art as collective illusion).

The preceding description of methodology and scope give rise to apparent problems which should be clarified. Roughly, they fall into four areas: genre/classic-film formulation difficulties; stylistics-as-commentary complexities; genre commentary in film history; and the intentional fallacy.

genre/classic-film formulation difficulties

Formulation of film genres and "subtext meanings" of individual films in what follows, as in all scholarship, is imperfect, and can be questioned. In the case of my own genre categories (e.g., the romance/love film, the outcast/outlaw/gangster film, the contest/success film), I acknowledge taking certain initiatives, but would argue that critical discourse by Pauline Kael, Andrew Sarris, Michael Wood, Robin Wood, and others which tends to support the formulations is also included. A genre is at heart a critical tool and category of thought, and if formulating one leads to new knowledge, it is in itself a valid scholarly activity, rather than something to be apologized for (e.g., I found the parallels of **Vertigo** and **The Searchers** as "love/romance obsession" films to be in themselves significant).

I acknowledge that I frequently discuss Altman's films in terms of their classic counterparts, as well as in terms of abstract themes, motifs, and other ideas — but this seems a more open, clarifying mehod of argument than working at one remove.

stylistics as commentary complexities

References to Altman's use of a distinctive individual cinematic style (camera, sound, and editing devices) in the following are perhaps less extensive than they might be. The reason is that while I see Altman as having a full command of cinema's stylistic techniques, I tend to see him using them primarily in the service of his genre-commentary, hence their being of only secondary interest in terms of advancing my analysis.

Thus, what many critics have pointed out as Altman's characteristic visual devices: the use of the zoom lens to call attention, and the floating camera which catches unexpected moments and details, are used more for genre style undercutting than for building a consistent point of view (as with the explicit visual undercutting via zoom of thriller visual conventions in **The Long Goodbye**, the detailed visual reprise of flight films in **Countdown**, and the deliberate viewer disorientation via zoom in **McCabe and Mrs. Miller**'s concluding gunfight). Likewise, other oft-noted Altman stylistic devices, such as overlapping dialogue and adlibbed lines and scenes, are also seen by me as well as other critics as primarily drawing the viewer's attention away from the conventional, strong, main plotline to the background characters and occurrences which are "equally" real (and hence undercutting traditional genre narrative conventions).

Finally, the visual look or mood of each Altman film I am considering also seems to serve mainly as a static consistent commentary on the orthodox genre. Thus, the "flashed" or brown-tinted old photograph scenes in **McCabe and Mrs. Miller**, for instance, appear to be a stylish counterpart of the "framing" of the past by the present via editing in **The Man Who Shot Liberty Valence**, while the bluish pastel look of **The Long Goodbye**, it has been pointed out, is a sort of bitter-sweet visual farewell to the 1950s crime thriller.

It might be argued that, in principle, *every* film is a genre-commentary on its predecessors and, in particular, the American films made in the same period as those I am discussing were often called anti-genre films or simply anti-films. Why then single out Altman's work as significant?

While many contemporaneous films evidence a certain awareness of genre history, critical analyses often show that this "awareness" reduces to a quick scrounging for devices, rather than an illumination of the genre. Consider the following comments by Pauline Kael on two such exemplars:

> . . . Other film students [watching **Judge Roy Bean**] may know what's coming in just about every scene, because they too have seen the movies [John Ford, Kurasawa, Jodorowsky] that have fed Milius's imagination . . . [But] the big scenes don't grow out of anything, and there are no characters, just mannerisms.[0.6]

> . . . [Mel Brooks] isn't self critical. And as his new [Western spoof] **Blazing Saddles** once again demonstrates, he doesn't have the controlling vision that a director needs . . . . Brooks' humor is intentionally graceless; he seems to fear subtlety as if it were the enemy of all he holds dear — as if it were gentility itself. Brooks has to love the comedy of chaos.[0.7]

Kael's remarks do not say anything about Altman's achievement, but they do indicate how any number of genre-referential or classic-film-referential works may make no contribution to critical understanding. I would reiterate that my concern is with how Altman's ten films are consistent, systematic, intelligent commentaries on significant film genres and classic genre works. That easy genre references were stylish during the period in which Altman's films were made seems to me to do nothing to decrease the significance of his achievement, and indeed, in the light of the Kael comments on possibilities for failure, tend only to increase it.

intentional fallacy

What follows is consistent with the critical principle known as the intentional fancy — that any data about the creators' intentions are extraneous to the critical argument. That is to say, I work only from the finished films, other films, and critical insights. That Robert Altman and the other participants in the filmmaking process deliberately planned a great deal of what I detail I cannot deny, yet for formal reasons I choose to ignore.

The value of the following critical discussion for film scholarship is discussed at some length in the conclusion. Very briefly, I see this book's value as threefold. First of all, it provides useful "critical tools" — completely thought out, integrated examples of the film-making-as-genre-commentary process. Secondly, it illuminates this process — how, via Altman's works, genre commentary can be a creative aspect of filmmaking. Lastly, it supports the idea that genre commentary, as a number of critics now suggest, is a significant evolutionary step in film history.

ACKNOWLEDGEMENTS

My special thanks to Brian Camp of E.F.L.A., Professor Michael Kerbel of the University of Bridgeport, Professors John Belton and Andrew Sarris of Columbia University, Mary Corliss and Charles Silver of the Museum of Modern Art Film Study Center

Photograph credits and acknowledgements: Metro Goldwyn Mayer, Columbia Pictures, United Artists, Universal Pictures, Warner Brothers Corp., Commonwealth United Entertainment, Paramount Pictures, Twentieth Century Fox, and Corith Films.

Stills from Cinememoribilia, Movie Star News, Museum of Modern Art Stills Collection, and Steven Salley.

Countdown (1968)

Robert Altman's **Countdown** exemplifies the tendency of his early films to comment on film genre conventions (in this case, those of the science fiction "adventure" movie). Though Altman was dismissed after shooting and the film somewhat re-edited, a basic consistency with his later work in this respect is clear. As Professor Andrew Sarris has intuited, "**Countdown** can be considered the first Altman feature film."[1.1]

Countdown begins with long static shots of gargantuan space hardware against the hard blue Cape Kennedy sky: 10-story-high radar antennas, immense red steel launching towers as big as high-rises, sullen concrete mission control bunkers. Behind the technological images is an odd discordant, jarring "industrial film" score that is powerful but never builds, just grumbles sinisterly. Images and sound together already signal a subtle mocking of science fiction genre figures of style. Susan Sontag has pointed out that, via monsters or space trips or apocalypse, S.F. genre films basically: "reflect worldwide anxieties . . . and serve to allay them. There is a sense in which all these movies are in complicity with the abhorrent."[1.2] In a remarkably subtle fashion, Altman's **Countdown** turns the genre inside out, revealing this accommodation of monstrousness by reversing key genre themes: dehumanization, anti-intellectualism, and reverence for asocial science.

The first sequence in **Countdown** suggests the genre themes to be questioned. The story opens up *in medias res*, with a three-man Apollo space capsule in earth orbit, supposedly one of the pre-moon-landing test flights of the late 1960s. Dramatic intensity is established visually by Altman's jamming his camera in with the astronauts, squeezed up against each other in their technology-packed little cabin. From the first, there is a lack of the genre's elaborate art direction or intricate models negotiating cosmic vistas; visually, **Countdown** stays in people-perspective, a genre reversal.

Almost at once, into this super-rational world of crisp commands and winking lights, a note of covert mystery and mysticism is injected.

The flight is abruptly terminated without explanation, over the objections of the film's protagonist Lee Stegler (James Caan), who wants to proceed. The anti-genre mood of human motivations and technology at cross-purposes is clear from the first.

The sequence also quickly sets up the key conflicting characters. The mission commander, obsessive astronaut Chiz (Robert Duval), accepts cancellation calmly, cued in by a secret in its phrasing. Subordinate pilot Lee-Caan is rebellious, arguing a touch humanistically "You didn't give us a chance . . . I thought that's why you had us up here instead of computers." Letting the Lee-Caan and Mission Control voices overlap, suggests, as later, a conflict that can't be settle, reversing the smoothly working space crew genre convention. The argument also ironically prefigures Lee-Caan's later "human" choices on the moon mission, taking him to the edge of death.

At Mission Control, emotionless project director Ross (Steve Inhat) and passionate flight surgeon Dr. Gus (Charles Aidman) also bicker. Mocking the genre again, none of these semi-stereotypes is allowed more than one name, and these can be seen as jokes — Chiz for schiz or schizophrenic, Ross for boss, Gus for fuss or gas, and hero Lee Stegler ("stabler").

Of all the tensions and types **Countdown** pops onto the screen, however, the most reverberating anti-genre symbol is the key word "pilgrim" in the recall order. Ross-Inhat's rumbling voice announces: "I know more about your mission, uh, pilgrim — *scrub it!*" Eventually, pilgrim is defined in technological detail. But, for a few minutes, the word ironically hints at all the discourse and human possibilities the genre rejects — a transcendental journey full of adversity made at great risk into a new realm, in a context of spiritual values. (By comparison, the genre exemplar **2001** *equates* soulless super-technology *with* God as man's creator.)

On the ground, the weary astronauts leave their exhausting debriefly, one muttering: "That couch still isn't right — it's breaking my back up there." Again, the human rattles and smears its brilliant but flat technological environment.

In the bright sunlight, Lee-Caan is met by his family, displaying affection for wife Mickey (Joanne Moore) while his young son demands they "cut it out." Here and later, the pre-adolescent son suggests the limited voice of the genre itself. By contrast, Lee-Caan mentions a feeling there's some secret behind their sudden return.

At home, Lee-Caan's "wholeness" is implied in his kidding yet sensitive repartee with his wife, which also reflects their pleasure with each other. One notes **Countdown**'s exceptionally sympathetic treatment of all characters' emotions, a very anti-genre approach.

That night, Lee-Caan, Chiz-Duval and a third man gather at a table, as the obsessed astronaut manipulates rocket toys (presumably

2

Lee-Caan's son's models) to explain Project Pilgrim. In opposition to the entire genre, particularly its most recent products, **Countdown** uses a minimum of model work — except here, where a certain mocking silliness is suggested about the whole convention by the Duval character's intensity.

The Pilgrim secret is a contingency plan for a one-man one-way high risk moon flight, should the Soviet Union dispatch a lunar landing mission. A Russian landing is now imminent, so Chiz-Duval was called back to finish up his preparations. His "pilgrim" will live in a shelter sent up from earth, until brought back by the familiar Project Apollo. Apparently confident, Chiz-Duval makes a Freudian slip, speaking of "you" as the moon astronaut, at which Lee-Caan demurs (an exchange hinting at the chosen pilot's lack of surety, in comparison to Lee-Caan's self-confidence.

A TV newscast instroduces space agency spokesman Larsen (Ted Knight), the character-actor mocking the genre's tendency towards pompous figures of authority (e.g., Raymond Massey in **Things to Come,** Michael Rennie in **The Day the Earth Stood Still**, even the monoliths in **2001**). He stresses the Soviet Union's silence regarding a current round-the-moon mission, though we've just been shown the Americans are in their way just as secretive (sinister Soviets are a genre motif, viz., **2001**). Here and later, authority is portrayed as hypocritical and self-righteous, the opposite of the genre's approving view of a society that promotes any science. As Sontag puts it: "In science fiction films the antithesis of black magic and white is drawn as a split between technology which is beneficial, and the errant individual will of a lone intellectual."[1.3] **Countdown**, by contrast, always favors the thinking-feeling individuals, notably Mickey-Moore's expression of sympathy for Chiz-Duval's wife, who must live without him for a year. Smiling, she seems to intuit the situation about to arise: "Yeah, well, we're all tough."

A sting of dramatic music, a stock shot of the White House, then the hardwood "corridors of power," with grimfaced project director Ross-Inhat and scholarish scientist Dr. Ehrman (Steve Coit) greeted by a White House staffer and aristocratic State Department official Seidel (Charles Irving). Rather than overlapping dialogue suggesting an emotional quarrel, conflict between these disciplined power wielders is portrayed in harsh staccato duels, as in this slashing exchange:

> Seidel-Irving: (The Russian) is a geologist.
> Ross-Inhat: That's untrue!
> Seidel-Irving: he's had no military training.
> Ross-Inhat: and no one knows that either!

The President's men come to the point: the anticipated Russian landing mission has a civilian crew. Is there a U.S. civilian who can be trained in three weeks, rather than using Air Force officer Chiz-Duval? Seidel-Irving also murmurs that the problem arose because his Department was not consulted. This and what follows is remarkable for again inverting the genre idea of larger-than-life, idealistic if pompous "scientific" leaders. Instead, this pair of careerist-hypocrites anticipate the mean-minded P.R.-conscious Watergate conspirators.

The technocrat project director argues that Chiz-Duval is the best pilot, adding grimly: "I'll put the man up there — you worry about the public relations." At once, **Countdown** completely inverts the theme of reverence for asocial science. As Sontag points out, "the notion of science as a social activity, interlocking with social and political interests, is unacknowledged. Science is simply either adventure (for good or evil) or a technical response to danger."[1.4] Here is science stripped of its myths and shown feeding off money and lives, bringing forth prestige and power, like any other social activity. In its way, **Countdown** is as disturbing and myth-shattering about science as **China Syndrome** is about technology a decade later:

> Seidel Irving: (sneeringly) Public relations is everyone's problem. What supports your program? Public relations! Public acceptance! Public revenues!
>
> Dr. Ehrman-Coit: And your programs — whatever they are.
>
> Seidel-Irving: We feel very strongly that even a technically military connection could be used against us.

The exchange restates **Countdown**'s anti-genre attitude, that the asocial space adventure is very much a political tool and strategem.

The end of the interview has an even darker implication — that the project is at heart a techno-fascistic gesture, the individual's actual survival chances being of less importance than what he stands for. The genre's hero-astronaut is portrayed chillingly as a human sacrifice to technological society, recalling Sontag's point about the science fiction genre being "in complicity with the abhorrent":

> Ross-Inhat: You're saying — come up with a civilian or the program is jeopardized. Is that correct?
>
> Seidel-Irving: Consider. The cost is enormous in money; there is risk of human life. To justify this, let us make more points — accomplish as much as possible. Our space program is non-military. We can demonstrate that.
>
> Ross-Inhat: Three weeks!
>
> Seidel-Irving: Some civilian . . . who could be trained . . . .

At this moment, the two anti-genre technocrats suggest the oldest literary images of scientists: Doctor Faustus and Shakespeare's Prospero. Project director Inhat-Ross is a Doctor Faustus, making his twentieth century black bargain, while scholarly Dr. Ehrman-Coit is an overdetached Prospero, only partly in control of the magic forces which he is investigating.

Many genre films (e.g., **Them!**, **Things to Come**) gloss over the ambivalent nature of the scientific enterprise by having their technologists save us from monstrosities, even though the horrors are often man-made or man-triggered (the monster as "McGuffin" or excuse). Altman's anti-genre **Countdown** repeatedly shows the technocrats as amoral; lying, risking, and rationalizing their way to "good ends." The bureaucrat Seidel-Irving's last speech about the enormous cost, risk of human life, and "more points" is not much different in principle from the notorious Vietnam directive about "destroying this village in order to save it."

Suggestively, **Countdown** leaves out the actual offering of the job by Ross-Inhat to Lee-Caan — often a genre highpoint, but in this anti-genre work a very dubious business. Instead, there is a morning kitchen discussion between Lee-Caan and Mickey-Moore, two perceptive, feeling adults who show they care for each other in the face of a risky, profound challenge. Lee-Caan concludes strongly: "I didn't say anything . . . there are no commitments . . . I haven't decided, Mick." The point of view is almost impossible to imagine in a genre science fiction film. Amusingly, a science fiction genre author has in bewilderment commented on the novel on which **Countdown** was based: "Such novels are not really science fiction at all, but books with spaceships in them."[1.5]

The next sequence, almost a parody of the couple's discussion, an angry Chiz-Duval confronting his grim superior. The two bicker like an unhappy love match (earlier the technocrat had called the astronaut "my choice"). The first choice mocks the White House arguments: "Why don't you send some big beautiful babe with big teeth and a stack of pop tunes!" The two voices crowd over each other, Ross-Inhat rumblingly concluding: "He's been asked — I just heard from him."

A night party for a few hundred space people follows, one casual guitarist making an ingenious story-genre comment via an updated "John Henry" folk ballad:

> When John Henry was a little baby
> Sittin' on his mama's knee
> He looked at the sky, and the moon got in his eye
> and he said: the moon is gonna be the death of me . . . .
>
> Now they put John Henry on the space team
> He got a pretty white pressurized suit
> they made him a major the very next day
> 'cause the colonel's wife whtought he looked cute . . . .

The colonel said: Johnny, we gotta make a moon shot
or the Russians will leave us behind
so get ready soon —
and we'll drop you on the moon —

Here the music is used in anti-genre manner, no inspiring "Thus
spoke Zarathustra" or "Star Wars Overture" to build mood and expectations, but rather the swift, direct injection of historical material
working against themes and motifs. Like the original John Henry,
Lee-Caan is shown as having accepted a degrading and suicidal task:
competing against robots that should do the job in a pathetic pub-
licity stunt — the genre in disgrace. Also, like John Henry, he's
promoted not so much for his ability but because he is "cute"
(black or civilian), a public relations quality that at root suggests a
"natural, free" soul's willing participation. The song shows him up as
a stooge and a pawn, which everyone at the party seems to accept.

It follows, and the last chorus of **Countdown**'s "John Henry"
suggests, that the rational masculine heroic mood of the science
fiction genre at heart conceals its opposites: self-delusion, insecurity,
irresponsibility, suicidal impulses and sado-masochism — all implied
in the behavior of "ideal astronaut," Chiz-Duval.

They took John Henry to the launch pad
He blasted off in a whirl:
And I heard him say, as the booster fell away
That man in the moon is a girl, oh yeah, the
man in the moon is a girl!

Emphasizing this subtext, Chiz-Duval and Lee-Caan confront
each other, and the "jilted" pilot bitterly tells the new Pilgrim astronaut that he won't be his "backup": "You'll just have to forgive me
about that!"

The John Henry ballad and the behavior of Chiz-Duval also im-
ply that **Countdown** is concerned with another genre motif, that of
the personality being "taken over" from outside, a la **Invasion of the
Body Snatchers** and **Children of the Damned** (half-human, half-
spacefolk). But here the anti-genre "takeover" is by the obsessively
rational project activity. As Sontag points out, they come to the
same thing:

Thus, science fiction films can be looked at as thematically
central allegory, replete with standard modern attitudes. The
theme of depersonalization (being "taken over") which I
have been talking about is a new allegory reflecting the age
old awareness of man that, sane, he is always perilously close

6

to insanity and unreason . . . . The image derives most of its power from a supplementary and historical anxiety, also not experienced consciously by most people, about the depersonalizing conditions of modern life.[1.6]

(A notable tension in the genre is that, in a number of films, a case is made *for* depersonalization and "artificial instincts" — tomorrow's inhabitants as efficient heroic semi-zombies (viz., Kubrick's **2001** astronauts, for instance). Indeed, the apparently depersonalizing "Force" in **Star Wars** (a fantasy genre film with science fiction trappings) as well as the "saucer possession" experienced in **Close Encounters of the Third Kind,** treat this "take-over" as *desirable*.)

In a noisy hangar, Lee-Caan, Chiz-Duval, and Director Inhat-Ross confront each other across a Volkswagen-sized Pilgrim space capsule, comparing its inadequacy to a toy. The dehumanized Chiz-Duval's explanations stress the unnaturalness of every part of the astronaut's task, the need to respond with *"artificial instincts,"* instincts Lee-Caan won't have time to acquire. He bitterly concludes: "When you find out how much you don't know, you won't want to go" (then, to Ross-Inhat) " . . . and when he cracks and you don't scrub him, I'll go over your head." In Chiz-Duval, passion and dehumanized rationality are hopelessly confused.

By comparison, Lee-Caan never loses his individuality: "When I figure out I can't make it, I'll get out so fast I'll blind ya — okay, teach!"

In a small auditorium, head scientist Dr. Ehrman-Coit sketches the mission on a blackboard, stressing the pilot's decision point, near the moon, when he can either maroon himself or return to earth. Flight surgeon Dr. Gus-Aidman angrily lists the medical risks: the astronaut could be broiled or frozen by temperatures, shattered by meteors, or seared and blinded by radiation. Formerly sarcastic over this fate befalling Chiz-Duval, he stomps out, upset, to protest when he learns the Pilgrim astronaut is instead his friend Lee-Caan, sitting beside him.

The moment suggests one more genre motif, not simple death, but incineration by radiation. The anti-genre point is that several science fiction films (**On the Beach, This Island Earth**) focus on the experts' guilt over atomic destruction. Here, closer to life, the vaguely humanistic physician tolerates the radiation risks as long as he's not emotionally involved. And when he wants to speak out, Director Inhat-Ross threatens the Navy doctor with court martial; if he won't work with them, he'll be relieved of all responsibility:

> Dr. Gus-Aidman (compassionately): How to you go about that on your t/o? He's my friend. How do you relieve me of that?

Inhat-Ross: (like a machine) Stop making friends.

In a momentary respite from training, Lee-Caan walks with wife Mickey-Moore. He speaks of the paradoxical "emotional flavor" of technology, as having a sort of affirmative sustaining quality: "(The capsule's) very much like a good woman, just like you." The attitude directly confronts the genre's glorifying attitude to technology (as opposed to people), with a reasonable centrist feeling, as if describing a good car or a good house. Lee-Caan also keeps his sense of proportion about the job: "Well, we made a bargain — if anything looked too rough, I'd get out."

Intense training follows. We watch a spacesuited Lee-Caan in a vacuum chamber, a hanging cable system called a "Peter Pan" reducing his apparent weight so he skips and glides around the tea-kettle-shaped shelter-vehicle, with its blinking red beacon. Outside, Chiz-Duval, Ross-Inhat, and Dr. Gus-Aidman observe; then as an emergency develops, they clash hysterically over whether to help or to let the "test" proceed. The sequence is comic in its treatment of the genre's familiar, smoothly-working, detached science team as frantic depersonalized zombies trying to figure if this death is worth it to their project. Never has the male cameraderie motif of American action films been so creepily mocked. Fortunately, Lee-Caan manages to save himself.

Later, the flight surgeon seeks unsuccessfully to turn wife Mickey-Moore around: "If Lee says we are going to the moon, then we are going to the moon until Lee says we are not going to the moon." The line sums up their "wholeness" against the project's "take over."

Next, amusingly, a brief scene shows a knowledgeable science reporter listing, for the doctor, hardware arrivals, schedule changes, odd silences, and other events which add up to a Pilgrim-like mission in the offing. This is notable as the only "scientific" investigation and deduction in **Countdown**.

In a dark hangar, a windowless cockpit-shaped flight simulator rocks and shudders in its framework, amid exhausted technicians tensed over control panels. The "simulation" races towards earth orbit departure, all equipment breakdowns and frantic exchanges between Lee-Caan's anxious voice and a shrill hovering Chiz-Duval. But when Lee-Caan, in control, "aborts" (correctly, a technician tells him), Chiz-Duval breaks and storms to Director Ross-Inhat's office, crying: "I'm the only one who wants it bad enough to make it!" The Pilgrim project boss tries to placate the obsessed, dehumanized astronaut: "I'd pass it on, disclaimed and disapproved. But they won't put you in. We'd just have to shut it down . . . it's not a question of who's the better man." But the balanced intellectual Lee-Caan isn't sweet enough to spare Chiz-Duval the truth: "You couldn't make this mission, Chiz — *you have the guts, but you haven't got the brains.*"

The sequence reverses another surprisingly common genre theme: anti-intellectualism. Sontag points out that:

> . . . the implication remains that other men, less imagina-
> tive — in short, technicians — could have administered the
> same discovery better and more safely. The most ingrained
> contemporary mistrust of intellect is visited, in these movies,
> upon the scientist as intellectual.[1.7]

Though seemingly a genre self-contradiction, the theme is surprisingly frequent: in **2001** and **Alien** the only "intellectual" characters go crazy and have their brains literally *torn out* by the film heroes. Significantly, the "intellectuals" in both cases are robots to begin with. Likewise, in **War of the Worlds, It Came from Outer Space, The Thing** and **Them!**, the scientists are all uniformly *in*effective when they are not mentally unbalanced.

In one more orchestrated wholistic respite, Lee-Caan plays catch with his son, charging the boy with caring for his mother. Next, newsreel footage shows the launching site, and the successful shelter-liftoff for the moon.

At a restaurant press dinner, newsmen inform Lee-Caan, Mickey-Moore and Dr. Gus-Aidman of a successful Soviet moonship launch. They ask about cancelling the Pilgrim project, as bankrupt propaganda, while the physician friend can now say that Lee-Caan won't be a martyr, just a possible suicide. Lee-Caan: "It's not suicide. As long as the decision stays with me, it's an acceptable proposition." In a fascinating anti-genre variation, **Countdown** keeps the story problem constant, but instead keeps finding new moral, social and psychological perspectives. The humanist-physician, for example, now involved, cannot understand the individual choosing an amoral risk: "I want you to survive, I value you." More upsetting for Lee-Caan is his wife's feeling of betrayal: "What happened to all the caution you promised? What do you expect me to do — smile?"

In one more anti-genre stroke, the hero-scientist cannot for the moment keep cool and rational. Angrily, Lee-Caan tells her: "Yeah, you smile. You got that? If it kills you to do it, smile! *Smile!*"

In another auditorium holding experts and newsmen, it's announced the moon shelter has landed successfully, but that its homing beacon is out. Lee-Caan, seemingly "taken over" by the project, commands the assembly: "The only thing that's added to the risk of survival are the odds — the odds of me aborting the mission when I get there. I accepted those odds." The intellectual's awareness of the realities of power is an anti-genre delight; by comparison, **2001**'s astronaut's confused defiance of his ship's "mad computer," stylized into a heroic triumph, is almost slow witted.

Ted Knight's TV reporter, seemingly the fraudulent voice of the genre itself, announces the Russian launch and the approach of the Pilgrim flight. Left out is the central emotional truth: that both heroic missions are taking on additional risks.

At their motel on the last night, Mickey-Moore comments on the stylized straightjacket of the news media (like the science fiction adventure genre), men who jam microphones in her face crying: "Do you really think he'll come back, Mrs. Stegler?" They work desperately to dramatize the event, yet are totally hamstrung by the government (and public) need for positive reports in familiar categories (what TV programmers call "happy people with happy problems"). In these remarks, Altman's film sketches in another concern of the decade-away **The China Syndrome**: news management. As Mickey-Moore sums it up, even if the newspeople dangled microphones into their bedroom all night, they'd still have to print: "Headline! Astronaut Takes Wife to Motel, Kisses Goodbye, and Blasts Off for the Moon."

The exchange dissolves, visually emphasizing the point, to the couple "after the kiss." Lee-Caan, half to himself, seeks to justify his decision.

> Lee-Caan: There never was a time when I had to weigh the mission on one side and you and Stevie on the other . . . I knew I'd be back, I never had a thought of not coming back. It's not fair, but that's the way it's gonna be . . . I spent years thinking of myself taking that trip. I always thought I would . . . . If I don't make this trip, then who the hell am I? Forgive me. Forgive me. Forgive me . . . .

In a sense, Lee-Caan *has* been subtly "taken over," dehumanized by the technological project. Yet he remains aware of his overwhelming involvement as something human, which he must balance against other aspects of his life. In this he is an anti-genre hero, still human compared to those who have mutilated their personalities to accommodate the "techno-intellectual life": obsessed leader Chiz-Duval, who ignores his alcoholic wife; the "Jewish mother" Dr. Gus-Aidman; the ironwilled director Ross-Inhat, who has "stopped making friends" (incidentally, the "admirable" character-types that run the **Star Trek** spaceship). In the end, Mickey-Moore accepts his decision, telling him softly: "Be sure to wave goodbye when you leave." In a modern anti-genre sense, the depersonalization of the techno-intellectual life and techno-intellectual world is illuminated as a very mixed blessing.

In the bright morning, to ominous music, Lee-Caan, in his silvery garment, ascends slowly into the spacecraft, Chiz-Duval respectfully assisting, Director Inhat-Ross murmuring: "God go with you, Lee." Symbolic tokens include his son's rubber mouse, a folded American flag, and a cross-shaped white light kickback on his helmet. "I can see I'm not going to be alone," Lee-Caan murmurs, and this "cross" *does* appear at crises on the mission. In fact, the sci fi genre thematically extends to "religious" films (e.g., **Teorama, Winter Light**) and monster/horror films (e.g., **Frankenstein, Dracula**), both about complicity with the abhorrent. The monster/horror films such as **Frankenstein, King Kong** and **Dr. Jekyll and Mr. Hyde**, seen as allegories of adolescence or uncontrollable libido, also edge into the fantasy genre (see genres chart, in Introduction).

Leaving, Chiz-Duval warns not to land unless he sees the shelter: "Don't get any cute ideas." In Mission Control, everyone waits as the countdown unwinds, then watch as, with an immense blowtorch roar, the Pilgrim begins the journey.

Rather than genre cliches, **Countdown** portrays the moon voyage as a recapitulation of the history of flight in movies. Liftoff has the flavor of James Stewart's **Spirit of St. Louis**, Lee-Caan riding in a small crowded vibrating cabin, shouting over the radio in exultant tones: "Altimeter up off the peg! . . . Comin' through the clouds! . . . Sun through the window — wow!" **Countdown** cuts from the lone figure to his narrow cabin to blue skies, white cloudbanks, a spear of sunlight shifting across the deck.

Moving forward in flight history in movies, the breakaway from earth orbit is stylized as David Lean's **Breaking the Sound Barrier**, the Pilgrim rocket vibrating wildly as if it is about to break up (Lee-Caan: "It's a wild horse, Capecomm . . . Right out of the ballpark!")

Continuing the historical reprise, a modern airliner carries the Pilgrim team to Houston, Ted Knight's newscaster grumbling that he can't get unlimited drinks (so much for the pioneers!). **Countdown** makes explicit the shared tension: Dr. Gus-Aidman requesting more medical data, Director Ross-Inhat dozing and starting up to ask about future problems. Chiz-Duval's ignored wife (Barbara Baxley) drinks, while Chiz-Duval and Mickey-Moore exchange guilts over trying to stop Lee-Caan. The sequence neatly inverts the anti-intellectual "individualist" theme. As Sontag points out:

> It is interesting that when the scientist in these films is treated negatively, it is usually done through the portrayal of an individual scientist who holes up in his laboratory and neglects his fiancee or his loving wife and children . . . . The scientist as a loyal member of a team, and therefore considerably less individualized, is treated quite respectfully."[1.8]

Here, it's those surrounding the protagonist, who have grasped and respect his individualistic decision, who suffer and are ashamed.

Tension clamps down during halfway maneuvers, instruments failing mysteriously. **Countdown** suggests the trip into the unknown with angled cabin interior shots, Lee-Caan's agitated face, eerie lunar terrain. As before, there is an anti-genre lack of model shots — the viewer must "sweat it out" with the people.

In another genre inversion, Lee-Caan's radio begins to fail, a reversal of space film's mysterious sounds and signals (e.g., **2001**, **Close Encounters**). Yet, this straightforward problem produces extraordinary drama and suspense (what was that message? How long till total failure?). The problem is power loss; the answer, cutting down all expenditures. Lee-Caan is talked into shutting down and trying to sleep, redfaced in the instruments glow, a released flashlight floating away — a single stylistic touch denoting his bizarre environment. Throughout, **Countdown** goes against the genre's glorifying attitude toward technology from Melies to **2001**; no limitations and unlimited expansion.

In Mission Control, Dr. Gus-Aidman and Mickey-Moore watch the automatic recorders which chart Lee-Caan's heartbeat, respiration, and other vital functions. The dehumanization motif is mocked in another key as Dr. Gus-Aidman speaks of his friend as "functioning beautifully," though Mickey-Moore replies: "But everything is all wrong."

Ted Knight's TV newscaster announces a successful mid-course maneuver, followed by radio silence — again omitting the key emotional crisis-facts. Increasingly, Knight's newscaster is used to mock the plot conventions of the science fiction genre itself, assuming that "*when* [my emphasis] Lee Stegler lands on the moon, he'll immediately make his way to the survival shelter." Knight's media reports grow progressively irrelevant and false, deflating the genre, as Sontag suggests, as a sort of conform-to-the-abhorrent propaganda. One grows disgusted with this smug bureaucratic lying.

The approach and landing sequence is handled filmicly as a series of brief overlapping scenes. Lee-Caan's voice grows tense but calm, repeating his messages to force them through. Failing power requires him to use eyes alone to spot the shelter signal light, calling out reports much as the characters landing in classic flying films. To brooding, sinister music, his face greenish in the lunar glow, Lee-Caan murmurs: "I believe I see it east of Hanstein." His message doubted, he angrily calls for a countdown, then fires his motor. A cry: "He's cut the cord, he can't come back!" is made, as the capsule's fuel is used up in the landing. The call for a countdown echoes the film's first one which brought him home and so, in a literary sense, suggests again an anti-genre view of sci-fi heroism as including dubious motives: social pressure, frustration, ambition, all piled in a tottering tower on inadequate technology.

Ted Knight's fraudulent voice reports that Pilgrim has just landed successfully on the moon, but a permanent mood of anti-genre bleakness now envelopes the film. Death symbols multiply: radio data indicating a pilot blackout, Lee-Caan's failure to answer radio messages or even speak again. One could even interpret his later movements about the moon as the wishful thinking of those on earth.

Inside the Pilgrim cabin, a low-angle camera shot makes Lee-Caan a faceless, unmoving aluminum-covered mummy. Finally, to solemn music, he rises and walks the lifeless rocky terrain in utter silence.

On earth, the other characters are gathered in a quiet Mission Control. Lee-Caan has three hours oxygen, and has not signalled his arrival. Far from genre triumph or terror, their speeches are a jumble of guilt and recriminations. Chiz-Duval tells them soberly: "he said 'I believe I have sighted' that's an old fighter pilot phrase — what you say when you fire into the dark and hope you hit a target."

The scientist character, Dr. Ehrman-Coit, in the end gives them the astronaut's case, an ignored aspect of the genre's "accommodation of the abhorrent": natural human intellectual curiosity about the unknown, abhorrent or not. He recalls Lee-Caan's very first line of dialogue — that a man was placed in the capsule to make the landing decision. For, in truth:

> Dr. Ehrman-Coit: That lunar surface is like clean snow, no one's touched it yet. The pull of the moon is very strong to the mind, to the imagination. That's why Stegler's sitting there now, waiting for his oxygen to run out . . . anyone with the courage to go would have landed, what's the mystery? There's no mystery, that's why Stegler's there.

At the same time, Altman's **Countdown** climax completely reverses Sontag's major genre themes — the *allaying* of worldwide anxiety over technological destruction, dehumanization, and so on. Instead, our worst fears are realized, the hero, our metaphorical representative, tricked by his own human curiosity, walks robotlike through an unlivable wasteland, with only the faintest hope of survival — the genre's anti-essence, the worst possible future. He finds an out-of-focus artifact, but it is only the crashed Soviet vehicle, one Russian propped against a rock on which rests a Russian flag. Lee-Caan places his own folded United States flag beside it. The moment of the doomed and dead enemies at peace mocks one more genre

The sci-fi genre film *Close Encounters* renders "complicity with the abhorrent" in lyrical, hypnotic images, the aliens' arrival suggesting the overwhelming experiences associated with religious or horror films.

In the genre-commentary film *Countdown*, complicity with the abhorrent is debunked: pushing beyond the limits of experience, skill, and reason leads to empty risk and futile death. Nevertheless, the intelligent individual endures.

motif Sontag discovers: "Science-technology is conceived of as the great unifier. Thus the science fiction films also project a Utopian fantasy."[1.9] But this Utopia is Necropolis.

On the stony lifeless moon, Lee-Caan walks about, seemingly with no hope. But when he pauses, he (and we) note a slight on-and-off reddening of his spacesuit. In an extreme longshot, we view him from atop the shelter vehicle, its rotating light beacon causing the reddening. Gratuitously, he has been given a chance to survive. The music swells up as he moves towards the lonely shelter in the dead landscape, but **Countdown** ends before we learn if he reaches it safely. Unlike the genre's familiar climatic motifs, the light show cosmic battles or saucer flights Sontag interprets as "the peculiar beauties . . . in wreaking havoc, making a mess"[1.11] **Countdown** ends as the anti-genre work began, with an isolated individual still struggling against an abhorrent universe.

Andrew Sarris has pointed out in conversation that Altman claims **Countdown**'s original "downbeat" ending was reshot and reedited after he left, and so has disowned it. Even if the intentional fallacy did not make this irrelevant, it seems to me clear how any hypothetical "followup" filmmakers were trapped by the mood and story Altman established into only the most tentatively optimistic ending; in fact more a barren respite than happy conclusion. By comparison, consider the end of the "ultimate" genre work: Kubrick's **2001**. A no longer human, charming scientific power fantasy figure is shown about to succeed to our home planet — versus Altman's **Countdown** ending — a vulnerable individual still trapped in the lifeless hostile wilderness of tomorrow. Sontag's "genre in complicity with the abhorrent"[1.2] was never so openly embraced, and never so bitterly criticized. Most central, **Countdown** realizes an always human intellectual who resists complicity with the monstrous.

That Cold Day In The Park (1969)

Robert Altman's **That Cold Day in the Park** can be seen as a cinematic critique of the most highly regarded love/romance genre exemplars — such films as **Vertigo, Letter from an Unknown Woman, Last Tango in Paris,** and **The Searchers** — in which love becomes an agonizing obsessional conflict impossible to resolve. Psychiatrist R.J. Stollar has argued sexual love requires rechanneling of unconscious hostility to our own sexual impulses: "Sexual excitement depends on a scenario . . . every detail counts for increasing excitement and a-voiding true danger or boredom . . . For many people sexual excitement is like threading a minefield."[2.1] Consistently, the genre's finest works — heroic tragedies — focus on imperfect management of this hostility — leading to such motifs as protagonists' psychological collapse, blocking, or obsessional behavior; *folie a deux* linking of love-aggressor and love-victim; and suicidal and homicidal impulses. A comment by de Rougemont seems definitive:

> Their oppressive fate . . . carries them away beyond the source of moral values, beyond pressure and pain, beyond the realm of distinctions . . . into a realm where opposites cancel out.[2.2]

That Cold Day in the Park commences with the tense, thirtyish Frances Austin (Sandy Dennis) hurrying through a damp, chilly Vancouver public garden, glancing at a babyfaced hip youth who significantly remains throughout a nameless Boy (Michael Burns), all to the poignant, nervous theme. In an ornate townhouse, she plays joyless hostess to four sexless, cranky old rich people and an oldish physician-suitor, glancing down periodically at the youth shivering on a park bench.

Genre films treat the life of sane moderation in an overly repressed, flat manner (the Midge-Bel Geddes career woman in **Vertigo**, the bookshop suitor in **Story of Adele H**, the grotesque Marriales in **The Searchers**) or in intolerable exaggeration (the stultifying bank in

The Collector). Altman's approach is to ironically stylize the genre by showing a number of possible "sane" worlds of greater or lesser carnalities. He starts with the old rich people's dinner party, in a way the worst of civilization's promise. Like Swift's Strullbruggs, these protected ancients are ugly, sickly, repellent. They disfigure the suite's elegance, can't identify their fancy cuisine, choke and gasp grotesquely. Like the pointless deaths at the start of **Vertigo** and **Last Tango**, they set the genre tone, undercutting a "reasonable life" as a contemptably blind shuffle towards oblivion.

Understandably, Frances-Dennis, at the end of youth, stares increasingly at the golden Boy-Burns shivering outdoors in a sudden downpour. Later, in the rainy, shabby park she calls urgently through a wire fence, asking him up to get dry. He accedes, smiling, but will not speak. In her luxurious bath, she turns away as he skins out of his clothes under a rich, thick towel.

At the kitchen table, Frances-Dennis repeatedly asks the silent Boy-Burns his name, without reply. In the living room, always silent, he chooses Greek folk music by scanning the album covers, a sort of a savage. His energy is a comment on the genre's convention of a passive victim-lover (e.g., Madeleine-Novak in **Vertigo**, the daughter-lover in **Obsession**). He does a wild kicking dance to her enthusiastic response, an ironic celebration of sexual energy.

When Boy-Burns becomes sleepy, she offers him a separate bedroom: "You don't have to — it's just an idea — ." Again, anti-genre, she initially appears healthy, not a sick personality awaiting obsession (e.g., **Vertigo, The Collector, Story of Adele H**).

In the bright morning, she brings in a sumptuous breakfast tray; then Boy-Burns wordlessly explores the richly furnished large rooms while she shops. A playful cherub, eyes bright, he tries on an expensive sports jacket, folding an ascot from a tower. Returning, a cheery Frances-Dennis gives him more clothes/gifts — a teasing of the "lover — re-creation" motif of the genre's **Vertigo** and **Obsession**, the gifts showered on the lover-victim in **The Collector**.

In a long speech, Frances-Dennis tells how her oldish physician suitor, a psychotherapist, treated a woman who couldn't walk until she could ride a bike. She then relates how as a child she played truant — biking with a friend for miles — but ending up back at the schoolyard just as the teacher came in: "You see, we had made a complete circle and ended up where we had started from." Together, the two anecdotes sum up a witty yet despairing selfawareness, mocking the genre films in which therapy is unthinkable (**The Collector**) or never works (**Vertigo**).

Left alone, the silent Boy-Burns abruptly snakes out the window, eventually reaching a rundown houseboat at a misty dockside. At a window, against the scarlet walls, his beautifully-made, blond, young

18

In Hitchcock's *Vertigo*, a twoshot of Scotty (James Stewart) and Madelaine/Judy (Kim Novak) suggests the one-sided relationship implicit in the genre.

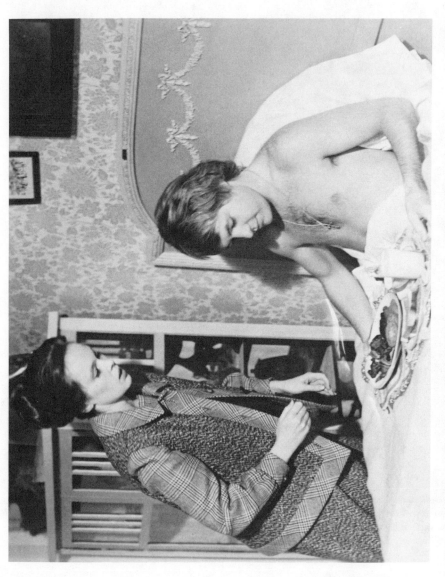

In Altman's genre-commentary *That Cold Day in the Park*, a counterpart composition of Frances (Sandy Dennis) serving The Boy (Michael Burns) restates the submerged potential for destructive obsession.

sister Nina (Susanna Benton) completes moaning sexual congress with bearded draft dodger Nick (John Garfield, Jr.).

The hippy milieu Altman now portrays again undermines the hermetic genre, a second sane alternative to ingrown, self-destructive love. At the same time, it mocks the protagonist by stylizing *uninhibited* behavior. The beautiful free-living orgasmic Nina-Benton is all poor Frances-Dennis is not: a savvy drug dealer against Frances-Dennis' stifled politeness; a family rejector versus Frances-Dennis caring for her dying mom. Yet in her way, she's as imperfect: shrill, teasing, kittenish, backtalking. In many ways the "free" Nina-Benton is the more unbalanced: immature, impatient, demanding, overbearing, Altman only partly concealing her instability behind her erotic allure. In this, he restylizes the genre's sinister lover-competitor figures (e.g., Tom Helmore's Gavin Elster in **Vertigo**, Henry Brandon's Chief Scar in **The Searchers**).

Boy-Burns odd silence is at last casually explained by his sister as a "number" he's used for many years, paradoxically his own response to an apparently unhappy home life:

> Nina-Benton: He's got this thing — he's been doing it since he was a little kid. *He doesn't talk!* I mean it — he doesn't talk *for days*.

To the trembly theme, Frances-Dennis, abandoned, wanders silent through her home's enormous, exquisite empty dark rooms: great mirrors, fine furniture, and windows of elaborately patterned translucent disc mirrors and clear lenses, all blocking off the outside. The camera often pans and focuses past her, framing elaborate mirrors or crystals, then rack-focusing to infinity. The effect, calling attention to itself, is an exaggerated counterpart of the genre's various visual suggestions of distorted emotions: the highly placed or smoothly pursuing camera in **Letter from an Unknown Woman**, the inhuman landscapes (Sequoias, surf) and vertigo-simulating-zooms in **Vertigo**: the claustrophobically-depicted basement love-prison in **The Collector**. Eerie tinkles and zithers accompany and further amplify Altman's visual madness-metaphors.

In the morning, smiling and silent, Boy-Burns suddenly appears at the door with a bag of scorched (drugged) homemade cookies, which they share. (His arbitrary appearances and vanishings comment on the genre's plot improbabilities, which unite and separate the lovers.) The two spend the day in the enormous draped living room, Frances-Dennis' hair undone, face youthfully exuberant. From here on, she is made up alternately as brighteyed, childlike, beguiling: then pale, exhausted, terribly strained — another visual genre comment.

This disjointed Dr. Jekyll and Mr. Hyde effect is only one of the interwoven comments on the film-genre's passionate insanity motif. The extreme dislocation of time is a second — the mental decline over weeks or months in **Vertigo, The Collector**, and **The Searchers** takes only six days in **That Cold Day in the Park**. Likewise, space and distance periodically dissolve; long lenses and extreme angles make the sealed off living room seem miles deep during the couple's eerie idyll.

The "games" the two carry out further mock and extend the genre's conventions. First, posing and teasing, they parody Frances-Dennis' claim of incompleteness: in one shot, the two seem to merge into an androgyne, with her head and hands, his lumpish feet. When he naps, she screams to waken him, a mouthed cigar suggesting a gender reversal.

Next, there is a sort of guessing game with a strip of cloth, the lovely Frances-Dennis giving coy encouragement to his (imagined) tries at identifying her old school tie. Her face is a naked, desperate exaggeration of female coquetry — grotesque, erotic, patheic. Finally, the beautiful woman blindfolds the boy, sounding a harmonica to lead him to her through the immense luxurious room, the woman calling him on until he grasps her. Then, in the dark red landscape, it's her turn to be blinded and spun and move cautiously through the emptiness, sensitive fingers touching fine possessions in stillness until she pulls off the cloth, to find herself alone in vast darkness.

Sexual "merging," guessing game, and hide and seek can be seen as poetic visual depictions of the genre's limits and form, the quest for ideal emotional fulfillment. As Robin Wood comments of the theme of **Vertigo**:

> [If the protagonist] represents an extreme case (we classify him by now, certainly, as a sick man) this rejection of life for an unattainable Idea is something fundamental in human nature, his sickness still, potentially our sickness.[2.3]

Sadly, the "games" also suggest the psychological case history side of the genre: implied irreparable sexual phobia, confusion and panic.

In the morning, Frances-Dennis taxies to a birth control clinic while her voice reads a note about going out and returning later. As she waits alone, the other women kid around. Tightlipped, hospital-gowned, she's fitted for a diaphragm, lying about an upcoming marriage. The dull but happy women ("You mean some men are bigger than others?" "Just like girls, they're all different!") are a third portrayal of rejected normalcy.

Meanwhile, the uninhibited, beautiful Nina-Benton, having trailed her brother, demands entrance to the apartment ("I want to see! . . . . Is this your room? *Not bad!*").

Their erotic childishness is cut against a funereal "date" of Frances-Dennis with the oldish doctor-suitor, a lawn bowling party for decaying, elderly rich. He seems to be a geriatric physician, the ultimate focus of rational civilization.

In the luxurious bath — thick towels, long tub, crystal contains of oils and bathsalts — the lovely, long-legged girl plunges into the bubblebath. Squealing at soap in her eyes, she drags the boy in jeans in with her, the two babbling about their childhood. These semi-erotic, yet innocent games are an extreme contrast to the exquisitely charged dance of frustrated yearning between Frances-Dennis and the boy. They reach their peak in the richly decorated bedroom, Nina-Benton temptingly smiling and purring to the youth: "I wish you weren't my brother . . . do you wish I wasn't your sister? C'mere — I have this stiff neck . . . . "

The boy retreats, annoyed-bewildered: "Jesus, Nina, you're really crazy!" The touch of incest is most meaningful as a clever comment on the genre; here are two people most likely to be obsessed with each other, yet both (in different ways) capable of handling the impulses consistently with their personalities. By contrast, tormented Frances-Dennis, blocked from the erotic, reflects this in her *"unnatural"* playfulness as well as adult behavior.

The moment of very attractive but lower class youth at play in an upper class bed also inverts another genre motif. Most of the obsessive destructive love films tend to the same economic context and focus: **Vertigo**'s love-object is an "imposter" millionairess mental case; a prestigious, wealthy family shaped the obsessed heroine in **Adele H**; in **The Collector** the suddenly wealthy lover-jailer at one point exclaims: "There'd be a bloomin' lot more of this if enough people had the time and money!" In ironic commentary, Altman dwells on the youthful "free" poor, showing how their own taboos and inhibitions begin to fall away when they're surrounded by the disorienting sumptuousness of wealth and class.

Outside at night, Frances-Dennis and the physician are two pure black silhouettes against the townhouse's three-story warm yellow glass center panel, a visual stylization of overcivilized emptiness (the motif recalls the use of doorways in **The Searchers** to indicate exclusion). The oldish physician tries to speak of his love, but her only response is flashes of images of the birth control clinic — her straining sensitive face, her feet in the stirrups, the physician's brisk: "Bend you knees and wiggle on down the table!"

Repeating how sorry she is, Frances-Dennis takes the blame, and when he leaves, turns her sensitive intelligent face to stare directly at the audience, as if to ask the viewer to challenge her decision. Such a moment comments on the genre, whose protagonists always have no doubts about their extraordinary obsessions. Yet, in her great seriousness, it also stylizes the way genre protagonists see life as pure Idea: the unattractive geriatric doctor is a symbol of compromising "sensible" twentieth century reasonableness, not simply one of the genre's sensible unwanted lovers (e.g., Barbara Bel Geddes-Midge in **Vertigo**).

At the guestroom door, Frances-Dennis speaks endlessly to a dim shape in the bed, blond hair peeking from the covers. Speaking of her loneliness and lonely dying senile mother, who also talked on and on, she suggests an anti-genre self-awareness of her growing instability.

> Frances-Dennis: Old people disgust me with their feelings, sometimes — I wonder, do you think I'm old . . . I wish I knew if you were really asleep, or just pretending. You are very clever at pretending not to understand. Do you mind if I lay down on the bed? . . . . I want to tell you something. If you feel you want to make love to me, it's all right. I want you to make love to me . . . . "

The sequence is an archetypical genre turning point, a mistaken or mistimed declaration of love which makes catastrophe certain. Molly Haskell skillfully analyzes the moment's counterpart in **Letter from an Unknown Woman**:

> The exquisite pain of this scene, of her humiliating surrender to a love that is so unreciprocated, is balanced in the Ophuls' vision and sublimely sensitive direction, by the sense of Jourdan's general depletion and decline, but mainly by the counterweight of Fontaine's obsessiveness, the stubbornness of her will to love this one man against all reason and logic, her certainty that she can "save" him; by that total defiance of social rules, she becomes not only the architect of her fate, but the precipitator of her downfall, and thus a tragic heroine.[2.4]

In **That Cold Day in the Park**, this key moment is not inverted via comedy or irony. Rather, it's stylized by the brevity of the affair, the woman's imperfect self-insights into her loneliness, the boy's ignorant good-heartedness — all sustaining both poetry and pathology. (Frances-Dennis: "You are very clever at pretending not to understand.")

Frances-Dennis brushes his hair — and screams, for there is no one in the bed, just a blanketed shape made from pillows, and a doll's head placed so blond hair shows.

The "betrayal" and pathological response point up this genre's characteristic plot device: the obsessed lover's apparent "betrayal," resulting in even more extreme pathology. This takes various forms. In **Letter from an Unknown Woman** and **The Story of Adele H**, the driven females simply cannot hold the love object's attentions; in **Vertigo** and **The Searchers**, the reciprocated love is distrusted or simply "blanked out"; in **The Collector**, the unloved mad protagonist interprets an escape attempt as a "reversal" of feelings. To make his particular anti-genre point, Altman's **That Cold Day in the Park** has a "betrayal" that seems simply a symbolic expression of independence. Later dialogue supports this interpretation. (At the same time, the doll seems the idea of the childish "competitor" Nina-Benton.)

The disturbed woman's prolonged screams, however, show that she has taken the mockingly empty bed as a terrible rejection and "betrayal." This is the genre's story-turning point, sytlized yet stressed — the inability of the obsessed lover to deal with the other's contradictory passions.

Screaming and shadowed doll dissolves to a bright, noisy coffee house, one table holding the Boy-Burns, Nina-Benton and Nick-Garfield. The three conduct a shouted, half-drunken conversation, Nick-Garfield reading a sex-aid ad in a croon: "for funloving people, it gives a slippery sensual effect." The impression of incompatibility of natures is heightened by the Boy-Burns dim understanding that: "She's got a very strange attitude towards sex. She makes a big deal out of it." The line is comic as an anti-genre comment, an attempt to restore proportions; one can ponder the lover victims of **The Collector**, **Vertigo** or **Letter to an Unknown Woman** using it to describe their obsessed pursuers.

A moment later, the young people quarrel, and the Boy-Burns runs angrily off, a black silhouette against the great colored plumes of the square's floodlit fountains. The shot repeats the civilization-drained-silhouette visual motif, paralleling the boy's sympathetic attraction for the sensitive, disturbed woman — the intermittent *folie a deux* idea of the genre.

In her home, the Boy-Burns doesn't notice the smashed doll, but lets the cool woman run a bath for him, his face bewildered at faint pounding sounds outside. Dressed, he finds new "inside" locks on the doors, the window frames crudely nailed shut. The two lovers confront each other, straining faces framed in her bedroom mirror. Abruptly, for the first time, two-thirds of the way through the film, he finally speaks to her:

> Boy-Burns: (harshly, defensively) . . . . Don't think I can't get out of here. I can get out anytime I want . . . and if you think by keeping me here, I'm gonna get in bed with you or anything like that you're wrong. If I want a girl I'll just go out and get one myself — and I might not come back.
>
> Frances-Dennis: (placating, frightened) I'm sorry . . . I'm so sorry. I don't want you to be angry with me. I want things to stay the way they are. You can understand that, can't you? I — I can't let you go. Not now.

Frances-Dennis then turns from him and goes out into the night, seeking a "girl" for him. The scene is a genre archetype, a conflicted protagonist seeking a grotesque "solution" in **Adele H.** and **Letter**, prostitute surrogates; in **The Searchers** a sibling as a mate, in **Vertigo** the guardian role. In melodramas, the conflict is "externalized" via blocking obstacles (e.g. **Love Story**'s disapproving father, who must be "won over").

In Vancouver's "sexual underground," the frightened, upper-class woman stammers and flounders, yet for all her undignified desperation gets help and soon a prostitute for the boy. The tour of the "Combat Zone" completes the film's casual profile of society's carnality: orgasmic irresponsible youth; repressed inhibited ruling class; matter-of-fact families "getting" birth control; the tormented, ground-down deviate underclass. This "tour" runs strongly against the genre's characteristic mood: in describing **Vertigo**, for example, Wood points out that "the film conveys a terrifying impression of external reality as a sort of fragile shell which we pierce at our peril; once beyond it, we are whirling uncontrolled in chaos."[2.7]

To the purple theme, Frances-Dennis' upper face is shown in the taxi's mirror, floating amid abstracted city lights. The image realizes the genre's mood, summed up beautifully by JoAnn Crawford:

> [The protagonist's] madness comes as no surprise; remarkable however is the strength of will which remains even as she becomes more detached from the world . . . she is the creator, not the victim, of a self imposed exile and tortuous obsession.[2.8]

Likewise, it is remarked of **The Searchers'** protagonist:

> What marks Ethan off is his intense pursuit of single linear goals. He refuses to enter complex societal relationships that include contradiction. Ethan is only good for "one oath at a time."[2.9]

The thin, raincoated young prostitute Sylvia (Luana Anders), with a simple-sly face under feathery blond hair, is led through the dark, sumptuous apartment, peering at the rich furnishings. Abruptly Frances-Dennis and the Boy-Burns are framed against the wall to one side of a door, the whore a totally black silhouette on the other — the society-drained husk visual motif. Frances-Dennis abruptly speaks in her apologetic whisper, and the other two are locked in the bedroom:

> Sylvia-Anders: (with alley-cat sophistication) She one of them voy-airs? . . . . But *you* look okay.
>
> Boy-Burns: (patiently) She's just a little mixed up, that's all . . . . Twenty dollars, very generous — I mean to me, not you.

Outside, Frances-Dennis sits blankfaced and alone among her fine furniture and walls of blind lens and mirrors, listening to their blurred voices and laughter. The moment mocks the vicarious "sexual participation" by the obsessed heroines in **Adele H** and **Letter from an Unknown Woman**. At the same time, the heroine's detached fascination with the couple, suggests Kael's summing up of the genre theme:

> She has given herself over to love so completely that the actual man doesn't exist for her anymore. She doesn't even know him . . . the craziness doesn't cancel out the romanticism — it complete it.[2.10]

Interestingly, it also implies the very opposite view: the self-destructive lover as *unable* to ever fully trust, to instinctively accept unvouchsafed love, as implied in the agonized climactic monologue of the **Vertigo** protagonist:

> Scottie-Stewart: . . . Did he *train* you? Did he *rehearse* you? Did he tell you exactly what to *do* and what to *say*? You were a very apt pupil, weren't you? You were a very apt pupil! But why did you pick on *me*? Why *me*?

Suddenly, screaming and laughing, Frances-Dennis is in the dark room, bouncing and crawling atop the lump of bedclothes that coves the other two. For a confused moment, she seems a delighted-hysterical child desperate to join in, but there is a big kitchen knife in her fist, and she jabs deeply and repeatedly into the shouting mass, killing someone. Then, the Boy-Burns reaches the door and throws on the lights, revealing Frances-Dennis blind-eyed atop the bedclothes and the dying prostitute. The murder is Altman's anti-genre commentary, illuminating the poetry pathology of the genre as the obsessed protagonist's desperate efforts to manage their enormous hostility towards the possibility of sexual love.

In fact, the outstanding members of the genre similarly transcend its theme and motifs, notably in **Adele H**'s "willing away" of the real lover, of **Vertigo**'s protagonist's terminal agonized-antagonism and its possible part in the death of Madeleine-Novak. But Altman's anti-genre work strips away the genre's carefully built up romantic tone: at heart this obsessed lover must have some mad, passionate release. In this, it resembles **The Searchers**, in which the protagonist, instead of grieving for his murdered real lost love, obsessively tracks down a loved innocent, in time intending to murder her.

In the conclusion, the Boy-Burns runs naked through the apartment's dark locked corridors, to the distorted theme: an accelerating zither and windchimes. Abruptly, Frances-Dennis stands facing him, eyes-wide and bright, a patient sweet child comforting another:

> Frances-Dennis: Oh, don't be frightened. Oh, I'm so sorry. There's nothing to be frightened of now. I've told that

girl to go . . . you don't have to be afraid, you can stay with me now, oh, please . . . I want to make love to you . . . .

Characteristically, genre films end either with the annihilation of the love object (**Vertigo, Letter from an Unknown Woman, The Collector, Adele H**), or the murder of the "competitor" as a sort of substitute (**The Searchers, Taxi Driver, Lolita**). This suggests the concealed heart of the genre is the murderous working out of the loveless obsession. By making the key death arbitrary (Frances-Dennis could have stabbed either), Altman reveals the cold heart of the love genre, flayed bare: *liebestod*. Perhaps de Rouchment has best summed up Altman's view of the genre:

Most people go after the kind of love that promises the most feeling . . . passion means suffering, something undergone, the mastery of fate over a free and responsible person . . . The way passion has persisted through the centuries should cause us to look to the future with deep despondency.[2.12]

M*A*S*H* (1970)

From its first moments, **M*A*S*H** throws into question the basic war film genre theme: the growth of individuals into community and conventional wisdom through hardship,[3.1] as in **The Big Parade**'s characters' "vitalism in responding to and affirming each other."[3.2] We begin in No Man's Land; silent low angle views of the battleground with its wounded and dying making any possible community appear futile. Sympathy-detaching longshots show the loading of rescue helicopters' exterior stretchers, as the film will view with detachment the genre's traditional motifs: combat as heroism, the bravely mad warrior, successful first trial by fire, generous G.I.s. Now, as the rescue machines skim over the landscape, the genre's traditional patriotic score is rendered with psychopathological skepticism:

> Through early morning fog I see,
> Visions of the things to be;
> The pains that are withheld for me
> I realize that I can see.
> That suicide is painless,
> It brings on many changes
> And I can take or leave it as I please.

Immediately, warfare as an education into the benefits of society is turned away from rejected. Visually and aurally, war is shown as the individual's mad choice of isolated death. Any social profundities are denied:

> A brave man once requested me
> To answer questions that are key
> Is it to be, or not to be
> And I replied — oh, why ask me?

The stretcher-bearing copters descend onto large pyramids of earth, up which hurry the army doctors and nurses. To the lazy piano theme, they offload the mutilated, placing them on trucks and jeeps, walking alongside to steady the stretchers of the ragtag convoy. The shots catch an instinctive, compassionate efficiency in the healers —

"medicine men," who wordlessly cooperate. The moment suggests a second anti-genre theme: war as bureaucracy, highlighted by the unnecessary clumsy orders of Col. Henry Blake (Roger Bowen), all of which are aniticipated by Corporal "Radar" O'Riley (Gary Berghoff) (their voices overlap), and all missed by Corporal Velmer (David Arkin). The anti-genre theme of war as the ultimate bureaucracy — communications failures leavened with E.S.P. — is recast with a long pompous quote from General MacArthur about leaving his Korean forces with high morale, followed immediately by President Eisenhower's anxious "I will go to Korea."

The film's title, **M*A*S*H**, an acronym for Mobile Army Surgical Hospital, reinforces both anti-genre themes; lifetaking and lifesaving are so mixed together the total enterprise makes little sense, and a clumsy obfuscating official way of naming things and doing them is neatly capsulized.

The film's main characters are introduced in ways that further undermine the genre theme of war as a journey to affirming social maturity. Told to wait for a motorpool jeep, tall gangling Captain "Hawkeye" Pierce (Donald Sutherland) removes the officer's bars from his fatigues, and pulls on a soldier's shapeless cap, so that handsome drawling Captain "Duke" Forrest (Tom Skeritt) mistakes him for their driver. With a Harpo Marx whistle, "Hawkeye"-Sutherland guns the jeep and, a la Marx Brothers fantasy, their angry pursuers blow a tire and begin socking each other. The brief scene helps build the anti-genre mood, comic anarchism overturning war movie motifs.

Arriving, "Duke"-Skerritt and "Hawkeye"-Sutherland are greeted by their commander in the mess tent, having already described them as very sharp surgeons. To confirm this, "Hawkeye"-Sutherland, in a few moments, gets the key details of the surgical setup. Yet, the two admit they've spent the day drinking, one makes a pass at a married nurse, and the other admits a theft (Commander: "I understand you stole a jeep," Hawkeye: "No sir, no, as a matter of fact it's right out there"). The effect is to undermine the genre's moral and characterological motifs; instead of ignorant recruits or weary wise veterans, the heroes are sharp, sexy, likable rascals.

Likewise, the war film genre landscape — dull, stable homefront versus chaotic, lethal No Man's Land — is replaced by permanently casual, temporary, camouflage-netted tentscapes holding relaxed fatigue-dressed men and women in shades of dusty brown and army greens. Together, characters and environment redraw the genre's "morally didactic terrain" into a sketchy, alternately relaxed or intense semi-chaos, held together by habit and routine, but allowing for comic rebelliousness and individuality. **M*A*S*H** has in its first minutes established the standard comic war genre film milieu

(**Operation Madball, No Time for Sergeants, Mr. Roberts**).[3.2] Shortly afterwards, continued careful preparation permit it to take an absolutely anti-genre position via four theatre-within-film set pieces.

In contrast to the mess tent camaraderie, the first shot of the protagonists' tentmate Major Frank Burns (Robert Duval) is one neurotic, bloodshot eye surrounded by darkness. Major Burns-Duval is teaching their Korean messboy to read English, using the doomiest part of the Bible (Korean teenage voice: "Though-I-walk-through-the-Valley-of-the-Shadow-of-Death . . ."). The warrior is shown doing the right thing in a negative context, a central anti-genre notion to be elaborated throughout the film. This key anti-genre device, the sanctimonious warrior together with his antidote, is shown here for the first time as the hip outsiders give the boy some girlie magazines to learn from instead. ("Duke"-Skeritt: "It's easier to read looking at pictures . . . ," Teenager: "May I leave now major!"). While incidentally mocking the genre's love of local children, the scene foreshadows M*A*S*H's cruel dissection of several motion picture archetype warriors, and the warfilm genre itself, as embodiments of destructive hypocrisy.

The war genre as hypocrisy is re-emphasized in a scene that has the two weary surgeons sipping cocktails while Major Burns-Duval repeats the Lord's Prayer on his knees, a teetotaler believing he can humiliate the social drinkers. He concludes by blessing "the supreme commander on the field" and even the one in Washington, associating the genre's patriotism and obedience with religious hypocrisy. In response, "Duke"-Skerritt and "Hawkeye"-Sutherland exit, raise a rake to the overcast sky, and parade with a growing crowd of soldiers chanting "Onward Christian Soldiers." The sequence not only emphasizes the war-as-sanctimoniousness idea, it prepares us to accept the heroes extremely subversive behavior. The sequence's last image is of Major Burns-Duval's bloodshot eye again hanging furiously alone in the dark.

A third, stronger anti-genre stroke against war's sanctimoniousness turns up in the surgical tent, brilliant white and full of bloody meat, with several surgeons at work and chaplain-Auberjonois administering last rites. Abruptly, "Duke"-Skeritt calls for the priest to help his team:

> "Duke"-Skeritt: I'm sorry Dago, but this man is still alive and
> that other man is dead and that's a fact. Will you hold it
> with two fingers, please? (to himself) Hell!

Thus, religion and warrior-spirit, already associated, are shown again to be anti-life delusions, this further emphasized by the sympathetic chaplain character's abandoning his rites to help save lives.

In yet a fourth undercutting of false feelings, "Hawkeye"-Sutherland and attractive WAC Lt. "Dish" (Joanne Pflug) make out briefly on the officer's tent pooltable, the nurse murmuring that she's married, for which the surgeon-officer has a response:

> "Hawkeye"-Sutherland: I'm married too, I love my wife, if she was here I would be with her, there is no question of loving someone, only of caring . . . those are the vows you make when you're with someone.

Significantly, they abandon the preliminaries to lovemaking when they're called on to help in a lifesaving medical emergency.

These beginning scenes are low key yet vital preparation for **M*A*S*H**'s attack on the war film genre, the undercutting of the whole array of film warrior treatments and film warrior virtues. At ths point, **M*A*S*H** still somewhat resembles the anti-war films of the 1960s[3.3] (e.g., **Dr. Strangelove, How I Won the War, Oh What a Lovely War**) in its military milieu, holding both sympathetic and hypocritical elements. Altman's film, however, wisely emphasizes the humanistic over the cheaply satirical.

As the loudspeaker pipes a Japanese "Chattanooga Shoeshine Boy," "Hawkeye"-Sutherland and "Duke"-Skerritt meet their new tentmate, surgeon "Trapper John" McIntyre (Elliot Gould). In a comic exchange, "Trapper-John"-Gould won't reveal his background or even true name, but delights them by magically producing an olive for his martini. The act exemplifies the anti-genre style and resourcefulness with which **M*A*S*H** replaces the conventional war film's courage and loyalty as virtues. Significantly, the three "heroes" of the anti-genre war film all have names from alien societies: "Hawkeye" (Native American); "Duke" (European royalty), and "Trapper John" (mountain man). The non-American names suggest the anthropological perspectives employed in undercutting genre themes and conventions.

The next scenes, brief anti-genre jokes and wit, build the mood: operating room kidding of hypocritical U.S. doctors ("An enlisted man? — Make the stiches big!"), G.I.s enviously peeking at a showering well-endowed dental surgeon ("Boy, I'd sure like to see *that* angry!"); mocking introductions in the middle of surgery ("How's the operation going?" "Are you kidding!")

In a quiet tent,the war-as-hypocrisy anti-genre motif is nailed down as Major Burns-Duval leans over a comatose patient, casually asks a young orderly for some help, then savages the boy. "It's too late, Boone, you killed him!" As Burns-Duval covers the man's face, the teenager bows and weeps. So, as soon as work is over, "Trapper John"-Gould knocks down the hypocritical sadistic officer. "Duke"-Skerritt explains to their commander:

> "Duke"-Skeritt: Frank Burns is a menace! Any time a patient croaks on him, he says it's *GAWD*'s will or somebody else's fault . . . . This time he blamed it on some kid who

was stupid enough to believe it.

The anti-genre point is not just that leaders may be sadistic or hypocritical, but that subordinates who submit to them are implicated in their own pain as well.

Not all of M*A*S*H is thematically focused. For example, the next sequence slowly pans the hospital enclave: fatigued figures amid the green-brown tents pitched seemingly minutes ago in the unbeautiful valley; Colonel Blake-Bower flyfishing; the loudspeaker giving a staticky Japanese: "I'll be Down to Get You in a Taxi Honey." Plotless moments like this one are orchestrated to let the viewer relax, and prevent the film from becoming an aesthete's fever dream.

Final preparation for the four large anti-genre set pieces to follow is a scene between "Hawkeye"-Sutherland and Chief Nurse Hoolihan (Sally Kellerman), already hinted to be a smug prude. Nurse Hoolihan-Kellerman is set up as a female counterpart to Major Burns-Duval ("I like to think of the *army* as my home") who admires the incompetent surgeon and criticizes "Hawkeye"-Sutherland for letting nurses call him by his first name. A hypocritical match for Major Burns-Duval, "Hawkeye"-Sutherland calls her "a regular army clown."

What follows is for many the film's highlight, a brilliant working out of the anti-genre view of the war film as hypocrisy. It commences when Colonel Blake-Bowen is called away, putting Major Burns-Duval in charge. Night is the occasion for a spontaneous drunken party: a mess tent crowded with yelling, beer-swilling medics; a P.A. system "Hail to the Chief" greeting "Trapper John"-Gould, carried in cockeyed in an Uncle Sam hat.

> "Trapper John"-Gould: No food — sex! I want sex! That one! The sultry bitch with the fire in her eye. (Points to Nurse Hoolihan-Kellerman.) Take off her robe and bring her to me!

The anti-genre treatment of war film as hypocrisy is comically extended, with the glum U.S. national patriot figure "Uncle Sam" revealed as an uninhibited sensualist-fraud, with overtones of a brutal harem master. This is a key moment, visually suggesting Altman's film's anti-genre strategy: illuminating the ridiculousness of the war film genre by parallelling it to society's sexual hypocrisy.

In a quiet tent, Major Burns-Duval and Nurse Hoolihan-Kellerman, nastyfaced, write the commanding general about the M*A*S*H's "unwholesomeness," using the party which he "runs" to prove the point. They clinch and mail the letter together, as the drunken brawl goes on in other parts of the camp. Together again, the pair's romantic attraction is couched in their hypocritical mindset:

Hoolihan-Kellerman: We've grown very close in a short time.

Burns-Duval: It's not just chance — *he* meant us to find each other.

Hoolihan-Kellerman: (embracing him) *His will be done!*

As they move clumsily onto a cot, shy corporal Radar-Burshoff peeks through the plastic window, then shoves a big silver microphone under the love bower.

At once, the supremely private act is made into a public spectacle, very much the counterpart of the war film genre itself (which deals, after all, with the individual's clumsy attempts to survive and accommodate his fellows in an intimate, emotional life situation involving extraordinary self esteem, one of the two basic "tests of manhood"). Shocked and surprised, although prepared by early sequences, the viewer can quickly join the film's other characters in their responses, at the same time being implicated by them.

In the almost pitch-black communications tent, for example, highlighted faces — a grinning Black sergeant, a seemingly sexually excited nurse, the purselipped Radar-Burshoff — listen to the lovers' murmurs and groans. The Chaplain fusses in, then retreats in embarrassment as he gradually realizes the broadcast is not "The Battling Bickersons" (Altman suggesting the unstylish moral view). Others treat the "sexual combat" as a sports event or as pure melodrama ("he's such a *sweet* thing"). In a few moments, the sex act, like the war genre, is stylized into crude spectacle, humiliating and insulting to both participants and audience.

In a final mockery, "Trapper John"-Gould puts the voices on the camp public address system, so the groaning, sighing and pleas hang over the misty tents in the darkness ("My lips are hot — kiss my hot lips!"). The lovers' intimacies penetrate cardgames, operating theatre and cafeteria, all to raunchy comments. At last, a feedback effect distorts the words into piercing, whistling echoes, and the pair finally catch on. To a Japanese-worded "My Blue Heaven," the sequence cuts off.

The "sexual combat" sequence is a unique anti-war genre statement, criticizing the mass media's "test of manhood" genre by creating its sexual counterpart, and showing us how quickly we take pleasure in its cruel mockery of imperfect individuals at their most vulnerable moments.

In the morning, Major Burns-Duval and Nurse Hoolihan-Kellerman try to breakfast in the mess tent as if nothing had happened. Here the war genre warriors, patriotic and brave (read sanctimonious and hypocritical) are laughed at anew. Nurse Hoolihan-Kellerman, nearly hysterical, is simply scared off by "Trapper John"-Gould bumping into her and pretending to be a homosexual ("What's the matter with *her* today?"). Traditionally a contemptible type, his "gay" successfully mocks her normal sexuality like a boor provoking a shell-shocked veteran. In the same manner, Major Burns-Duval is savaged for hypocrisy about his concealed stateside marriage as well as his "battlefield experiences":

> "Hawkeye"-Sutherland: Does that big ass of hers move around much, or does it kind of just lie there? Would you say she was a moaner, Frank? (Clenches teeth, works lips) Does she go huh-huh-huh-huh?

Unable to accommodate his exposed sensuality and daylight dignity, Major Burns-Duval leaps at "Hawkeye"-Sutherland and must be subdued.

In the next sequence, to a mocking Japanese "Sayonara," a straightjacketed Major Burns-Duval is loaded into a jeep. "Duke"-Skerritt, "Hawkeye"-Sutherland, and "Trapper John"-Gould stand by their tents, grimfaced, arms crossed on chests, proud alien tribesmen watching the casting out of a brave who has failed the "test of manhood." For a moment, the jeep pauses; Burns-Duval sits behind the pale flames from a garbage can, a U.S. flag flapping overhead, a labored visual metaphor of the war movie genre archetype's hellish role. Then, he is taken away.

This key sequence, unlike anything in the war genre's tales of combat and conflict, metaphorically demolishes its central theme. Most basically, war is not shown as a bloody but meaningful education into maturity and wisdom in a supportive society. Rather, the survivors are those canny outsiders who can maintain their own style and savvy, and collaborate to deal with the self-deluded non-survivors. Courage and loyalty, the genre hero's touchstones, are shown up in this anti-genre fable; rather, the real soldier would do wiser to cultivate stoicism and style to endure grim war's mortification.

In passing, it is as a profoundly "guilt relieving" metaphor for the warrior's life-or-death real struggles that the "sexual combat" and several other sequences in M*A*S*H obtain their comic force. The comedy lies in the humiliating circumstances being extended to the edge of real unbearable permanent degradation, then the tension being "relieved" as merely cruel joking. As I've written elsewhere:

> A sense of humor starts with a finely developed sense of proportion; comedy, by exquisite exaggeration, makes us laugh by showing when we've gone too far. Bergson sees this as when the gap between body and spirit become grotesque; Freud as when we "save out emotional energy" by neatly handling emotional situations. Both would agree that war and death have enormous comic potential. To the tough minded, death itself is the body's funniest trick, about which the

noble spirit can do nothing. The spirit proclaims: "Ah, next I'm going to – " and the body keels over like a big dumb animal. "How grotesque!" Bergson would say. "That sums it up!" Freud would comment. Thus war comedies are a fine laboratory for exploring the many species of the comic muse.[3.4]

Altman's film next goes on to mock and deride a second war film genre motif: the film warrior treated as madman/suicide (e.g., **The Steel Helmet, The Halls of Montezuma, The Dirty Dozen, Twelve O'Clock High**). This sequence commences when "Hawkeye"-Sutherland is approached by mild Chaplain-Auberjonois, faced with a problem he cannot even discuss involving the hospital unit's "sexual athlete," dental surgeon "Painless" Walt Waldowski (John Shuck).

The "Dental Don Juan of Detroit" is mock-suicidal, his slab-featured face despairing: "I got these three girls I'm engaged to, (But) if a man isn't a man anymore . . . . " A single failure to perform and some fat psychiatry texts have convinced him of his lifelong coverup: he's a latent homosexual. His self-claimed irreversible pathology is an anti-genre comic counterpart of the many war films built around a hero's battle madness. (Again in Altman's film, sex and fighting are the "tests of manhood"). Mocking the genre film's self-destructive mad heroes, "Painless"-Shuck strolls into a poker game and announces: "I know you fellows have been talking about me. I came in to tell you I'm going to commit suicide . . . . " With equanimity, "Trapper John"-Gould immediately offers him a "black capsule" ("it worked for Hitler and Eva Braun!").

Within the war film genre, the mad warrior is often treated as both a tragic and romantic figure, his indifference to survival allowing him to take suicidal risks and accomplish prodigies of heroism. Altman's film, in a comic anti-genre turn, reverses this motif, making us applaud the mad hero's return to society. This comic rite commences when, in surgical gowns and stethoscopes, their wine in laboratory flasks, their tables arranged in a Last Supper tableau, (lifted from **The Dirty Dozen**) a dozen medics pose in the misty night with the dentist. "Hawkeye"-Sutherland announces gently that they have come to make a final farewell to "Painless"-Shuck; "Duke"-Skerritt next praises the suicidal hero's decision to "Do a little recon work for us all." "Hawkeye"-Sutherland adds, mock-admiringly, that: "Painless volunteered – that's what we give the highest medals for. That's what being a soldier is all about."

Again turning the genre upside down, the film's theme now justifies suicide as suicide, not hidden as heroism:

The game of life is hard to play
I'm going to lose it anyway
The loser's card I'll someday play
And that is all I have to say.

The only way to win is cheat
And lay it down before I'm beat
And given another man my seat
For that's the only thing I leave.

For suicide is painless
It brings on many changes
And I can take or leave it as I please.

Mockingly, as in some pre-Christian or non-Western culture, Altman's film has "Painless"-Shuck's friends place gifts — whiskey, sex magazines — in the coffin in which he lies sleeping and smiling, as they give their farewell regrets (e.g., young orderly: "Wasting your whole education!"). The anti-genre implication that nobody, least of all his friends and fellow soldiers, wants a madly brave (read suicidal) hero instead of their familiar companion. As with the "sexual combat" anti-genre playlet, this one, too, is carried out as theater-within-film, the audience encouraged to identify with the "reasonable" participants in the ceremony.

Still later, vapors rising into the purplish-black sky over the seemingly deserted camp, "Hawkeye"-Sutherland stands before a redlit medical tent. Lovely WAC Lt. "Dish"-Pflug, leaving the next day, murmurs in his arms: "You're just gonna have to stop using logic about why I shouldn't go to bed with you." But "Hawkeye"-Sutherland offers instead a "rare privilege" that will beautifully complete the anti-genre rite: a chance to restore a human being's life. "Painless needs you for therapy — and it certainly wouldn't do you any harm either!" In the candlelit tent, to exultant organ music, he lifts the sheet so that she can observe the "Dental Don Juan," the music rising to a religious crescendo, a comic tabernacle of anti-genre sexual valour.

At dawn, the brisk nurse jeeps to her copter, even as "Painless"-Shuck announces cheerfully that he " — can't waste time, got two jaws to rebuild!" The leggy "Dish"-Pflug is visible behind the copter's scratchy plexiglass — as she ascends, so does the theme — and the camera zooms to her smiling face.

The third sexual metaphor for a war film genre motif is perhaps the most imperfect: several of the outsider heroes deciding to "test" if nurse Hoolihan-Kellerman is a "true blond" by exposing her in the shower. The incident can be viewed as an anti-genre mockery of the "trial by fire" motif in the genre; examples include the No Man's Land rescues (viz., **Birth of a Nation, The Big Parade, Air Force**), and "Last Stands" (**Wake Island, The Steel Helmet**).[3.5] In this comic anti-genre counterpart, we watch the lonely, detached hero-to-be-figure strolling with the other **M*A*S*H** nurses, all of whom are diverted from the showers to sit with the doctors as Hoolihan-Kellerman goes inside the crude wood and canvas structure (more theater within film). With a drum roll and a clash of garbage-can-top/cymbals, the canvas wall flies upwards revealing a naked, soapy Hoolihan-Kellerman sprawling on the wooden boards in embarrassment — as the nurses run towards her, now sympathetic; it's clear she has at last won acceptance.

The central (and anti-genre) point of the sequence — without which it would be merely cruel, sour and only slightly humorous — is not her embarrassment. Rather, it is the following moments, with a furious Hoolihan-Kellerman storming into Colonel Blake-Bowen's tent shrieking: "You let them get away with everything! If you don't turn them over to the M.P.s, I'm going to resign my commission!" The commander character, in bed with a happy nurse ("More wine, dear?"), disgustedly tells her to go ahead and resign. The anti-genre point is that even the high command doesn't much believe in war film ideas of the valorous and responsible officer-gentleman; it's up to the individual to learn how to protect his own dignity (and life) as best he can. This is suggested by Hoolihan-Kellerman's crying-mutter: "My commision, my commission . . . . " as she turns away, shocked at the facts but self-possessed enough not to actually give it up. Not prominent in the last third of the film, Nurse Hoolihan-Kellerman is shown in a few glimpses which suggest she has assimilated her anti-genre "trial by fire."

Next, a brief sequence has "Hawkeye"-Sutherland medicating his Korean messboy so he'll be judged 4-F by the local draft board, until a shrewd native physician notes that the youth worked in a **M*A*S*H** unit and smilingly informs the Americans: "You'd better say goodbye to him now." The anti-genre point is the reversal of the cliched "childish or monstrous natives" of the genre. While waiting in the jeep, "Hawkeye"-Sutherland is filmed by a spunky patronizing woman combat reporter, the idiotic, superficial interview format (she yells questions as she films from a passing jeep) suggesting a directorial awareness of the medium's limitations. The director's own constant grating awareness of genre conventions is suggested by the braying hospital public address unit, which is constantly, crudely plugging old war movies to be shown in the camp (e.g., "This week's movie will be **When Willie Comes Marching Home** — the biggest parade of laughs of World War II!").

Still another anti-genre sequence follows, this one mocking the "benevolent U.S. soldiers" motif (a la **A Bell for Adano**). It starts with "Hawkeye"-Sutherland and "Trapper John"-Gould playing comic golf on the helicopter landing field (another sendup of heroic physicians who can't get out of their plutocratic habits). A flying machine comes tornadoing in with an urgent request: a Congressman's son lies seriously wounded in an Army hospital in Tokyo, and stateside experts have convinced the politico that "Trapper John"-Gould is the best physician to save him. The idea is an anti-genre joke on the upper class genre G.I.s, notably the hero of **The Big Parade**, but also members of the "ethnically balanced" World War II squads, who insist on being treated "the same as everyone else."

Briskly, in brilliantly-colored golfing clothes, the two as "silly ass" Englishmen sweep into the hospital. Putting down the pompous administrator, Col. Merrill (J.B. Douglas), they promptly save the patrician G.I., who is never characterized (rather the ugly prerequisites of the powerful are taken as a fact of life). At the same time, between comic bits ("Hawkeye"-Sutherland: "I am Dr. Jekyll — this is Mr. Hyde"), their anaesthetist asks their help for a prostitute's sick illegitimate Japanese-American baby. Again, the symmetrical grim truth of lower class mixed-birth, abandoned children is given with a minimum of melodrama, a reversal of the genre's cliche of local adoring kids being adopted by soft-hearted U.S. G.I.s.

Instead of bleeding-heart Americans, "Hawkeye"-Sutherland must win over the stodgy nurses ("We got him, we don't want him, but we don't feel we can back away"). The two physicians spend a cheery night at the whorehouse, incidently mocking the glamorous hygienic "nightclubs" of the Korean war epics (e.g., **The Bridge at Toko-Ri, Men of the Fighting Lady**). When bureaucrat Col. Merrill-Douglas finds them in the operating room with the Asian-American baby and objects, the anti-genre opposite of the tough but sympathetic occupation leaders (e.g., **A Bell for Adano**), they sedate him, then take blackmail-potential snapshots of the fat, bewildered officer waking up in bed with a smiling young Korean whore.

At this point in the film, there is an unstressed but very powerful and suggestive shot. As the two surgeons' helicopter unloads at the M*A*S*H, we see their absurdly brightly clothed legs stepping from the helicopter, while on the ground nearby are two stunned casualties in torn dirty khaki. The shot seems to sum up the film's anti-genre attitude: death is inevitable, but individual honest style and craft are what will sustain each of us. Supporting this, there are no scenes showing the grateful beneficiaries of the physicians' lifesaving work; like idealized artists, they make their efforts for their own sake.

Upon their return, "Hawkeye"-Sutherland and "Trapper John"-

Gould find "Hot Lips" Hoolihan-Kellerman has indeed been "blooded." In their tent with "Duke"-Skerritt, she zips out in a Groucho crouch covered by a big towel as the two doctors make scolding finger motions.

The last part of the film is devoted to a fourth anti-genre metaphor, a football game whose progress parallels the war film genre's gradual corruption and decline. It starts with a visit by tough worldly General Hammond (G. Wood) (to his aide: "Check this place out — see what the nurses are like"). The sly, bluff, old warrior is interested in getting Colonel Blake-Bowen to set up a hospital unit football team, then betting on it.

> General Hammond-Wood: Special services says it's one of the best gimmicks we've got to keep the American way of life going in Asia.
> Colonel Bowen-Blake: Betting?
> General Hammond-Wood: No — football!

The brief comic exchange suggests the corrupting nature of any "entertainment" in both shaping minds and extracting dollars.

The two officers' conversations all stress one of the film's anti-genre motifs: war as a bureaucratic game rather than a courageous struggle, the high command so mixed up and/or indifferent that even victories or alarming reports of possible defeat don't hold their attention:

> General Hammond-Wood: Henry, you were so concerned about the battle of Old Baldy. Well, it's all over.
> Colonel Bowen-Blake: Oh, that's great, General! Who won?
> General Hammond-Wood: Oh, by the way, I have a report here from your chief nurse. I find it hard to believe.
> Colonel Bowen-Blake: Don't believe it then, General!

In fact, the Colonel is shown to spend most of his time flyfishing (another rich U.S. doctor joke), while the general is mostly busy coaching the football teams, the anti-genre opposites of the war movie's obsessed and driven commanders (e.g., **Command Decision, Twelve O'Clock High, In Harm's Way**).

"Hawkeye"-Sutherland sees the football idea as a way to make some easy money, and uses the bureaucracy to insure victory, requesting a particular surgeon who is also an ex-professional football star. Practice with the Afro-American Dr. "Spearchucker" Jones (Fred Williamson) mocks the "integrated" war film of the 1950s (Col. Blake-Bowen: "We're all the same on the playing field — uh, officers and men alike!"). Quick cuts of the grotesque padded uniforms, clumsy non-athletes, rah-rah music, here and later suggest the ugly "stylization" of "entertainment." Likewise, there is a sort of aesthetic-moral decline of the Panlike-Chaplinesque outsider heroes to clever, money-hungry "team players." These elements implicitly

40

parallel the genre film's treatment of warfare.

Once the game begins, the subtle parallel of this entertainment to the war film genre is maintained. The team strategy, like the dramatist's, is to leave out the "pro" or reversal factor till half-time, rolling up the odds so the audience's judgment causes them to bet more heavily against the chances of success. Almost at once, the team learns the opposition has a similar plan, comically suggesting the medium's tendency to limit story possibilities to a few mechanical but "safe" entertainment strategies.

Still other parallels with the war film genre's development and decline are implied. The game begins, for example, with at least some elements of honest realistic combat and confrontation (**The Big Parade, What Price Glory, Wings**). Gradually, however, the emphasis shifts to "hardware as heroes," such as the hypodermic the M*A*S*H unit uses to immobilize the other team's "ringer" (**I Wanted Wings, Flight Command, Dive Bomber**). The stress is next placed on team play, clumsy cutting and blaring music de-emphasizing the individual's style (**Air Force, Bataan, Sahara**). The nurses employed as grotesque cheerleaders parallel the drawing in of women to the genre to whip up enthusiasm (**Cry Havoc, So Proudly We Hail**).

Race also comes in as a goad, one Black player being insultingly called a "coon," then coming back with a cleverer insult that gets him chased off the field (**Home of the Brave, Between Heaven and Hell**). As the game goes on, a charging ball carrier is forced out of bounds, tumbling into several innocent wheelchair-bound spectators, suggesting the genre's late tendency towards pointlessly upsetting bloody savagery (**Sands of Iwo Jima, Halls of Montezuma, Beachhead**).

The two commanders, supposedly sportsmen and gentlemen, wind up cursing each other across the field like competing generals (**Bridge at Remaggen, The Longest Day**). The game concludes with what is termed a "semi-legal play," a complicated ruse which depends on hiding the ball until it's over the goal-line. The semi-legal play suggests a parallel with contemporaneous war-is-for-suckers genre works of the late nineteen-sixties (**The Americanization of Emily, The Dirty Dozen, Catch-22**). As if to comment on this "entertainment strategy," the ball carrier, the absurdly anti-heroic Sergeant Major Vollmer (David Arkin) becomes completely confused, not knowing which way to run. The M*A*S*H wins the game by a fluke, though also to mechanical rah-rah music.

As a metaphorical critique of the war film genre, the football game sequence is both clever and comic. Moreover, the sequence, which implicates us through our pleasure of competition according to rules, is so easily and quickly "corrupted" into one where our pleasure is derived from comic interventions which systematically violate the rules, and is a subtle comment on the idea of genre itself. In addition, the football game sequence artistically balances the "sexual combat" sequence early in the film; together they show how readily an emotional event can be stylized into a form of entertainment, and how swiftly genre can be stylized and/or reversed. I believe it is these concealed genre-theoretic concerns that are the "long bones" of the film, the mysteries that the audience dimly perceives and is enthralled by, as much as by the humor or characters.

Triumphant, the M*A*S*H staff gathers up the cash in a heady mood — the first "victory" in the film, and a crooked, ignoble anti-genre one at that. As General Hammond-Wood predicted, games and betting have re-established a corrupt "American Way of Life." Returning to camp, the protagonists count the money, puffing movie moguls' cigars, and Nurse Hoolihan-Kellerman poses on the table like a cheap producer's chorine/mistress, completing the football game as a war genre metaphor. The moment suggests the filmmaker's own self-conscious genre awareness that he's come up with a neat, safe upbeat way to end his war film.

Being an anti-genre film, M*A*S*H does not end. Instead, "Duke"-Skerritt and "Hawkeye"-Sutherland go back to surgery, until they are abruptly informed that their tour of duty is over. In a flash-forward, "Duke"-Skerritt images his home airport arrival, with a small crowd and his plain wife and children running to him, a completely unsentimentalized, anti-genre image.

Asked to await a driver, "Hawkeye"-Sutherland instead wheels their jeep away, giving the same anarchistic Harpo Marx whistle he did at the start of the picture, emphasizing once again, as the anti-genre work does almost continuously, its rejection of the basic genre motif of war as a bloody education. Rather the protagonists remain totally unchanged, as savvy and sexy as they were when they arrived, the anti-genre reason that they have prevailed.

As well as its protean protagonists, M*A*S*H ends by stressing a second intermittent anti-theme, war as a bureaucracy rather than a path to glory. For when Commander Blake-Bowen asks about the stolen jeep the two men came in, the all-knowing Corporal Radar-Burghoff murmurs that he gave them the very same illegal vehicle.

M*A*S*H ends with its always inflamed anti-genre self-consciousness kicking up again: the characters appearing to a P.A. system movie trailer narration like those already heard: "Tonight's movie has been M*A*S*H! Follow the zany antics of our combat surgeons as they cut and stich their way along the front lines. . . . "

Brewster McCloud (1970)

Brewster McCloud has special interest as a provocative inversion of the critically neglected fantasy film genre. Stuart Kaminsky has rather succinctly defined this type of film as:

> . . . usually presented as a personal, dreamlike childhood exploration of our less-than-conscious thoughts. Fantasy films almost always take on the form, or appearance, of a self-contained dream. Quite often, in fact, the fantasy is presented as a dream of one of the characters . . . . Invariably, the fantasy theme is one of reinforcement of the world outside the fantasy, an acceptance of the real world as a less interesting but safer place to be.[4.1]

In terms of this definition, Altman's **Brewster McCloud** denies and comments on the basic genre themes and motifs, while playfully inverting the dramatic devices of the more successful films (mainly **The Bluebird, The Wizard of Oz**, and **Eight and a Half**).

Brewster McCloud commences with the M.G.M. trademark; but Leo the Lion forgets to roar, suggesting from the first modern self-conscious skepticism, shared by artist and audience alike, which makes the sustaining of Kaminsky's "self-contained dream" almost impossible.

As Tag Galleger has written of the most recent **The Bluebird** (1976): "Was it too much to hope that a good fairytale movie could be made . . . and even if [the director] had pulled it off, could today's audience become involved enough — *with any film*[?]"[4.2] Even 16 years ago, Fellini's **Eight and a Half** was greeted scornfully by many critics.[4.3] (Significantly, **Star Wars** is a "frameless" fantasy.)

In a sense, Altman's anti-genre fantasy film is more concerned with an exploration of this audience response than with the genre itself. Suggestively, a baleful-eyed, twitching Rene Auberjonois in feather-trimmed sweater delivers a provocative classroom lecture on the fantasy of flight, which also dissects the fantasy genre:

> Lecturer-Aberjonois: Flight of Birds. Flight of Man. Man's similarity to Birds. Birds similarity to Man . . . the desire to fly has been ever present in the Mind of Man. But the reality has been long in coming. Has Man truly realized his dream? To answer that, we must isolate the dream. Was the dream to attain the ability to fly, or was the dream the freedom that true flight seemed to offer?

Instead of beginning the business of setting up the fantasy, Altman's anti-genre work starts by questioning its basic nature: giving the viewer a fantasized counterpart of reality, or the experiencing of a fantasy of pure liberation?

The Wizard of Oz is clearly the first sort of film, a fantasized rendering of adolescent development. Harvey Greenberg points out that: "the opening sequences of Wizard adroitly capture Dorothy's central preoccupation with whether the adult stirring within her can dare to leave the nest."[4.4] Fellini's Eight and a Half exemplifies the second subgenre, dealing with the artist's creative freedom to fantasize.

In Brewster McCloud, the two fantasy subgenres are jarringly combined, as well as being reversed, both processes puncturing the self-contained dream. Taking place mostly within the collossal Houston Astrodome, the film's beginning shows the dominating dowager Daphne Heap (Margaret Hamilton, the Oz film's Bad Witch) leading a chorus of subservient black singers (Hamilton-Heap: "I want everything just exactly the way it should be . . . . That's why I bought you those uniforms!"). The Bad Mother figure of the Oz film, Heap-Hamilton demands the Blacks sing again, and the film repeats the identical shots, a comic mocking of fantastic "evil powers."

Intercut with the Blacks' repetitious rendering of a dreary spiritual are our first moments in the quiet Astrodome sub-basement workshop of colorless, innocent-seeming youth Brewster McCloud (Bud Cort). The reverse of the fantasy genre's plucky children (e.g., The Bluebird, The Wizard of Oz) who acquire wisdom by facing a variety of challenging monsters, this never-developed character only sees Heap-Hamilton on TV, and is passive when he meets the anti-genre film's other grotesques. Rather, Brewster-Cort focuses on his obsession, glimpsed as a drawing of a feathered/mechanical contraption, eventually revealed as a pair of man-powered, man-carrying wings resembling those of Icarus. Brewster-Cort suggests the active fantasizer/artist of the second sub-genre but, in this anti-genre work, all his dreams end in persecution, betrayal, and death.

Likewise, the genre's characteristic idea of having the protagonist's fantastic adventures and meetings lead to wisdom (e.g., "The Oz film suggests everyone wants a Wizard during adolescence, but the wanting will cease when the younster begins to tap his own unique abilities"[4.5] is mocked. For instance, we next see, sprouting more feathers, bulging-eyed, the Auberjonois-lecturer in his classroom, cawing and then speaking of bird social behavior and social hierarchies: "Within a flock . . . there is this definite order of social distinction . . . one invariably has precedence." But, unlike the very didactic Wizard of Oz, Altman's dream creatures all tend to be simply contemptible — some more powerful than others.

Thus, through a bright green Houston, Texas suburb, a mild young Brewster-Cort chauffeurs cackling, wheelchaired, ancient Abraham Wright (Stacy Keach) in a gleaming Rolls Royce (license plate: OWL). Stopping at the nursing homes he owns (Feathered Nest, Blue Bird Rest Home, etc.), avaricious comic villain Wright-Keech makes his collections (Wright-Keech: "If Mr. Saunders did die . . . he still owes me!"). The comic irony of pastoral rest home names versus moneygrubbing business realities is perhaps less interesting than the anti-genre treatment of death itself. Death in the fantasy genre is always treated very carefully: in **The Wizard of Oz**, Dorothy kills her two enemies only "accidentally," as when her house lands and crushes the Wicked Witch that tyrannized the Munchkins; in the successive versions of **The Bluebird**, Tag Galleger points out, the dream treatment of death is progressively toned down:

> In every other version, when the children visit their dead grandparents in Memory Lane, the old folk fall back into sleep-death when the children leave. No doubt this was considered too scary for modern kids, and so now the grandparents are still animate at the end.[4.6]

Altman's version inverts and mocks the careful stylizing of death: one horrible old monster preys on the other pathetic ancients in their last nests.

Moreover, when leaving one home so the wheelchair accidentally spills Wright-Keach into the grass and his greenbacks fly from his cigarbox, the old man pulls out an enormous .45-caliber pistol and whispers fiercely: "Don't you ever lay a hand on my money!" Kidding the genre's birds-for-people metaphor (e.g., **The Blue Bird**), Brewster's crow releases apparently lethal droppings on the murderous old man.

The story device in **The Bluebird** of having the "Bluebird of Happiness" change color, escape, or otherwise vanish is mocked as, slumped in his wheelchair, the dead Wright-Keach corpse coasts rapidly down a thruway ramp, cars swerving and impacting as the chair zips through a Houston intersection. There's another wreck, and the sound of smashing glass, as a guitarist sings:

> And all that funny money

> It won't get you milk and honey
> So ride, ride, ride, Abraham ride!

The loaded wheelchair strikes the curb and the dead old man flies to the ground, his whitestained face encircled by dollar bills.

Here and later, Altman's film playfully provides what, for some critics,[4.7] is the fantasy's basic pleasure, a coherent, witty "alternative" to such disagreeable realworld norms as wealth-as-dignity. (Successive episodes cover law and technology as well.) Hence, while aspects of the genre "dream world" are mocked in passing as **Brewster McCloud** proceeds, its skeletal "alternative" design is built up until the end, when it is smashed.

Continuing to use the genre's episodic structure, **Brewster McCloud** next introduces another fantastic archetype: "supercop" Frank Shaft (Michael Murphy), a cool fashion-plate parody of Steve McQueen's policeman-character in the film **Bullitt**. The Auberjonois-lecturer, still more birdlike, caws of the visual grandeur of this species: "everything that can delight the eye and contends to place it in our highest esteem." In some ways resembling **The Bluebird**'s seductive Queen of Luxury, Altman's parody of the fantasy-seducer is only loving towards himself, unpacking in his motel room a seemingly infinite wardrobe, only pausing to absurdly match the color of his concealed shoulder holster with the right turtleneck pullover and custom slacks.

Intercut with "cool" detective Shaft-Murphy's arrival is the death of dowager Heap-Hamilton, the **Oz** film's wicked old witch; dying (like Wright-Keach) offscreen, the corpse splattered by Brewster-Cort's crow. Roberta Rubinstein[4.8] has suggested that Wright-Keach, Heap-Hamilton and other victims are "caging figures" who dominated gray Americans, Afro-Americans, and so on. While this is so, Brewster-Cort, in a reversal of the genre's frightened-but-brave children heroes, is only involved in their destruction when he notices they are possible obstacles to his obsessive artist's flight/fantasy. By contrast, Dorothy "accidentally" crushes the Wicked Witch and is embraced by the Munchkins, while the Black chorus here has to liberate themselves.

At the mansion of the deceased Wright-Keach, Shaft-Murphy learns that Brewster-Cort has stolen a secret ancient pioneer text by the dead man's brothers, Wilbur and Orville! In his Astrodome workroom, Brewster-Cort is shown studying the ancient browned drawins of man-powered wings. As Rabkin suggests,[4.9] the complete fantasy even has its own "alternate" technology, in this case human-scale flight as opposed to the conventional technological aerial transport with which we are familiar. In the same way, Oz has its crystal ball and magic balloons, while the **Star Wars** series takes this genre aspect to its limit.

In a cool green city park, the cawing voice of Lecturer-Auberjonois introduces yet another fantastic co-mingling of man and bird: cruel, dishonest policeman Greene (Burt Remson), a nasty old man who hobbles with a cane and whose cowed wife has suggestive cigarette-end-sized marks on her arms. Greene-Remson, spotting Brewster-Cort photographing birds with an expensive camera, tries to extort it by threatening a drug arrest (mocking the Wicked Witch of Oz with her passivity-inducing poppy field).

The passive Brewster-Cort is saved by a fourth bird-fantasy, the beautiful mysterious raincoated Louise (Sally Kellerman), whom we have glimpsed at the murder sites, so, almost immediately, Green-Remson lies dead and birdbesotted. Here suggested to be a mother figure, (Lecturer-Auberjonois: "When an Intruder disturbs or endangers the nest or the young . . . some may attack the intruder . . . . "), Louise-Kellerman's role in the film seems at first a stylized counterpart of the fantasy female protector/teachers: Aunt Em/The Good Witch in **The Wizard of Oz**, or The Mother/Witch/Maternal-Love-and-Life of **The Blue Bird**.

The investigation of Greene-Remson's death brings out the Houston police, who both suggest and invert the genre idea of "dream companions" (e.g., **Oz**'s Scarecrow, Cowardly Lion, and Tinman): impatient, grim, old captain Crandall (G. Wood); smooth, cold politician Haskell Weeks (William Windom); and, bright, vain Shaft-Murphy. Like the immature Dorothy's companions, "each lacks some crucial portion of their spiritual anatomy."[4.10] Unlike them, they are not good at heart, nor "learn they really have within what they thought they lacked."[4.11] Instead, they are killed off as they get in the hero's way, or seek to destroy him.

As with the **Oz** film's companions, so with the film's protagonist Dorothy (Judy Garland), whose lookalike, a teenager named Hope (Jennifer Salt), visits Brewster-Cort during his flight exercises. In her pigtails, patent leather shoes, and freckles, Hope-Salt proposes that the **Oz** film's heroine's extreme sweetness was a product of total sexual repression: sweet on Brewster-Cort, she sublimates by spurt-in stadium-dispenser mustard on two immense hotdogs, then hides under a blanket to apparently masturbate enthusiastically, which the innocent Brewster-Cort ignores. The character comically illuminates the genre's highly stylized treatment of sexuality, notable in **Belle de Jour**; the harem sequence in **Eight and a Half**, and the **Star Wars'** protagonist's:

> father's laser sword, the ultimate phallic weapon (you carry it in your pocket until you need it, then press a button and it's three feet long and glows in the dark).[4.12]

In his underground workroom, the complex feathered/mechanical wing array taking shape in one corner, young Brewster-Cort is visited by the lovely-mysterious Louise-Kellerman. Their dialogue gradually makes plain the central anti-genre focus of **Brewster McCloud** as when the eerie woman warns against the ordinary teenager Hope-Salt as a threat to his flying:

> Louise-Kellerman: People like Hope accept what's told them. They don't think they can be free. Their sex is the closest thing they have to . . . flying.

The fantasy film genre, as Kaminsky points out[4.13] at heart reinforces acceptance of the safer but less interesting "real world"; thus, Dorothy and the children seek the "Bluebird of Happiness." Then, older and wiser, they return home. Even the artist-hero of **Eight and a Half**, in the end, retreats from his fantastic Ideal:

> . . . . Later, when Guido has embraced his new life, (the Ideal) walks away, not directly from the camera, but across the screen in the opposite direction from that taken, in other shots, by all the others. She has no part in the final circle. In this sequence the different elements in the film are brought together, as there come flooding toward Guido all the people who have ever meant anything in his life.[4.14]

Likewise the minor fantasy genre films all eventually turn away from the dream fantasy: **The Secret World of Walter Mitty** has the dream girl of the different fantasies turn out to really exist; **The Five Thousand Fingers of Dr. T**'s piano school Inferno and **Alice in Wonderland**'s fantasies disappear when the protagonists wake up.

In Altman's anti-genre work, however, the masterful female teacher/protector demands throughout that Brewster-Cort reject the real world and real desire for the fantasy. When Brewster-Cort asks if "they" wanted to fly, she replies:

> Louise-Kellerman: Oh yes . . . at first . . . but something happens to them as they grow, and then they turn more and more toward the earth. And when they experience sex, they simply settle for it, and procreate more of their own kind . . . .

Louise-Kellerman tells the youth he must focus all his thoughts and energies on his flight fantasy, and this anti-humanistic anti-genre view of existence has its visual counterpart in a sexless, nude bathing scene that follows. The Louise-Kellerman anti-genre character thus combines the worst elements of the **Oz** film's Good Witch and Bad Witch; she seduces him into passivity so he can fulfill *her* goals. As Greenberg suggests:

> The Bad Mother has attempted to lull the children into fatal passivity . . . while the Good Mother allows her children to go down the path towards fulfillment . . . [their two images

fusing in the Crystal Ball] is peculiarly troubling to most children, no doubt because it captures so effectively our archaic terror of the mother's destructive potential.[4.15]

In the anti-genre **Brewster McCloud**, this destructive potential is fully realized, Louise-Kellerman suggestively crooning the mockingly prophetic nursery rhyme "Rock-a-Bye Baby" in the bath with the boy. In another sense, the anti-genre film uses the song to subtly call our attention to the basic fears that the genre tries to calm.

In addition, the scene reveals Louise-Kellerman's lovely naked back, which is shown to carry large symmetrical marks, as if great angelic wings had been removed. While a teasing joke on the movie's central metaphor, the image also helps to complete Rabkin's "alternates" to the real norms of the world,[4.16] also suggesting an actual heaven from which Louise-Kellerman has descended — or been thrust, her obsession suggesting a satanic drive to storm it at any cost, yet another anti-genre implication.

The bath sequence dissolves to lovely images of fluffy cloudtops as seen by someone soaring above them, to charming but fatalistic lyrics:

How the bird sings,
When she is flying;
And how the bee stings,
When he knows he is dying . . . .

Perhaps halfway through the film, the fantasy fulfillment is here associated with a voluptuous catastrophe in an inhuman milieu.

The anti-genre reversal is in the context of **Eight and a Half**'s director's deliberate rejection of elaborately confected fantasy sets, and the temptations of being driven:

Having once made this rejection, he unhesitatingly orders the demolition of the [launching pad] structure, unafraid now to confess that there is no film. He accepts his want of inspiration, accepts himself as he is, and gives up the pretense that there is something behind his indecision and silence.[4.17]

In Altman's anti-genre film, the fantasizer-protagonist cannot turn away from the flight dream; instead, the flier goes out of control, and makes an Icarus-like plunge into the sun and down to earth, ending as a dead dove ignored on the grass at officer Breen-Remson's funeral.

The understated funeral, with the police chaplain reading "his favorite poem" according to the cigarette-scarred widow ("How Do I Love Thee? Let Me Count the Ways . . . ") is the film's anti-genre

49

turning point. Tag Gallagher[4.6] has pointed out that while fantasy genre films include much death, they treat it in a carefully stylized way, to either clarify or disarm our edgy awareness of mortality. Here, death is shown as simple, bleak, total obliteration: the wife already has a new lover; the friends present snipe at each other and ignore the ceremony; even the poem reading is broken off because the rain runs the ink. The whole genre mood of light-hearted, suspended disbelief is replaced by a bleak awareness of easy empty transience.

In the same rainstorm, Brewster-Cort steals the sports car of Suzanne (Shelley Duval), a scrawny-beautiful Astrodome tour guide with enormous eyes. Jumping in, she hardly seems to mind, a slyly anti-genre mistress-companion. Instead of lacking only a brain like **Oz**'s sweet scarecrow, or courage like **Oz**'s loyal lion, Suzanne-Duval seems a completely birdbrained sociopathic innocent:

> Suzanne-Duval: Anyway, one night this guy offered to take me home. So I said okay. Only instead of takin' me home he took me to Memorial Park. I mean, wow, he tried to rape me! Anyway, I hit him with a lug wrench and drove home. I haven't seen him since, so . . . I've got this neat little Roadrunner!

After having picked up some wildlife photographs — part of the flying project — the two go to her apartment, where she mentions a special fascination with artists like himself, though she doesn't manage to seduce him. The scene inverts the artist/mistress relationship in **Eight and a Half** in which the mistress keeps spoiling the romantic mood by chattering about her dull husband ("He's serious, not pushy at all, that's his tragedy"). Finally, leaving, Brewster-Cort triggers a fourth murder, the end of the beefy redneck owner of Suzanne-Duval's car, sprawled and splashed like the rest. These quick deaths of an artist's enemies are incidentally mocking updates of **Eight and a Half**'s director's way of swiftly disposing of critics:

> Guido listens courteously, as always, then [beginning of shortest fantasy sequence] raises one finger. Two assistants take the critic by the arms, lead him into the aisle, put a black hood over his face, a rope around his neck, and hang him. Back to reality; shot of Guido with his collaborator, undamaged, still sitting behind him.[4.18]

In **Brewster McCloud**, the wished-for-deaths are not retroactive, they are an anti-genre actuality, the ease and casualness with which they are achieved adding to and mocking the death-fears which the genre films work so hard to relieve.

To increase the narrative tension, the scenes in and around Suzanne-Duval's home are intercut with the police running down more clues, including a security camera photograph of Brewster-Cort which Louise-Kellerman prevents from being developed. In a long comic auto chase, Brewster-Cort and Suzanne-Duval get away in their vehicle (license: DUV-222), while Louise-Kellerman diverts Shaft-Murphy's car so it dives into an ornamental pond. The handsome, vain officer's legs are crushed, one blazing blue contact lens lost, and the peacock supercop suicides with his own gun. The anti-genre reference is perhaps to the many fantasy film characters, notably the Wicked Witch in **The Wizard of Oz**, who are "accidentally" destroyed in efforts to save a sympathetic character. As Greenberg puts it:

> She takes up a torch and sets the scarecrow alight . . . . By virtue of his flimsy construction, he is the most vulnerable to total annihilation; our deepest fears of death center around this awful sundering of the self by a titanic, overwhelming force, symbolic of the catastrophic power of the Bad Mother . . . Dorothy flings a pail of water over Scarecrow. The Witch is drenched too, and shreiking piteously, she dwindles away to nothing . . . . Once more, Dorothy has unintentionally committed an ambiguous murder of a Bad Mother, and in the bargain, become a kind of Good Mother herself.[4.19]

The loss of Shaft-Murphy is a very different matter; he harmed or threatened no one, and his enormous vanity indeed suggested an equally great vulnerability. In this, he was more sympathetic than the shallow Brewster-Cort and Suzanne-Duval. It's as if Dorothy in the **Oz** film simply executed the Bad Witch (or the Scarecrow!) with a landmine.

In passing, the police, with their endless analysis and dull speculations on the bird droppings ("Could tell you what it ate, but I don't believe we could determine what kind of bird it came from. Besides, it might not have been a bird") are comic counterparts of the pestering, foolish critics in **Eight and a Half** ("Is it that you cannot communicate? Or is that merely a mask?").

At the Astrodome basement workshop, situated in a fallout shelter (a modern counterpart of the tornado storm cellar that Dorothy hid in in **The Wizard of Oz**), Louise-Kellerman humiliates teenager Hope-Salt so she will leave the film's hero alone. The sweet teenage character, in pigtails and polka-dot dress and patent leather shoes, suggests the **Oz** heroine, Dorothy, in whom sexuality is sublimated, unable to deal with the ruthless, anti-genre, directly sexual Bad Mother character.

In Suzanne-Duval's apartment, Brewster-Cort has meanwhile been seduced. As he speaks with Suzanne-Duval in bed, their faces to the overhead camera, her's upside down with respect to his, we have a visual counterpart of opposite and irreconcilable outlooks:

> Suzanne-Duval: Fly away?! Brewster, you could be a millionaire! . . . I've gotta get you a good lawyer, to protect you. And you'll need a patent . . . . You could get a limousine − and a chauffeur . . . everything! . . . You could get a house on River Oaks Boulevard!

Intercut with their conversation in bed, we see his later bitter meeting with Louise-Kellerman in the Astrodome catacomb:

> Brewster-Cort: I think I'm capable of picking my own friends. . . . Why'd you lie to me? . . . It's not like you said it would be at all, Louise.

The reversal in this sequence is of the genre's treatment of the artist's relations with mistress and wife, shown in **Eight and a Half** and suggested in **Alex in Wonderland**. Dwight McDonald describes Fellini's approach:

> After his wife and mistress have disastrously collided, Guido leans back in his cafe chair, closes his eyes (behind dark glasses), and revises the scene so that the two . . . are presently waltzing together; since this works so well, Guido's ending goes all the way, and we have the lovely and witty harem fantasy, which poetizes Freudian ideas about the libido even as it parodies them.[4.20]

In Altman's anti-genre fantasy, the opposite happens: as soon as Brewster-Cort simply *has* a "wife" and a "mistress," both turn on him and attempt to do him in. In tune with the fantasy genre's "alternatives," this anti-genre "negative magic," a nightmare of guilt, is shown to have been in force all the time:

> Brewster-Cort: But we have to fly away.
> Suzanne-Duval: Why can't we stay here? This is my home. I love it here.
> Brewster-Cort: They'll put me in a cage . . . . You know all those people who died?
> Suzanne-Duval: You mean the ones who were strangled?
> Brewster-Cort: Uh-huh . . . . I'm responsible . . . .

Brewster-Cort is here revealed as the anti-genre reverse of **The Wizard of Oz**'s Dorothy and the children in **The Bluebird**, who only kill "by accident," and the hero of **Eight and a Half**, who brings his victims back to life a second later. Brewster-Cort kills for keeps, and solely to advance selfish dreams. In this anti-genre work, fantasy is viewed by Kaminsky not as leading to acceptance of the real world,[4.1] but as a flight from it and/or effort to destroy it, and so multiplier of guilt. Note that the viewer never has any evidence that

Brewster-Cort kills anyone: the anti-genre point is that he takes all the blame. On another level, the Brewster-Cort character is the opposite of Fellini's blocked director; he goes ahead and finishes his artistic project, at the price of manipulating (killing?) actual people. But, by explaining what he is doing too soon and in the wrong way, he wrecks it.

Enormous-eyed, the left-alone Suzanne-Duval, to a female chorus chirping the song "I Promised Not to Tell," hysterically calls her old boyfriend Bernard (William Baldwin), secretary to sinister politician Weeks (William Windom):

> Suzanne-Duval: He says he's got wings he made himself. He probably swoops down on people and strangles them!
> Weeks-Windom: Uh-hmm. Looks like she's deranged also!
> Bernard-Baldwin: Suzanne is very gullible, Mr. Weeks.

As the three rush to the Astrodome, so Weeks-Windom can "bring in the confessed killer," the politician is shown as a sort of anti-genre Wizard of Oz, a good magician (i.e., politician) but a bad man. (Oz's Wizard: "Oh, no, my dear, I'm a very good man. I'm just a very bad wizard . . . "). In The Wizard of Oz, the Wizard rules a happy city and wittily heals the "defects" of Dorothy and her friends. In opposition, Weeks-Windom is shown as a shrewd politician-magician hosting a party of foolish celebrities, but also a trigger-happy individual eager to advance his career.

The sweatered Auberjonois-Lecturer appears once more in his classroom, fists in armpits and arms pumping, chest puffed out, cawing and blowing, maintaining the genre's birds-for-people metaphor:

> Lecturer-Auberjonois: Waaakk! Courtship activities have the further function of regulating the timing of sexual readiness so that the reproductive physiology of a pair may be synchronized . . . .

As the Weeks-Windom politician goes into the stadium ramps with his gun, the two young people attempt clumsily to mate. Following this, they find the Bad Wizard Weeks-Windom dead and birdsplattered. The two look up to see Brewster-Cort, frightened-faced, the immense folded feathered mechanical wings on his back. They let him go past, Suzanne-Duval guilty-faced, Brewster-Cort not reacting to the betrayal in this sequence, the anti-genre work mocking the quest motif, which Tag Gallagher calls in The Bluebird: "Perhaps less a mystic's quest for "God" than a scientist's quest for certain knowledge of the ineffable.[4.21] The pair of young people, faced with Mystery, couple and then turn away in shame and fear.

Far away, Louise-Kellerman strides under the dome towards a great brilliant white opening — so white the edges bleed out — and seems to ascend into the glaring rectangle, having abandoned

Brewster-Cort. Playfully, the anti-genre fantasy leaves her method of departure ambiguous: did she walk out or fly away? Rabkin's system of "alternatives" is maintained, but the mood is one of wrong choices, a perverse logic grinding to a fatal conclusion. The music matches the slow, apologic "Last of the Unnatural Acts":

All of the rain that falls on the earth,
Cannot cleanse away what's been done.
And all of the winds, can't blow away the curse,
Nature has provided that will come.
These are the unnatural facts;
This is the last of the unnatural acts.

Now, bright blue ululating Texas police cars race towards the colossal dome, helmeted riot-gun-bearing cops taking the ramps into the grandstand. But the guns will not be used, the police will not touch the hero. Rather, following the fantasy genre's dream format, Brewster-Cort hunches under his wings, waddles into a private box, leaps — and flies!

As with Dorothy in **The Wizard of Oz**, he must learn alone, as if in a dream. Greenberg quotes Glinda the Good Witch, comparing the motif to psycho-therapy: "No, (Glinda repeats) she had to find out for herself — and not by an act of sheer intellect. As in analysis, the head must be connected to the heart."[4.22] Of course, Dorothy's insight is to "fly" home, the genre convention (" . . . if I ever go looking for my heart's desire again, I won't look any further than my own backyard"). (**Star Wars**' youth's flight is his attempted destruction of his Bad Father (Darth Vader).)

Blowing and flapping, the elaborate white plume system twice the length of arms and legs scissoring, Brewster-Cort soars across the dome. His sweating straining face is intercut with longshots of the flight, the neutral-faced policemen watching from the ground. Altman's film has him gasping and desperate, a reversal and anti-genre mocking of the flight fantasy at the beginning and end of **Eight and a Half** (viz., the "spaceship set"). As Budgen describes it:

> The [**Eight and a Half**] sequence represents . . . the soaring of Guido's spirit, liberated from the suffocating prison of daily affairs and of his own frustrating perplexities, and its sudden plummeting down to earth, tied and controlled by the financial and other interests within which creative work in the cinema has to be done.[4.23]

Completely free, the youth circles and soars, viewed against the elaborate radiating slots of the dome design, the stands, the scoreboard blinking with an electronic American flag. Tracking shots and clever editing make him appear to turn and glide as he pumps frantically, a cunning small *tour de force* of cinematographic skill like **The Red Balloon**: the fantasy of manpowered flight as a beautiful illusion. It is, however, an anti-genre illusion, as Brewster-Cort is shown to fly ever more desperately, screaming and grunting, wings spasming as he hurtles past the dome supports and banks of floodlights, a cruel mocking of **Oz**'s smug Good Witch ("She had to find out for herself"). Meanwhile, the Auberjonois-lecturer comments on the fantasy genre:

> Auberjonois-Lecturer: Man's insatiable mind, goaded on by a handicapped body, will undoubtedly invent subtleties and refinements for his present clumsy progress in the air. But he will never attain that mastery of the air which is the result of the development of millions of years, acting on a self-contained mechanism of a living body . . . waaak!

The anti-genre point being that the fantasy genre is unnatural, no matter how much thought is applied.

Despite all his genius, Brewster-Cort must circle round and round inside the dome/form, like the circular journeys of Dorothy in **The Wizard of Oz** and the children in **The Bluebird**. Likewise, even an *un*tethered Guido from **Eight and a Half** would soon become exhausted and fall back just as Brewster-Cort, flapping and screaming desperately, eventually pauses in midair, then seems to crumple and plunge — hitting with a thud, a crushed dead figure under the nodding white plumes.

In the stands, those incidentally present break into ignorant applause; and, as the Astrodome scoreboard gives the film's cast, the different actors in circus attire (politician Weeks-Windom as ringmaster, Louise-Kellerman as snakecharmer, etc.), emerge and pose. The sequence, a parody of the end of **Eight and a Half**, mocks the complete genre. For the circus finale of Fellini's fantasy genre film is obviously an effort to fit together the dreams and nightmares with the reality. As Budgen puts it:

> The last sequence, in other words, contains and reconciles all the separate elements in the film, showing the integration in Guido of everything that has been dividing him. Only in this one sequence is he wholly present in body, mind, and spirit.[4.24]

But in Altman's film, the actors and actresses wear the costumes and play the parts assigned by Fellini, rather than the American director or his fantasy-film protagonist, still sprawled "dead" on the ground in his wings. Instead of learning to accept the real world, in proper genre fashion, the dreamer/protagonist has perished, and the dream elements now belong to somebody else, symbolizing a shattered, chaotic artistic vision.

McCabe And Mrs. Miller (1972)

McCabe and Mrs. Miller is perhaps Altman's most deeply felt and pessimistic anti-genre film, a reversal of the classic Western dealing with the "taming" of the frontier. In the themes it inverts — the rediscovery by outcasts of community, and the challenging of that community by civilization — it is in many ways an anti-genre counterpart of John Ford's **Stagecoach, My Darling Clementine**, and **The Man Who Shot Liberty Valance.**

McCabe and Mrs. Miller commences as almost a pictorial parody of the western form, with moving crane shots of a horseman in furs leading a pack animal through the misty, richly-forested Northwest Territory in the first years of this century. The soft greens and browns of the verdant "wilderness" support the genre-mocking of one of Leonard Cohen's gentle ballads:

> I know that sort of man, it's hard
> To hold the hand of anyone
> Who's reaching for the sky, just to surrender
> Who's reaching for the sky, just to surrender.

In a few moments, with a minimum of narrative, Altman's film has set mood and tone as well as anti-genre stance. If the master antimony in John Ford's classic westerns is, as Peter Wollen suggests[5.1] "between the wilderness . . . and the garden . . . from the wilderness left in the past to the garden anticipated in the future," **McCabe and Mrs. Miller** will suggest that the lovely garden was in the past, and "progress" a seeking out of a lethal wilderness. In addition, the title links a loner hero with an unavailable heroine, two of the genre conventions — knowing prostitute, fated romance, range war, big shootout — included yet inverted.

Topping a low rise, the rider comes upon the film's again comically inverted western town: not a dry, dusty outpost but clustered canvas tents and clapboard shacks, blue-gray in the endless rain like the just-drained bottom of an aquarium. Rather than a center of ranching or sheepherding, it's a mining camp called Presbyterian Church, the actual incompleted steeple in the background. Again, rather than colorful cowboys and gunfighters, the crude loding hotel, with its low-ceilinged barrom, holds only listless, suspicious miners in shapeless workclothes and beards, the primal clay of a proto-society. The contrast with the figures of a classic genre film such as **Stagecoach** — arrogant banker, drunken doctor, outlaw cowhand — is an aesthetic shock.

From the start, Altman's western "hero," shabby/stylish gambler/entrepreneur John G. McCabe (Warren Beatty) is almost as unfamiliar a genre element. Calling for a light and a bottle, Beatty-McCabe, in fancy vest and bowler hat, spreads a bright orange cloth on a table, grinning past his cigar and gold tooth. As the bearded, stumpy shapes gather for a cardgame, the mean-faced owner Sheehan (Rene Auberjonois) tries to swindle him (Miner: "Three dollars a bottle? Yesterday it was two!"), yet the jokester McCabe-Beatty talks him down:

Sheehan-Auberjonois: I supply the place!

McCabe-Beatty: I supply the customers!

Again, in only a brief moment, Altman's film has suggested the uncouth McCabe-Beatty's special social talent. In a genre dominated by isolated protagonists, it is a revealing anti-genre treatment of the western hero-outcasts who:

> . . . have always fascinated Ford not so much for their rebellion as for the subtle ways they are linked to the society which scorns them. They act *for* society in ways society cannot see, and they understand society better than society understands itself.[5.2]

At the bar, miners murmur over McCabe's revolver, pointing up that as a sensible if anti-genre fact, no one is armed. When Sheehan-Auberjonois provokes the gambler again, he mutters: "Businessman, businessman — what's the matter, Sheehan, got a turd in your pocket?" Rather than the genre hero's strength and directness, this anti-genre hero will continually seek conventional success, yet let his individuality out in a frontier version of a hipster's absurd banter-baiting. As the game goes on, Beatty-McCabe raises the men's spirits as he raises the pot, one chiming a cheery tune on a Jew's harp, Altman's film rendering the frontier gambler as more gameshow host than coldblooded cardsharp.

Rather than the typically skittish, metaphorical genre treatment of the role of women on the frontier, **McCabe and Mrs. Miller** immediately shows sex as a main industry of the West, and its hero an aspiring whoremaster-entrepreneur. Taking his winnings, McCabe-

Beatty is soon bargaining for whores, the comic contrast of the roostery little man arguing with a bearded giant distracting us from the stricken faces of the women. The anti-genre sequence cruelly tests the audience: to the insensitive it is a scene of hilarious frontier haggling, yet at the same time a vision of a virtual slave-trade in women as dumb pleasure animals. Still, there are hints McCabe-Beatty retains a sort of innocence, as in the professional's last yell: "You don't know nothin' about it!" As the gambler and his three whores ride slowly into Presbyterian Church, the cross is raised and placed atop the steeple by the solitary churchman, working completely alone, a sly anti-genre comment on the town's new potentials, holy and unholy. It also specifically mocks the way the self-appointed, vengeance-seeking sheriff in **My Darling Clementine** brought order and so facilitated the building of a church by the whole community.

Significantly, all ordinary construction work in the town halts on the prostitutes' arrival, a sort of primal social crisis, the counterpart of the entering strangers in Ford's westerns who ask: "What sort of town is this?" (**Liberty Valance**) and "What sort of community have I come to?" (**My Darling Clementine**). The shabby artisans stare stunned at the unbeautiful prostitutes, in a wordless expression of love and greed, broken when one tries to speak, then somehow is grappling with one woman on the ground.

In a comic genre reversal of **My Darling Clementine**'s Wyatt Earp (Henry Fonda) and **Liberty Valance**'s Tom Doniphon (John Wayne), both of whom maintain the west's rough justice, it is the cheery pimp-gambler-businessman runt, McCabe-Beatty, who here and later in **McCabe and Mrs. Miller**, preserves order and maintains community. Here he pulls the mild, lust-dazed worker to his feet, and sets the men to work again by claiming that finishing the job will get them women who "can do more tricks than a Goddam monkey on a hundred yards of grapevine." Yet, alone with his whores, he is shown the opposite of John Ford's strong secure westerners, facing them as bewildered as any of the workers: one child-woman's request to "go potty" is followed by a zoomshot to his totally perplexed expression.

The next sequence, with McCabe-Beatty wheeling and dealing with the greedy, repellent simpleton Sheehan-Auberjonois, shows him secure again, and by implication makes another comment on the Western genre's strong but static heroes. For, by sketching McCabe-Beatty's projects, it illuminates the genre convention of the *unchangeable* physical Western habitat, the eternal cactus and saloon and false-front stores. In this anti-genre work, the town will expand and develop, and McCabe-Beatty will be the principal agent behind this anti-genre dynamicism.

By comparison, a minor mystery of the John Ford Westerns was how *anything* got accomplished. Two critics speculated that: "Wyatt (Earp) has powers which verge on the magical; he seldom carries a gun and seems to be performing his peacekeeping duties by remote control, slouched in his chair and issuing languid remarks."[5.3] More than the forgotten peacekeeping rancher Deniphon-Wayne in **Liberty Valance** or temporary sheriff Earp-Fonda in **My Darling Clementine**, McCabe-Beatty will be both the hidden motor behind the frontier's innocent first growth and the formalizer of its idyllic community. In this way, Altman's anti-Western is more wholistic than Ford's classic Westerns: it emphasizes the audacious, necessary *vitality* of the frontier, as well as its profound spiritual crises and thus, in a way, makes the loss of its first energizer more tragic.

The genre's "iron horse," suggesting the coming ordering of civilization to the frontier, is mocked by the image and screech of a huffling steam tractor rolling into the village, a sort of freelance locomotive churning along any trail on wide, hollow, iron wheels, towing freight wagons with people crouching atop them. The passengers include the frightened young mail-order bride Ida Coyle (Shelly Duval) and the gaunt frizzyhaired beauty Mrs. Constance Miller (Julie Christie), a masterstroke of anti-genre characterization.

Mrs. Miller-Christie reverses the archetypical genre dichotomy of whore and good woman, exempliflied by **My Darling Clementine**'s apparent prostitute Chihuahua (Linda Darnell) and pure nurse Clementine (Cathy Downs). In addition, this anti-genre free spirit is brainy, charming and assertive, immediately asking the bemused entrepreneur: "Have you anything to eat? I'm bloody starvin'!" When McCabe-Beatty kids that she'll get the bloody horse she wanted, she returns with cool intelligence: "A frontier wit, I see," then embroiders the impression by kindly remarking, eyes bright, that to come across as a fancy dude the gambler should "try something besides that cheap jockey club cologne."

Moments later, the wonderful anti-genre character is shown as McCabe-Beatty's spiritual counterpart, making her own "business proposition." A whore who knows "an awful lot about whores," Mrs. Miller-Christie wants to be his partner in a first class bordello; instead of tents, "a proper sportin' house — class girls, clean linen, and proper hygiene!" The scene mocks again the Western genre's classic opening of having a stranger enter the west, to speak of a future "where boys like you can grow up safe" (Earp-Fonda in **My Darling Clementine**) or "to practice law in the territory" (Stoddard-Stewart in **Liberty Valance**). Instead, the anti-genre heroes arrive with the "idealistic" hopes of setting up a gambling den or a first class house of prostitution. Yet, paradoxically, these entities turn out to be the bases of a more believable western community than any of John Ford's mythic commonalities.

Mrs. Miller-Christie's subsequent speech is fascinating in many respects, most simply for its illumination of a major part of frontier life totally bypassed by the genre during its seventy-year history (one thinks only of dance hall entertainers and saloon girls): In staccato phrases, Mrs. Miller-Christie gives the case for her expertise:

> Mrs. Miller-Christie: What do you do when one girl fancies another? How to you know when one girl really has her monthly, or when she's just aking a few days off? And what do you do when they don't get their monthlies — 'cause they don't! What're you gonna do then? And what about customers? Who's gonna skin 'em back and inspect 'em? You gonna do that? Cause if you don't, it's gonna be clapped up inside of two weeks, if it isn't already. And what happens when business is slow? You're gonna just let the girls sit around on their bums? Cause I'll tell you something Mr. McCabe. When a good whore has time to sit around and think, four out of five times she turns to religion, cause that's what she was born with. And when that happens, you wind up stuffing the bloody church down there instead of your own pockets. Now I haven't got a lot of time to sit around talking to a man who can't see a good proposition when it's made to him — do we make this deal or don't we?

Mrs. Miller-Christie's speech signals **McCabe and Mrs. Miller**'s major device for reversing the Western genre. By focusing on the whorehouse and whores, Altman turns the Western inside out; instead of archetypical manly activities and triumphs in the wild, the film's center is the providing of sexual and emotional gratification to frontiersmen whose work is neither shown nor seems to be of much interest to anyone, especially themselves.

The subsequent partnership agreement between McCabe-Beatty and Mrs. Miller-Christie leads to a character revelation about the gambler which is one more playful genre reversal. When he "goes partners" with the prostitute, McCabe-Beatty is shown laughing in amused awe and agreement. But later he appears very drunk and disturbed, drunkenly telling his workmen that *he* and not Mrs. Miller makes the decisions: "The girls come up here when I tell 'em to . . . so you'll have something else to do at night besides play with Mary Five Fingers!" Later, he reels drunk and alone into the night, muttering: "Money and pain . . . pain . . . pain . . . . " Here and later, McCabe-Beatty plays Doc Holliday to Mrs. Miller's Wyatt Earp. For, as J.A. Place points out of these two **My Darling Clementine** characters:

61

Doc acts as a foil to Wyatt . . . Doc fails where Wyatt succeeds . . . the cause is his personal failure to act morally in his life. What links him with Wyatt is that the boundaries of "moral behavior" are the same for both of them, setting them apart from the rest of the characters in the film.[5.4]

In **My Darling Clementine**, the Doc Holliday "good/bad man" is obscurely tormented by his past in society and present life on the frontier; in the anti-genre **McCabe and Mrs. Miller**, this tension's source is more explicit: McCabe-Beatty cannot deal with the emotional stresses of his contradictory intimacies with Mrs. Miller-Christie. In one scene, visiting the bordello, he watches from afar as she matter-of-factly sells herself to a miner ("Five dollars for Mrs. Miller – Jesus Christ, shit – let's go!"), and immediately begins arguing with his mild foreman. Later, when she visits his empty saloon-casino to find him grumbling over expenses, she delivers half of her receipts, but he continues grousing, prompting her to tell him shortly: "You have to spend money to make money! I don't like small timers screwin' up the business!" In passing, the genre motif of criminality on the frontier is mocked: the two keep their money in plain boxes without locks.

Simultaneously, the scenes re-emphasize the film's anti-genre treatment of frontier women. In discussing **My Darling Clementine**, which he calls "a classic western," Alan Lovell points out that: "the heroine . . . represents the already mature civilication of the East; her function in the film is to highlight the Westerner's lack of social graces."[5.5] In **McCabe and Mrs. Miller**, Mrs. Miller-Christie's role is a genre inversion: she coolly, and cheerfully continually reminds McCabe-Beatty to keep his eye on the dollar.

Altman's ironic anti-genre western "community" is summed up in **McCabe and Mrs. Miller**'s Christmas Eve sequence. In the bright, clean whorehouse of Mrs. Miller, all fine wood panelling and scrubbed, white-muslined charming girls, the polite washed miners dance gravely to tinkling rhythms from an immense clockwork music box. Here and earlier, Altman's film has set up in the bordello an ambience of warm heartfelt neighborliness, which combines the best of civilized east and straightforward west.

By contrast, out in the rude dark frontier street an old man gets into a stupid fight and is killed, while two shrewd business agents talk with a drunken McCabe-Beatty about buying out his holdings for a pittance on behalf of an enormous mining cartel. In a playful anti-genre gesture, the two are directed as living anachronisms, moving and talking like bland treacherous corporate henchmen, while the drunken naive McCabe-Beatty is the archetypical frontier gambler-entrepreneur, all whiskers and swagger. His period conundrum that "if a frog had wings he wouldn't bump his head so much," which bemuses contemporaries, is ignored by the corporate "hardguys" like a disturbed executive's neuroticism. The anti-genre confrontation is punctuated by one agent's referring to the town's moving spirit as "a real smart-ass," a bit of 1970s Hollywood slang out of **The Long Goodbye**. If Ford's **Liberty Valance**'s title character suggests the frontier was a sort of barely tamed jungle, Altman's anti-genre work here implies that same of the civilized future, which is of course our present.

By contrast, Mrs. Miller's girls are holding a birthday party for one of the whores; the modest rite — gentle unbeautiful women and bearded simple men smiling over cake and candles — emphasizing again the community spirit emanating from the bordello. The moment also suggests how Mrs. Miller has fulfilled the women, who were shown as little more than penned-up pleasure-animals when McCabe-Beatty bought them. Yet, the kind madam leaves the party to read and smoke opium in painful isolation and awareness in her room; like an ironic anti-genre feminine version of Ford's Wyatt Earp, she:

> . . . is halfway between the fanatic and the common man; rigid and gentle, taciturn and forceful, demonstrative and aloof, keeping all [her] conflicting facets in perfect harmony.[5,6]

When the adolescently romantic McCabe-Beatty taps on her own door, she receives him delightedly, fanning the drug smoke out into the night. But when the gambler-entrepreneur naively tells her about the corporation henchmen, her quick wits and worldliness cause the gaunt-faced beauty to stare bleakly at her mirror, instantly evaluating the situation:

> Mrs. Miller-Christie: Think . . . I should have known . . . . Your had better bet they come back here McCabe, 'cause they'd just as soon put a bullet in your back as look at you . . . .

The corporate agents appear again with a very slightly better offer, embroidering the anti-genre image of a western future which is not John Ford's civilized garden, but a poisonous corporate desert.

In Ford's **Liberty Valance**, the psychopathic, evil outlaw Liberty (Lee Marvin) early-on meets innocent lawyer Vance Stoddard (James Stewart) and, screaming "I'll teach you law — *Western Law*!" whips and bludgeons him to the ground. In a sort of anti-genre comic counterpart, one corporate agent starts teaching McCabe-Beatty *"civilized business"* via a speech glittering with hypocrisy, hyperbole and murderous suggestions:

> Ernie Hollander (Anthony Holland): John — may I call you John? I have a son named John, not unlike you. You've

done a wonderful job here, you've built up a beautiful little business from nothing at all. Now here we are willing to offer you a substantial gain in capital — an offer from one of the most solid companies in the United States — and you say no. Frankly, I don't understand. I guess I don't have to tell you some of our people are going to be quite concerned — *you know what I mean?*

All the speech's overtones are missed by the drunken McCabe-Beatty, including the comic attaching of patriotism and virtue to an immoral enterprise, while puritanically leaving it nameless. He does, however, manage to agree to an unconsummated meeting next morning, before going up to Mrs. Miller-Christie. McCabe-Beatty undresses to long underwear, suggesting his innocence, as the "high" Mrs. Miller-Christie smiles impishly, eyes glowing. Yet the business ethic even holds *them* in thrall, the woman gesturing to the cashbox he must fill before crawling in with her. McCabe-Beatty: "You're such a funny little thing — sometimes you're so sweet — other times . . . . "

The new community spirit the title figures have generated is demonstrated again in the ironic frontier funeral sequence (the deceased slipped, fell and died naturally). As Philip French has pointed out:

> Good or bad, a Westerner is entitled to a Christian burial and his passing is marked. That life may be easily taken does not mean that it is cheap and of no significance. Scenes of dying and the rituals of burial on the plains or in the frontier cemeteries abound and constitute some of the most poignant sequences in the genre.[5.7]

The burial is nicely staged as an adlibbed affair: on the steep, muddy hillside in the rain, the miners and whores cluster around a raw grave and crude coffin holding the old man who died naturally in a foolish fight. The tavern fiddler plays hymns, while the prostitutes sing "Asleep in Jesus." But instead of **My Darling Clementine**'s Earp-Fonda pledging a gentler future west, his counterpart, Mrs. Miller-Christie, locks eyes with the young new widow Ida (Shelly Duval) across the grave, offering her sanctuary.

Abruptly, McCabe-Beatty is called away to his own special genre ritual: a possible gunfight with an approaching lone rider over the sale of hs holdings. The gambler strides downslope to face a slim youngster (Keith Carridine) in fleecy chaps and a ridiculously tall sombrero (an icon of innocence from **Stagecoach**). Hand poised over holster, McCabe-Beatty asks what he wants, receiving a childishly enthusiastic reply:

> Keith-Carradine-Cowboy: I heard you had the fanciest
> whorehouse in the territory up here. Gee, it's been so
> long since I had a piece of ass!

The comic moment is an anti-genre masterstroke, mocking seventy
years of pathologically disturbed gunfighter-killers.

By turning a tense apparent shootout-in-the-making into a joke,
Altman's film also slyly exposes the genre's armed confrontation
motif to be mostly a matter of style. As Robert Warshow has pointed
out:

> Really, it is not violence at all which is the "point" of the
> western movie, but a certain image of man, a style, which ex-
> presses itself most clearly in violence. Watch a child with his
> toy guns and you will see; what most interests him is not
> (as we so much fear) the fantasy of hurting others, but to
> work out how a man might look when he shoots or is shot.
> A hero is one who looks like a hero.[5.8]

The mocking of style is part of the genre inversion of the following scene: in an exquisitely beautiful golden sunset, three silent
armed horsemen are shown moving on Presbyterian Church: death
prowling through spilled flame to ominous music. But instead of
grim riders in darkness, these evil presences are photographed as
heroic gilded knights against the sun, mocking genre conventions.
Simultaneously, they are a comment on the film cliches of "civilization": power figures so typical of commercials and industrial shorts,
here visual anachronisms bringing only destruction to the frontier.

As the anti-genre **McCabe and Mrs. Miller** repeatedly suggests,
the coming civilization is little but a treacherous killer-engine, so
the crude frontier community is treated with more than Fordian
sentimentality, and at times a mood approaching indulgent hilarity.
McBride and Wilmington have commented that in **My Darling Clementine**:

> The town is so removed from civilization that it does not
> seem to have a working mayor . . . ; governmental affairs are
> conducted either in the saloon or on Main Street. Adolescent
> boys would be especially attracted to the theme because the
> Earp brothers run the town as if it were their club-
> house . . . .[5.9]

Carrying this to its logical anti-genre extreme, Carridine's cow-
boy-innocent in Altman's film is shown in long underwear like a
pyjama-ed child, wandering through the bordello's bright parlour,
grinning at white and Oriental women alike as he looks them all over,

crowing: "Oh, hell, don't make no difference, I gotta have you all!"

Another aspect of the genre's theme of the "taming" of the West through community, the special "practical" western education, is meanwhile inverted in a scene upstairs in the bordello. In the film **Liberty Valance**, for example, the old westerner Doniphon-Wayne educates the young easterner Stoddard-Stewart:

> Doniphon-Wayne: I know those lawbooks mean a lot to you — but not out here — out here a man settles his own problems.

In an ironic anti-genre mocking of this motif, Mrs. Miller-Christie speaks with the new young widow, helping her accept the idea of prostitution. The madam removes the young woman's rough home-spun, replacing it with the soft linen the house women all wear, as she explains softly that the sex act really means nothing, the girl should learn to take her mind off it ("count the roses on the wall-paper"). She should relax and perhaps she'll even get to like it. The speech concludes by comparing marriage unfavorably with her new profession:

> Mrs. Miller-Christie: It wasn't your duty, Ida — you did it to pay for your bed and board — and you do this to pay for your bed and board, too — only you get to keep a little extra for yourself . . . . You don't have to ask nobody for nothin' — it's more honest, to my mind.

This speech again suggests that Mrs. Miller-Christie is Altman's anti-genre feminine Wyatt Earp out of Ford's **My Darling Clementine**, capable of "dealing" with both crude western "community" and avaricious corporate "civilization." That she is Ford's hero transposed into an ironic anti-genre treatment becomes apparent by reading J.A. Place's description of the source character:

> Earp passes between the best values of East and West with no real problem, . . . Earp is a man of the West with no conflict in his character — no nostalgia for the lost dreams, no naive looking forward to lost futures. He is self-contained and capable of partaking from either culture or of combining them to the very best advantage.[5.10]

Mrs. Miller-Christie's keen awareness of cross-cultural conflict, notably in her early pleas to McCabe-Beatty to make a deal, is dramatically realized in the scene of the arrival of the three company killers. Their mere sinister presence is enough to break up the child-ish skating-dancing of the frontiersmen on the frozen stream. Again she insists that the gambler-entrepreneur make some bargain before "he has no business and no money at all!"

Like a conflicted Doc Holliday, McCabe-Beatty insists calmly that the three are company timeservers only anxious to work things out. His apparent mastery of the situation is immediately shown up when an emissary races in to tell him before the woman that: "They said there was nothing to talk about!" Miffed, he goes to see them himself, ignoring Mrs. Miller-Christie's idea of escaping hidden in a supply wagon, responding: "I guess if a man's fool enough to get into business with a woman, she ain't gonna think much of him!" The line is an interesting interpretation of the **My Darling Clementine** character, as well as of the genre archetypical Western's attitude towards women, as seen by Warshow:

> The westerner himself, when an explanation is asked of him (usually by a woman) is likely to say that he does what he "has to do." If justice and order did not continually demand his protection, he would be without a calling . . . .[5.11]

In this anti-genre work, however, it is not abstract "justice" that is being maintained, but its shabby materialist counterpart, a "fair" business deal.

The first meeting of McCabe-Beatty and the company death squad clarifies Altman's anti-genre vision of the West: a fragile Eden to be poisoned and perverted by technological/capitalistic "civilization." The three killers wait in Sheehan-Auberjonois' ancient saloon, still dingy, dark and crudely furnished, like the primordial beast-brain of McCabe-Beatty's evolved community. Butler (Hugh Millais), the buckskinned giant hunter-killer, tells all, with enormous delight, how advanced explosives carried by sacrificed Chinese laborers will permit high efficiency mining (Butler-Millais: "The company inspectors say four out of five times it's an *accident*! You could do it here! Up to the rock face — CRASH!"). His companions, a stiff halfbreed and a meanfaced blond youth dressed as Little Lord Fauntleroy, watch grimly. The three recall the genre's "clans" of villains, exemplified by the perverse, evil Clanton family in **My Darling Clementine**; here they are rendered as Anglo-Saxon technological imperialism mated to race defilement, somehow having bred the detached amoral sadism of a child.

McCabe-Beatty's response stylizes the genre's clumsy dude (e.g., Stoddard-Stewart as a "waiter" in **Liberty Valance**) — he even picks up Butler-Millais' ashtray. The gambler-entrepreneur lets himself be ridiculed and humiliated, apologizing and backing off, losing all dignity, virtually surrendering until the sadistic killer tells him, laughing, that: "I don't make deals!" At this point, Butler-Millais asks about the man McCabe-Beatty supposedly shot, claiming the deceased was his best friend, so McCabe-Beatty relinquishes any credit for the death ("He went for his gun and he got shot, that's all − "), and gets out. At the end, Butler-Millais says he never knew the dead man and "that man never killed anybody!" The sequence, painful to watch, is anti-genre in the bleakest sense: McCabe-Beatty realistically letting himself be humiliated before the town rather than be destroyed by overwhelming forces.

The following sequence is crucial to understanding McCabe-Beatty as a complex, subtle anti-genre figure not, as many critics have described him, a weak unworthy fool, but as a heroic, flawed individual whose own contradictions illuminate the genre. As noted, J.A. Place has pointed out that **My Darling Clementine**'s Doc Holliday's problem is:

> . . . his inability to come to terms with himself and the various aspects of his life . . . the kind of power he wields and yet hates . . . [represented by] the women in his life − Clementine Carter; Eastern, fair, respectable, and virginal; and Chihuahua; dark . . . wild, unrefined, perhaps a prostitute.[5.12]

As Warshow has pointed out, such inner conflicts are a basic aspect of the "westerner" (see 5.11).

In the anti-genre **McCabe and Mrs. Miller**, Altman illuminates these motifs through mocking inversion. Mrs. Miller-Christie seems to combine the "best" aspects of Clementine and Chihuahua (see above), but she is not accessible to McCabe except on her terms. Unable to deal with this, McCabe-Beatty, like John Ford's Doc Holliday, grows romantically self-destructive. As Doc Holliday recites Hamlet's suicide speech, McCabe-Beatty acknowledges his own crisis in the comic/ironic mode, his conflict not so different from the western genre archetype who must pick up the gun as the only way to show who he is:

> McCabe-Beatty: . . . I keep tryin' and a tryin' to tell ya in a lotta different ways − if just one time you could be sweet without no money around I think I could − well I tell ya somethin', I got poetry in me − I do, but I ain't gonna put it down on paper, I got sense enough not to try. Can't never say nothin' to *you*! If you'd just one time let me run the show, I'd − freezin' my soul, that's what you're doin', freezin' my soul!

Altman's anti-genre western in fact has explicitly transposed the westerner's key conflict into sexual terms for, as Warshow points out:

> What he defends at bottom is the purity of his own image − in fact his honor . . . the image the Westerner seeks to

maintain can be presented as clearly in defeat as in victory; he fights not for advantage and not for the right, but to state what he is, and he must live in a world which permits that statement. The Westerner is the last gentleman . . . .[5.13]

In Altman's anti-genre work, it is not only the heroine who has no use for the Westerner, but the entire civilized future that proves to be his enemy. Riding to the mining company offices to make a deal and save his life, McCabe-Beatty finds the company agents gone, and only a young pompous lawyer, a comic inversion of the genre frontier attorney. Unlike John Ford's Stoddard-Stewart character, who speaks sincerely if naively of the coming "power of the little man," Lawyer Samuels (William Devane) prattles ingratiatingly about "the little guys like you" and "bustin' the trusts," an incompetent opportunist who ignores McCabe-Beatty's mumbling about just not wanting to get killed.

The same character can be seen in a more sinister anti-genre light: as combining the worst aspects of Ford's idealistic young Stoddard-Stewart, and the same older worldly politician seeing the McCabe case, whether the man lives or not, as a broad road leading to Washington, DC. The sequence also includes another bleak genre reversal: in **Liberty Valance**, the idealist Stoddard-Stewart and tough Westerner Doniphon-Wayne acted in concert to bring about the "taming" of the frontier. In **McCabe and Mrs. Miller**, the lone Westerner is opposed by a host of civilized yet soulless specialists not open to communal empathy: an opportunist lawyer; corporation agent/henchmen; a death squad under orders — who will all apparently chillingly disembowel and then normalize the sloppy but warm frontier community.

McCabe-Beatty's anti-genre Westerner, his locked-up personality made to seem ridiculous, returns to Presbyterian Church, where the comic treatment of his archetype Westerner's behavior goes on. Giving Mrs. Miller-Christie some lawyer talk about bustin' the trusts, she screeches that he's got to sell out and go some place where people are civilized. When he tries to comfort her, she shouts that she just wants her percentage, so she can make a deal with them.

The next sequence gives a grisly anti-genre preview of the coming "civilization" which will replace the western community. In sheepskin coat and comically tall hat, cowboy-Carradine warmly says goodbye to Mrs. Miller-Christie's girls, Ida-Duvall in high black stockings waving with a wistful sensuousness while the others turn to cheerily welcoming new patrons. Leaving the center of the community, he pauses on the slackroped wooden bridge when the youthful company gunman insults him, then taunts him into reaching for a pistol he admits he doesn't know how to use (Carradine's eyes show a dawning terror). As he touches the weapon, the evil boy blasts him off the bridge, so he seems to sit, tailor-fashion, in the water, hat over his face, his figure dissolving in soft focus while the townsfolk stand frozen and the company killers grin.

The murder and fall, chilling in its own right, is more upsetting for being the anti-genre opposite of the earlier-depicted death and internment. As French points out[5.7]: "That life may be easily taken does not mean that it is cheap and of no significance" in the genre. By contrast, this sequence does not simply suggest the opposite point of view, but identifies it with the forces of civilization. Indeed, the company death squad talk and behave less like western badmen than like knowing transplants from more contemporary genres: science fiction aliens with deathrays, Nazi storm troopers, Mafia "enforcers," C.I.A. men "terminating with extreme prejudice." The visual depiction of the death and its aftermath is also in opposition to the genre: instead of a tragic inevitability followed by emotional ritual, as a cruel whim the cowboy-Carradine character is punched off the bridge in abstract slow motion, then seems to disassociate materialistically back into atoms through the use of the visual dissolve. Death is not a spiritual transformation, but simply total annihilation.

In three separate encounters — McCabe-Beatty meeting the Carradine-cowboy, McCabe-Beatty meeting Butler-Millais, and Butler-Millais meeting the Carradine-cowboy — Altman's film creates expectations of a ritual genre gunfight, then rewards them with comedy, pathos, and horror. Yet, the inevitability of a final shootout becomes greater with each sequence, not only via the dramatic rhythms but through growing evidence of characters with both irreconcilable viewpoints and the willingness to kill.

First, however, in a genre figure of style, western hero and heroine, McCabe-Beatty and Mrs. Miller-Christie, have a final lovers' meeting. Altman's anti-genre directorial choice is to simply have McCabe-Beatty visit the woman, warmly state his well-intentioned hopes ("I've only tried to put a smile on your face"), and break down weeping, not perhaps so much at doom as at his own limitations and contradictions as a genre character ("I don't know what it is . . . I guess I never been this close to nobody before."). Her amusingly modernist response is to simply, smilingly welcome him under the covers ("Come 'on . . . you don't have to say nothin' "). But he awakens alone, with no sign of where she has gone.

The gunfight is likewise treated in an elaborate anti-genre fashion, taking place not in nature or in a dusty, raw frontier village, but among the large wooden buildings of the built-up community adrift in winter white under a bright blue sky, a Christmas card of mature frontier America. The anti-genre point is that the fullgrown western community, ready to be "civilized," has no place or use for McCabe-Beatty; he will fight and die alone, the town's citizens hiding from him or denying his peril. The banner on the casino — The House of Fortune — has a mocking double implications: success has only endangered McCabe-Beatty, and the "successful" community he created is conservative and won't help him.

Likewise, the anti-genre heroine, Mrs. Miller-Christie, responding with the enlightened self-interest she cultivates as the ironic "best" of society and community, will not support him. The Leonard Cohen ballad suggests his acknowledgment of this as he plods alone with his rifle through a light snowfall:

> Traveling lady, stay a while
> Until the night is over.
> I'm just a station on your way;
> I know I'm not your lover.

The elaborate stalking, feinting and murdering of the gunfight which follows also includes much knowing anti-genre mockery. In **My Darling Clementine**, the scene on the foundations of the incompleted church with its charming formal dancing, is "the physical expression of the society the West can support, with all its ritualistic connotations."5.14 In the anti-genre **McCabe and Mrs. Miller**, McCabe-Beatty runs lightly over the snow like a child to the lonely, unwanted, dark, incomplete church, from whose steeple he watches the company killers split up to cover the town. Moments after, he's forced out of the sanctuary by the bigoted preacher, who's built it alone, and we watch the religionist shotgunned by the sadistic giant Butler-Millais: Ford's jerky unifying square dance rhythms replaced by a slow-motion blood explosion. (The dances in this film are held at the bordello.) The lantern he was carrying sets the church ablaze.

In the next anti-genre stylistic figure, the half-breed company killer is shown walking through the slummy Chinese quarter of Presbyterian Church, a complex comment on the "pure" frontier, showing it had its own ghettos from the first. We also see one minority's detachment at another's abuse, mocking the loyal Afro-American servant Pompey (Woody Strode), who helps Doniphon-Wayne in **Liberty Valance** "tame" the town. Here, the racial minorities have always been pushed around, and furthermore are willing to use weapons against the sympathetic characters.

In one more anti-genre moment, McCabe-Beatty skitters through the snow to crouch in the bordello's bathhouse, hiding and then shooting the blond young killer in the back so he slides into a full tub, though he does wound the gambler. The death is the visual counterpart of and revenge for the cowboy-Carradine, the image again dissolving into soft focus, but even fighting the civilization murder-engine, it also implies, reduces the West's death rituals to the enemy's spiritless annihilation of matter shaped like people.

The church fire can be seen as an anti-Ford parody of the burning down of "town tamer" Doniphon-Wayne's ranch in **Liberty Valance**. The genre point of the Ford film fire is that "in doing away with Western Law, Tom also destroys the only way of life he can accept, and literally tries to destroy himself in the flames of his home."[5.15] In the anti-genre **McCabe and Mrs. Miller**, the church, until now shunned as a symbol of civilized repression and hypocrisy, is "saved" through the town's newfound social cooperation, even as the shady individual responsible for all this "progress" is being hunted down and freezes in the snow a few hundred yards away. In the Ford film, the structure signifying Old West values must be destroyed; in the anti-genre Altman film the incomplete building which stands for civilized stifling of feeling and insincerity is saved. Mockingly, this is done with all the "progress" at the town's disposal: an assembly-line bucket brigade, the steam-train acting as an industrial waterpump, the temporary calling in of the shunned Afro-American couple to provide more labor.

A final anti-Ford touch follows at once: McCabe-Beatty conceals himself in the town's barbershop, which in **My Darling Clementine** represents "Eastern values struggling to make themselves felt in the west . . . !"[5.16] In **McCabe and Mrs. Miller**, however, McCabe-Beatty's only use for the barber's chair is as an object to crouch behind until he can shoot the halfbreed member of the company killer squad in the back.

The conclusion of Altman's anti-genre gunfight is fascinating in its visual audacity. The archetypical western shootout has long been critically noted for its special pictorial-moral correlates. In **My Darling Clementine**: "the town's moral schematization is echoed in the town's topography . . . squares and planes, like a chessboard or a battlefield . . . , especially [emphasized in] the use of fences in the gunfight."[5.17] In opposition to this, the **McCabe and Mrs. Miller** shootout concludes amid deep snowdrifts and snowfalls which cause the eye to become disoriented, the visual counterpart of the contradictory social and moral forces which Altman's characters represent. Fleeing up a snowy slope, McCabe-Beatty is blasted by the sadistically-grinning giant Butler-Millais. The company murderer staggers through the drifts towards the gambler-entrepreneur, who drops his pistol and slides down the snowbank. After wading through the whiteness towards the sprawled form, who has already shot two men in the back, Butler pauses over the shape with the same slumped-over posture as the two dead youths. As if in visual revenge,

McCabe-Beatty's figure abruptly straightens and discharges a tiny extra handgun into the monster's forehead, confirming this anti-genre gunfight as a sly, dishonorable business won by the man with the most tricks . . . (and no Wayne-Doniphon to help).

Altman's conclusion is a bitter anti-genre treatment of the subtle genre paradoxes in John Ford's later westerns. Ford's "town tamers," Wyatt Earp and Tom Doniphon, leave quietly or die later in obscurity, ignored, forgotten transition figures. McCabe-Beatty dies almost under the ignoring eyes of the townsfolk whose lives he has transformed, while they foolishly celebrate the empty victory of saving the unwanted church. Alternately, the acquisitive McCabe-Beatty can be seen as a less heroic, flawed character who set the stage for future abuses, as much Doc Holliday as Wyatt Earp, as much lawyer Stoddard as Tom Doniphon, now dying and dissolving into the snow as he will be ignored in the town's later respectable "civilized" history.

Mrs. Miller-Christie's anti-genre female Westerner is likewise shown dissolving away in her own fashion — in an opium den in the town's Chinese quarter. **Stagecoach**'s prostitute Dallas goes off with a good outlaw; **My Darling Clementine**'s prostitute Chihuahua is killed and Clementine herself becomes a schoolmarm; **Liberty Valance**'s Hallie marries the territory's new Senator. But Altman's anti-genre pioneer woman can join neither community nor civilization, and rather chooses bouts of oblivion from the cruel limitations of both. The film's final image, the solarized ceramic jar that holds her drug "works," schematizes her anti-genre West: golden brown ceramic, edged with blue-white light, and beyond that, blackness: the illusionistic warmth of community, bounded by lovely indifferent natural sky and snow, and beyond that — death and oblivion.

Images (1972)

Images is Robert Altman's anti-genre exploration of what might be called the theme of madness. This genre includes such critically revered films as **Psycho, Repulsion,** and **Persona**, all typified by insoluble puzzles and ambiguities, deliberate multiple interpretations, and participation in major psychopathology. Their theme, broadly speaking, is madness as a possible way of life.

To wind chimes, a dissonant cascade of piano notes, and shivering electronic sounds, the camera pans across a fine home's brick front, then zooms in past rich furnishings, expensive cameras and lenses, expensive bric-a-brac, to the lovely blond Cathryn (Susannah York) sitting tailor fashion at a writing desk. Her husky voice begins a Tolkien-sounding tale, *In Search of Unicorns*; she is writing to wind chimes and climbing electronic notes, the soft disjointed cacophony of ululating music, fantastic imaginings, and luxurious eroticism together suggesting and mocking the austere, disoriented beginnings of **Psycho, Persona,** and **Repulsion.** The title **Images** appears, pointing up a deliberate detachment from the awareness of medium by filmmaker; in fact, the working title of **Persona** was **Film.**

As Cathryn-York keeps writing, the film's mood and tone are clarified as treatment of an individual's gradual retreat into fantasy and delusion. The plotline is nailed down as the lovely Cathryn-York reaches a highpoint in her narrative, both mocking the genre's tendency to let the viewer know the kind of material to expect, and suggesting he can leave his attention free to pick up on the ambiguities, ambivalences, and genre reversals:

> . . . In the pit the water rose round her . . . . Bother, blast, she said, I bet I'll drown! . . . Suddenly, the sounds of *something* came crashing through the forest — stretching a long arm down into the pit in the pouring rain. It's no good! I can't see anything, not even your hand! *I'm too deep!*

The opening fairy story thus directly mocks the genre's tendency to use small subliminal harbingers of the storyline. At the start of

Persona, for example, the disturbed actress watches a TV show with a slow-motion burning Buddhist priest, backing terrified away from this "entertainment"; while in the motel tryst in **Psycho**, the male rejects respectability ("Send sister to the movies, turn Mama's picture to the wall.").

The next sequence commences in the married Cathryn-York's luxurious all-white urban condominium; its elegant, mirrored walls and creamy, thick carpets bring to mind Andrew Sarris' comment that: "American admirers on the arthouse circuit were . . . ripe for Bergman not only because his concerns were more relevant to the *angst* of sheer affluence but also because he seemed immune to the corruptions of mass taste."[6.1] Throughout, sets and characters are almost comically upper class.

The lovely highstrung Cathryn-York receives a series of increasingly upsetting phone calls. The first caller is simply a gabby, self-concerned divorcee with alimony problems, the second a mysterious throaty female voice that could even be her own, laughing cruelly and asking if she knows where her husband is tonight. Her husband's call that he'll be late is followed by the too-similar voice laughingly telling how he's in bed with her. The series of calls is a counterpart to the one in **Repulsion**, ending with not one but half a dozen phones in the fancy apartment all off the hook and buzzing eerily as husband Hugh (Rene Auberjonois) arrives. Hugh-Auberjonois' is a skinny, weak and insensitive British aristocrat ("Jesus Christ, Catherine!" is his characteristic petulent response). To her accusations of adultery he smilingly replies: "There is only you," a pun — Hugh/you) — which prefigures the film's visual style: deliberate visual ambivalence.

The genre storyline, involving an early-on transition to an isolated "sanctuary" which proves a terrifying trap, is parodied in Cathryn-York's anguished cry that they go to the couple's "home" ("I want to go to Greencover!"). Similarly, the **Repulsion** heroine is abandoned alone in the apartment, as are the two protagonists in the cottage in **Persona**, and **Psycho**'s isolated "hero."

Characteristically, the genre storyline next has a transition to an extreme psychopathological state by a sympathetic protagonist. In **Images**, this happens in stages: the couple's expensive roadster climbs gentle red-brown Scottish hills, plump clouds move in the bright sky, wind whimes murmur, Cathryn-York voice-overs her fantasy. From the hillcrest, the couple looks down on a lovely cottage beside a lake, high waterfall, and browsing miniature horses. Eerily, the camera zooms from crest to cottage front, where a blond female figure stands — our first view of Cathryn-York's Alter Ego. The real character "still" stands with her husband atop the hill. A little later, while the young woman is preparing dinner, she meets and speaks with a second hallucination, suave, balding, deceased lover Rene (Marcel Bozzuffi): "Remember when John and Sherry came up for the weekend at Boscowich?" Kissing, smiling, he hands her the wine bottle she's been looking for: "Spaghetti without wine is like a ship without a rudder!"

The introduction of the Alter Ego and dead lover hallucinations also make plain the extreme visual stylic devices characteristic of the genre. In the case of **Images**, deliberate visual ambivalence. Butler[6.2] discusses the counterpart in **Repulsion**, total identification with the subjective point of view of the mad protagonist:

> [Carol] then goes to the kitchen for a drink of water, and hears a grinding crackling noise in the wall . . . . A few minutes afterwards we also see the figure of a man leaning against the bedroom wall — something which . . . definitely does not really exist. These twin events herald a fundamental change in our subjective connection with Carol — the entry, so to speak, into her mind . . . . From now through until her final collapse, however, our relationship will be an integral one, the change indicated not by any alteration in our viewpoint . . . but by the fact that even while watching her from apart, we see what only she can see.

In a third example, **Psycho**, the visual convention (misleading, partial information) is introduced during the shock of the shower death, (viz., the seemingly innocent clerk Norman Bates (Tony Perkins) is shown to be only an eager "accessory" to the shocking motiveless murders).

Images mocks the extreme visual stylization convention of the genre by its choice of devices: deliberate *objective* visual ambivalence, which constantly calls attention to itself. It is in contrast to the other films' visual styles which allow us to identify and "sympathize" with the protagonist: misleading incompleteness in **Psycho**, subjective viewpoint in **Repulsion**, and the ambiguity of "fact versus fantasy" in **Persona**.[6.3]

The deliberate ambivalence shows up again in an early scene, in which Cathryn-York rebukes the ghost of the stocky, thin-haired lover Rene Bozzoffi: "Stop, you're dead!" To rising electronic music: "You weren't on that plane! You weren't in that crash! Somebody else took your plane, somebody else died, not you!" Struggling, stabbing him with a kitchen knife, triumphantly: "My-my-my, ghosts bleed!" But within seconds, Hugh-Auberjonois tears his hand in his shotgun breech, so the bloodstains on the floor have a second "reasonable" explanation.

Deliberate mockeries of genre conventions follow. Various

In Altman's psychopathology genre-commentary *Images*, the protagonist's child lookalike Susannah (Catherine Harrison) mocks the genre's characteristic visual devices, here parodying Bergmanesque image and mood.

In the psychopathology film *Persona*, extreme visual stylization is used to merge reality and fantasy/hallucination; here, the two protagonists seem to be alter egos, furthering the confusion and blending process.

dialogues suggest Cathryn-York's problems are due to her *lack* of a child, the reverse of the mother-child and sexual traumas in **Persona, Psycho** and **Repulsion**. Fiercely confronting the Rene-Bozzoffi ghost-lover, she tells him: "Let me tell you something – all I ever wanted from you was a baby! I did not cheat, I did not cheat!" The locale is also the opposite of the stifling motel in **Psycho**, the maddening bleakness of **Persona**'s seashore, the shabby squalor of the apartment in **Repulsion**; rather Cathryn-York writes in a lovely natural park-garden, all rich gold/green heather, with a stupendously tall waterfall off a vertical stone face, and delightful dwarf horses.

The deliberately ambivalent visual style quickly becomes a convention, as when the enormous smiling artist Marcel (Hugh Millais) and his blond girlchild Susannah (Cathryn Harrison) visit, the presexual double for Cathryn-York hiding and popping out of a cupboard, like another hallucination. Getting them drinks, Cathryn-York is smoothly handed the bottle by the just-out-of-sight Rene-Bozzoffi illusion, who murmurs: "You want it – take it!"

This key visual style convention – psychopathology rendered as deliberate visual ambivalence rather than by misleading incompleteness (**Psycho**), subjective point of view (**Repulsion**), or fantasy vs. fact ambiguity (**Persona**) – is visually developed in the next sequence, the dreamy end of an impromptu drinking party to the eerie rattling electronic music. Marcel-Millais' massive artist murmurs bitterly of his wife's adultery: ". . . screwing everything she could find . . . a year and a half's evidence with sixteen different men . . ." triggering tension among the sprawled figures in the luxurious, low-lit room. Leaving a dozing male, Cathryn-York helps another carry the child to the car, the man making a heavy pass ("Bitch!") by holding her against him, she pulling away and crying how she loves her husband: "I know I'm sick but I love him – so just keep away!" A male – shown as Marcel-Millais, but never clearly the sexual aggressor – does not pursue her. Neil Feineman stresses how the whole scene is deliberately visually ambivalent and clearly confusing, the stylistic counterpart of the shower scene in **Psycho**, which is misleading through suppression of key facts:

> Regardless of how many times the scene with Hugh, Marcel, Cathryn, and Susannah talking after dinner is watched, the tracing of who is laughing and kissing Cathryn and who is sleeping is impossible . . . . Like Cathryn herself, we have no way of knowing; also like her, we want, even need, to know. Because we cannot, our own feelings of frustration, dislocation, and confusion are further intensified.[6.4]

Staggering inside, the woman clutches at her husband, begging for him to make love to her, but numb, tired, drunk, he pushes her away and plods upstairs.

With his visual style convention established, Altman's **Images** proceeds with its anti-genre story treatment. The genre he will comment on has a characteristic three-step thematic development: the justification of madness, the madness strategy thrown into question, and the final mystery/retreat. For example, early in **Psycho**, the protagonist Norman Bates (Tony Perkins) "justifies" with quiet dignity what turns out to be total madness:

> Norman-Perkins: You know what I think? . . . We're all in our private traps, clamped in them, and none of us can ever get out. We scratch and claw, but only at the air, only at each other . . . I was born in mine. I don't mind it anymore . . . . We all go a little mad sometimes . . . haven't you?

In the same way, the early voice-over of the psychiatrist in **Persona** cleverly "justifies" the mute actress' mental illness as a desperate "defense through art" against unbearable stress:

> Psychiatrist: . . . you are forced to react. Nobody asks if it is true or false, whether you're genuine or a sham. Such things matter only in the theatre, and hardly even there . . . I understand and admire. You should go on with this part until it is played out, until it loses interest for you. Then you can leave it, as you left all your other parts, one by one.

In **Repulsion**, the justifying of Carol's (Cathryn Deneuve's) retreat into insanity is clearly, though much less explicitly stated: the total bleak isolation from which she chooses to withdraw. As Ivan Butler puts it:

> And there is loneliness. The whole world of **Repulsion** . . . is lonely. No one in the last resort, understands or can help anyone else. "We all have our own lives to lead, you know."[6.5]

In the anti-genre **Images**, however, insanity is never justified, never even accepted as a necessary evil for survival. For instance, soon after the drunken party Cathryn-York is shown in bed with the Rene-Bozzoffi figure, making love, the two rolling over, so she's abruptly in the massive embrace of Marcel-Mallais, equally ecstatic, rolling again so she's shown in lonely fulfilled closeup, followed by ravishing images of flames, excited eyes, rain on windows, and other orgasm-conventions. Standing nude, she turns to contemplate the ambiguous lover/illusion — and screeches, for it is her bitterly smiling Alter Ego in the nude. At her screams, her frantic husband brings her back to bed, the conclusion tending to suggest it was Hugh-Auberjonois all along. More important, the sequence suggests that irrationality, even momentarily unleashed, will make survival for Cathryn-York more agonizing rather than easier. Here and elsewhere, Cathryn-York's lapses into madness are sources of immediate pain and stress; in a genre reversal, we're never allowed to luxuriate in irrational impulses.

Once justified, the psycho-thriller protagonist gradually comes to question madness as a life strategem. In **Psycho**, **Persona**, and **Repulsion**, this thematic development comes after much story exposition. The anti-genre **Images** uses the same screen time to mock and reverse a number of lesser genre motifs. Typically, Marcel-Millais' arrival at the cottage next morning is signalled by an ironic: "Had a hell of a time getting out of bed!" mocking his earlier appearance in Cathryn-York's sexual fantasy. Taking the child Susannah-Harrison to the lovely fairy-tale park, Cathryn-York speaks to the girl of her own broken home and isolated growing up, suggesting a special mystical communion and understanding between the look-alikes, as in **Persona**. But the child only reacts in a warm, conventional manner; there is no psychic blending.

At the same time, the anti-genre **Images** never collapses into a simple clinical case history. For instance, later on, Cathryn-York seems to be in bed with a gleeful Marcel-Millais, who attempts a parlour psycho analysis:

> Marcel-Millais: You started this, now you're going to finish it . . . . You know what you are? You're a sick girl. One moment you're fighting like a tiger — the next all love and kisses! . . . I understand about you!

Her response is to stab the hallucination repeatedly with a knife, suggesting once more a full awareness of and rejection of her condition.

Characteristically, the psycho-thriller concludes with a questioning of madness as a life pattern. In **Psycho**, this is made explicit by the police psychiatrist's diagnosis of the now catatonic protagonist, proposing that the protagonist has no more reality as a personality:

> Psychiatrist: He was never all Norman, but he was often only Mother . . . .

There is in fact a counterpart speech late in **Persona**:

> Alma: Don't you think one improves a little even by letting oneself be as one is? . . . People like you can't be reached. I wonder whether your madness isn't the worst kind. You act healthy — so well that everyone believes you. Everyone but me. Because I know how rotten you are . . . .

Robin Wood argues that **Persona**'s narrative rejects the viability of madness as a way of life, in terms of the genre protagonist's mysterious retreat:

> The second half of the film conveys a sensation of sinking into a dark, perhaps bottomless abyss of uncertainties, both for the women and for the spectator. Elizabeth's withdrawal is no solution: we see her defeated at every turn . . . . Her very refusal to take part in life becomes, however unwittingly, a positive action with unforeseeable and uncontrollable consequences. In fact, she finds it impossible just to do *nothing*. [In several incidents] her silence preserves the ambiguity and thereby inflicts further pain.[6.6]

In **Repulsion**, the questioning of madness as a life tactic is much less explicit; rather, it is suggested by Carol-Deneuve's gradual disintegration, ending with her unconscious, having concealed herself under the bed where her sister made love, the focus of her attraction-repulsion.

In the anti-genre **Images**, Cathryn-York's madness is not faulted as fatal life plan, but "controlled" by her via its own special rules. Alone at the cottage, she encounters the suave European Rene-Bozzuffi illusion: "Do you want me dead?" he smiles: "Make me dead!" In response, she discharges the shotgun, concealing the "corpse" while explaining shakily that the gun fired accidentally.

Increasingly bewildered, Cathryn-York next gets a message that she must drive her husband to the train (he's needed at work for a day). At the station he makes another terrible pun but powerful portent:

> Hugh-Auberjonois: What's the difference between a rabbit?
> Nothing — one is both. The same.

She watches the train go, drives past her smiling Alter Ego, and finds the Marcel-Millais illusion at the cottage, having already checked that he is "really" elsewhere. She stabs him, the two "dead" hallucination in dark pullovers, trousers and bloodstains sprawled on the floor.

In an anti-genre victory, she has "mastered" her own unwanted madness. To reinforce the film's deliberately ambivalent storytelling, she is shown leading a neighbor through her home, though he apparently never glimpses the imaginary corpse.

The anti-genre **Images** then goes on to complete its reversal of themes and motifs. Characteristically, the film of madness ends with a final mystery-retreat. This is suggested in Raymond Durgnat's perceptive analysis of the climactic moments of **Psycho**, with Norman-Perkins seated in his cell, his face full up and fully mad, cackling in the voice of his mother:

83

[Norman's] ricocheting self punishment is so total that — well, we can hardly pity him, for there's no one left to pity . . . . Nothing to the nth degree has killed real people whom we sympathized with . . . . Each is still alone. This is the sanity that balances the diabolical nothing which is the human soul. Only Norman has defied society and superficiality and found 'rest.' Only Norman has found himself, and lost himself.[6.7]

In **Persona**, the retreat/mystery genre climax, because of the film's many ambiguities, has been interpreted differently by various critics. I favor the analysis of Robin Wood:[6.8]

. . . the breakdown consstitutes Bergman's admission that he can't resolve the problems the film has raised. The last third of **Persona** gives us a series of scenes of uncertain reality and uncertain chronology; all are closely related, thematically, to the concerns established earlier in the firlm, and all carry us deeper into the sensation of breakdown due to full exposure to the unresolvable or unendurable . . . .

In **Persona**'s conclusion, however, we see the nurse depart and there is a mood of calm if not resolution. We also see the actress on stage, leading critics to suggest her health has returned, or, an equivalent subtext, that the body of the film is her momentary fugue during a single performance.

The final retreat-mystery of **Repulsion** is perhaps best suggested by the moment in which the mad girl is picked up by her sister's lover, whom she seemed to have hated:

. . . . The look he gives her as she lies in his arms wide eyed, expressionless, like a child, . . . touches something hidden deep in us all . . . Alastair McIntyre, the editor, interestingly suggests that Carol has really been in love with Michael all along in a curious, disguised way, and that now, at last, she is where she has always longed to be — in his arms.[6.9]

In a genre reversal, the climax of **Images** exchanges mystery and retreat for the clarity of explicit painful ambivalence. Driving on the moor after "disposing" of her hallucinations, Cathryn-York encounters a lonely plodding figure, apparently her adult self, her Alter Ego. Shouting through the window, the voice female and familiar but using Hugh's expressions, the figure pleads: "For Christ sake, open the door and let me in . . . . For Christ sake, Cathryn, it's me."

Cathryn-York [to herself] I know it's you. But I've found

out how to get rid of you — just like Rene and Marcel, I can get you out of my mind forever.

She drives towards the figure, knocking it down a ravine and out of sight, the last problem solved.

She then drives to her town apartment, entering the elegant rooms, the shower already roaring and misty, picking out a female shape in the spray, who purrs: "See Cathryn — it was easy." It is her blond Alter-Ego, and **Images** cuts from Cathryn-York's horrified eyes in the roaring shower to the immense waterfall in the fairyland park, panning down to her dead husband still releasing blood into the foot of the falls. The neat ending, however, is more apparent than real, as Feineman[6.10] and Falonga[6.11] both seek to show, there is as much evidence that Cathryn-York only "killed" a third hallucination.

The evidence that the last death was just one more fantasy is actually considerable: Cathryn-York fantasizes often but has never really killed; her cliffside speech, because "Hugh" and "you" are homonyms, is coyly ambiguous; the real steamy bathroom suggests Hugh is alive and present; finally the much-too-late death, mocks the genre's tendency to use murders to make us take the descent into madness seriously. Interestingly, Feineman has pointed out that whether the last murder is real or a hallucination, **Images** works as an effective genre film, with a hopelessly mad protagonist.

In fact, the shower scene seems most significant as a final definitive genre comment. To begin with, it recalls the famous shower death in **Psycho**, in which Hitchcock makes clear his formal device of concealing the protagonist's mad nature, here Altman reemphasizing his own formal use of deliberate ambivalence via protagonist Cathryn-York and her Alter Ego. In this, it points up how all genre protagonists (in **Psycho**, **Persona**, **Repulsion**) withdraw into mystery, and the viewer regains a normal perspective. For, at the end of **Images**, the opposite holds: Altman forces on us again Cathryn-York's permanent inability to separate facts and hallucinations. In doing this, he reemphasizes her special pain and terror, the nightmare chaos into which she advances. In this solipsistic chaos, she and we must constantly face more terrifying possibilities, the precise opposite of the final withdrawals of the genre protagonists from us, and our own thankful return to normalcy. Altman thus suggests that the genre avoids the terrible core of madness as a way of life: unending, expanding isolation, confusion and despair.

The Long Goodbye (1973)

The raucous "Hooray for Hollywood," together with the Raymond Chandler title, at once signal that Robert Altman's **The Long Goodbye** will be a self-conscious anti-genre treatment of the detection film. Just as its title suggests the classic detective film **The Big Sleep** (Howard Hawks, Humphrey Bogart), so much of Altman's **The Long Goodbye** can be viewed as stylizing or comment upon that particular realization of Raymond Chandler's detective theme: the honorable search for moral behavior in a corrupt world:

> But down these mean streets a man must go who is not himself mean, who is neither tarnished nor afraid . . . . He must be, to use a rather weathered phrase, a man of honor — by instinct, by inevitability, without thought of it, and certainly without saying it.[7.1]

Two more genre themes are also treated: the "doppelganger" or character double of the detective, and the distrust of sexualized human relationships. Both are implicit in the anti-casting of a slack-jawed, gawkily sweet Elliot Gould as detective Philip Marlow, first shown staggering through his shabby bachelor apartment to feed his finicky cat. Mood and tone set are immediately clearly comic — implying that this archetypical movie sleuth character is in truth a comic figure struggling to meet various ridiculous obligations. The idea of the detective genre as foolishness, which Chandler himself was always aware of, is both made explicit and modernized when Marlow-Gould, absurdly questing after a particular cat food, is also asked to pick up "hash-brownie" mix for his drugdazed, half-naked girl neighbors. Both the tower-and-drawbridge layout of his building and druggy "ladies-in-waiting" mock his knightlike idealism. "Mr. Marlowe, you're the nicest neighbor we ever had," a shapely girl murmurs blurrily. "Got to be the nicest neighbor," Marlowe-Gould responds, a morally driven archetype: "I'm a private eye. It's okay with me." The exchange sums up and sends up Chandler's genre hero.

Against the film credits and a "blues" film theme, the shopping trip of Marlowe-Gould in his twenty-year-old Lincoln Continental is edited together with the freeway-jockeying journey via sportscar of the handsome brutish Terry Lennox character (Jim Bouton). The intercutting of the two characters suggests some linkage or affinity, though Lennox-Bouton, with his half contemptuous voice, bruised fists and facial scratches suggesting brutality against a woman, appears the opposite of Marlowe-Gould. The film theme, to appear genre-mockingly in about twenty different tempos and arrangements, adds an ambience of loss and pessimism:

> There's a long goodbye, and it happens every day —
> When some passerby invites your eye to come her way —
> Even as she smiles a quick hello, you've let her go
> You've let the moment fly —
> To late, you turn your head . . .
> (. . .) There's a long goodbye; can you recognize the theme?
> On some other street, two people meet
> As in a dream —
> (. . .) It's too late to try, when a missed hello
> Becomes a long goodbye.

Home again, Marlow-Gould's comic try to substitute another brand for the favorite doesn't work; his cat leaves, never to return. The moment reemphasizes a view of the genre as a detective's attempts to meet various people's unreasonable and unrealistic desires.

Arriving, the sexy/brutal Lennon-Bouton and Marlowe-Gould are linked by wordplay, male camaraderie, and scratched cheeks (by cat, by wife), suggesting a major Chandler and genre theme, the *"doppelganger"* or character double. In the Chandler novel, *The Big Sleep*, as well as the film, the double is the Bacall character's husband, who is "beyond the law . . . Marlowe's alter ego, an adult version of the detective's adolescent, solopsistic Romantic."[7.2] Lennox-Bouton asks for and gets a ride to Tiajuana, no questions asked, suggesting the detective's honor towards friends (see 7.1). One notes that, as first presented, Lennox-Bouton is bright, charming and masculine — a reasonable object for friendship.

Next morning, police detectives question Marlowe-Gould about his trip to Tiajuana, the exchange mocking the cliches of mass-produced TV crime dramas:

> Marlowe-Gould: Oh, is this where I'm supposed to say —
> 'What is all this about?' and you say, 'Shut up, I ask the questions.'
> Detective: (bored-annoyed) Yeah, yeah.

The genre mockery goes on as the police read off the detective's rights even as they haul him out of his home; it continues in the interrogation sequence in which Marlowe-Gould playfully claims to be a homosexual, makes faces at the poorly hidden one-way window in the "interrogation room," and uses fingerprint ink as makeup for a Jolson imitation. When tough lieutenant Farmer (Steve Coit) starts grilling him, a black officer intuits that: "*He's* the cutie pie, lieutenant — *you're* the smart ass!" The distinction points up that the police, and others, are clever but let it show, while cutie-pie Marlowe-Gould has a couple of extra "sly" motives hidden. Altman also parodies the rapid-fire exchanges in Hawkes' **The Big Sleep**, as here:

Marlowe-Bogart: How'd you happen to have one?

Eddie Mars (John Ridgely): Is that any of your business?

Marlowe-Bogart: I could make it my business!

Mars-Ridgely: I could make your business mine.

Marlowe-Bogart: You wouldn't like it, the pay's too small.

A counterpart in **The Long Goodbye** runs:

Marlowe-Gould: (sighs) He's always splitting up with his wife.

Farmer-Coit: Was he cheating on his wife?

Marlowe-Gould: Are you cheating on your wife?

Farmer-Coit: Maybe — but my wife's not dead. Was he cheating on her?

Marlowe-Gould: Is your wife cheating on you?

Lt. Farmer-Coit reveals that Lennox-Bouton's wife was murdered that night, and "not a nice death." Upset but honorable, Marlowe-Gould still won't talk ("I don't like the way you ask questions, and I don't know what you want to know."). Released, the detective is told of Lennox-Bouton's Mexican suicide, but won't believe he killed either his wife or himself.

Marlowe-Gould's next case, concerning unbalanced writer Roger Wade (Sterling Hayden), typifies Chandler's genre work in being a sort of "diversionary mystery" that leads back to the root problem, a counterpart of how Bogart-Marlowe in **The Big Sleep** at first defends the honor of the partly corrupt Sternwood family. Here, the link-up and misdirection is clumsily mocked, the vanished writer's beguiling aristocratic wife (Nina Van Pallandt) supposedly hired Marlowe because of the newspiece linking his honorable silence and the suicide. But Mrs. Wade-Van Pallandt lies on the phone about her husband, then suggests and at once denies she was actually a friend of Lennox-Bouton.

The meeting sequence also mocks the genre's convention of tough duplicitous characters: Wade-Hayden is alluded to as a masculine Hemingwayesque creator turned alcoholic and self destructive;

Mrs. Wade-Van Pallandt is a ravishing longskirted 1950s neurotic who gives herself away. The community's security guard does imitations of *film noire* period movestars — all pointing towards the genre's exhaustion.

The visual elements also seem to mock and otherwise invert genre conventions. Director of photography Vilmos Zsigmond reduced color intensities to pastels because:

> . . . . We did not want to recreate the fifties, but to remember them . . . . [We] put the picture into pastels, with a shading towards the blue side. Pastels are for memory.[7.3]

The camera style also undermines the genre. Critic Manny Farber has written of **The Big Sleep**:

> All the unbelievable events in **The Big Sleep** are tied together by miserable time jumps, but, within each skit, there is a logic of space, a great idea of personality, gesture, where each person is . . . Hawkes, in another special gem, gives the spectator just enough to make the scene work. One of the fine moments in 1940s film is no longer thank a blink: Bogart, as he crosses the street from one bookstore to another, looks up at a sign.[7.4]

By comparison, Altman's film's visual style has the camera constantly in motion, in such a way as to edgily undercut the action. Critic Michael Tarantino[7.5] points out that the movements draw in the viewer, but during the action highpoints work towards ironic distancing and disjunction (e.g., pullbacks occur just *before* violence, and the shot sequence doesn't help the viewer prepare himself for it). The special logic of the drama is thus mocked and parodied. For example, in the scene in which the gangster strikes his mistress, the camera starts the zoom in *before* he swings, then *pulls back* early so the consequences are obscured.

Genre story conventions are kidded when Marlowe-Gould's detective finds the disturbed writer almost immediately, the halfwilling drunken prisoner of extortionist-quacktherapist Dr. Verringer (Henry Gibson). The result is to make sly fun of the basic business of investigation, in the genre a serious matter of bravery, experience, shrewdness and connections. In contrast, both here and later in **The Long Goodbye**, the criminals are so disoriented by society's chaos and silliness, it's easy for Marlowe-Gould to outthink them, as he "explains" to Mrs. Wade-Van Pallandt:

Marlowe-Gould: Well, Dr. Verringer denied being Verringer.
He pretended he didn't even know your husband's name

and wouldn't even look at his picture on the dust jacket
— so I'm reasonably sure that's the place.

In solving this "diversionary" case, genre conventions of technique
are also reversed. Instead of a tough Marlowe-Bogart, Marlowe-
Gould won't use force ("Well, I'm supposed to bring you home if
that's where you want to go").

The genre motif of the hero's "double" becomes important again
when Marlowe-Gould is visited by Altman's film's satirical nineteen-
seventies mobster, Marty Augustine (Mark Rydell), a roostery tanned
egomaniac with a lovely shy girlfirend, and an ethnically balanced
goon squad (Jewish, Mexican, Italian, Irish). The gangster's explicitly
Nixonish lifestyle (he lives across the street) is summed up in its
circle of futility:

> Augustine-Rydell: . . . I got to have a lot of money so that I
> can juice the guys I got to juice, so I can get a lot of
> money so I can juice the guys I got to juice.

Augustine-Rydell needs a large amount of money stolen by Lennox-
Bouton, and shows Marlowe-Gould that he must help via a knowing
anti-genre demonstration of violence. The gangland chieftain speaks
adoringly to his lovely moll, mesmerizing the others ("I sleep with a
lot of girls, but I make love to you — "), then suddenly swings a coke
bottle to smash her face to red ruin. Amid her screams, even the
henchmen's faces clearly shocked, the mobster snarls to Marlowe-
Gould:

> Augustine-Rydell: See that! Now that's someone I love. You
> I don't even like. You have an assignment, cheapie. Find
> my money!

Most obviously, the scene mocks the crime film's mobster-moll
iconography (grapefruit in face in **Scarface**, a Hawks film; boiling
water in **The Big Heat**). More abstractly, it stylizes the crime boss
figure (e.g., Eddie Mars in **The Big Sleep**), turning him inside out.
He's plainly revealed as stage managing an aesthetic creation of
orchestrated attitudes, psychopathic impulses, and theatrical effects
by which he maintains control, gaining his ascendancy by being
more detached and designing than others.

Third, and most pessimistically, this moment is the anti-genre
counterpart of the main motivating incident in **The Big Sleep**, in
which:

> . . . Gallantry is again the key to Bogart's renunciation of
> disengagement. Bogart unwittingly observes the murder by
> poison of a smalltime hoodlum played by Elisha Cook, Jr.,
> . . . When Bogart discovers that Cook shielded an unworthy
> mistress even in the moment he faced certain death, the
> detective is transformed into an avenger. The most violent

denouements never obscure the director's commitment to the decencies of human behavior.[7.6]

In the bleak anti-genre universe of **The Long Goodbye**, there is no opportunity for romantic commitment, no chance for affirming gallantry. Rather, the violence is carried out as a sort of detached demonstration; the criminals even look after the brutalized girl themselves, and later on she's shown to be back with the mob chieftain, and indifferent to it.

Much of our fascination with the detective genre is linked to the characters' possibilities for individual style, as in **The Big Sleep's** Bogart and Bacall (personal style linked to "moral style"). By comparison, Altman's anti-genre film always tries to *undercut* or otherwise deny gestures of authenticity. For instance, when two thugs beat up Marlowe-Bogart, they're praised by a third for their professional skill, an opinion **The Big Sleep** hero even grudgingly accepts. By contrast, Marlowe-Gould must *give* the apprentice hood tailing him the address he's driving to, as he must constantly mutter "It's okay with me" to get cooperation, then say the clever remark to himself (personal style as now futile).

The anti-genre **The Long Goodbye** also works against the detective's special qualities when he visits the Wade beachhouse the next day, having learned they're connected with Augustine-Rydell. The couple, charming, rich and aloof on the brilliant beach, point up the detective's asexuality and immaturity. In a visually extraordinary sequence, Altman's film shows the handsome adults quarrelling soundlessly behind a glass wall, on which Marlowe-Gould's image skips back from the surf like a child. The shots suggest a whole ocean of deep exquisite emotions of which the genre figure can never know; in fact, the couple's dialogue is an agonized lover's quarrel, yet the passionate exchange eventually descends to old crankiness and insults. When the two men talk, there is no quick empathy as with Bogart's Marlowe and dying General Sternwood in **The Big Sleep** ("I enjoyed that cigarette almost as much as you did."). Rather, the morose, disturbed old novelist speaks of suicide and "more dignified" professions than writer or detective.

A brief sequence revives the Lennon-Bouton "double" mystery, the detective visiting the Mexican suicide site to get the plausible details. Wittily, he refers to himself in accented English as "a friend of the diseased." Next a scene at a glary, druggy beach party at the Wade residence includes a mocking of the ambience of the genre. Not in dark, shadowed, puddled, mean streets but on a bright expensive beachfront the diminutive quack therapist Dr. Verringer-Gibson abuses the weeping, clearly disturbed Wade-Hayden, while hangers-on stand unmoved, and detective and wife are indifferent (though they have their reasons).

In a night scene, Altman's film parodies the distrustful yet romantic byplay during **The Big Sleep** (Mrs. Wade-Van Pallandt: "Call me Eileen." Marlowe-Gould: "Okay, Eileen, what was Marty Augustine doing here the other night?"). As he obsessively interrogates her, each to one side of a beach house window, the writer can be seen staggering into the sea, a cruel mocking of sharp detective technique.

The death scene itself is poetically rendered, exaggerating the expressionistic aspect of the genre: hissing purplish waves, a black sky, Mrs. Wade-Van Pallandt's soaked orange silk gown making her a pathetic drowned butterfly, the writer's big Doberman trotting from the surf with the dead man's walking stick after Marlowe-Gould fails to save him. The mood of eerie futility and loss is immediately broken by the police team sequence: floodlights glaring on turquoise water, crackling intercoms, flat unintelligent voices repeating questions, boats and helicopters gunning motors, crouching shivering figures on the sand, Marlowe-Gould and Mrs. Wade Van Pallandt sodden and semi-hysterical. The two sequences visually sweep across the spectrum of genre treatments of oblivion, from agonized poetry to bodybag routine. Here, in a few moments, is the tension between the fearful mystery and social rituals which fuels our fascination with the genre: art about the death mystery. Staggering over the sand, Marlowe-Gould's detective articulates the central genre paradox and limitations: "Yeah, everybody's here, everybody's having a party *now*!" — attacking the genre directly by disparaging its frivolous artifice.

The scene concludes with the obligatory "lay off the case" exchange. In **The Big Sleep**, the detective's motivation has switched to Vivian-Bacall:

> Marlowe-Bogart: Bernie, put yourself in my shoes for a minute. A nice old guy has two daughters. One of them is, well, wonderful. And the other is not so wonderful. As a result, somebody gets something on her. The father hires me to pay off. Before I can get to the guy, the family chauffeur kills him! But that didn't end things. It just started them. And two murders later I find out somebody's got something on wonderful.

In **The Long Goodbye**, the anti-genre approach allows the investigator neither amour nor determination. Marlowe-Gould confronts and drunkenly questions a hysterical Mrs. Wade-Van Pallandt, so she blubbers she feared her husband was the killer. Facing tough cop Farmer-Coit, Marlowe-Gould is told that idea has been tested and rejected, so: "Why don't you go back to your gum shoes and your transom peeping and leave us alone!" Discredited, ineffective and drunk, the genre figure has reached his lowest ebb.

A final anti-genre view of the mob as pathology triumphant follows. Shown in a swank executive suite high over the freeway traffic (through the long windows, the headlights are tinted to abstract processions of eerie blue candles), undersized brighteyed mob boss Augustine-Rydell commences his compulsive theatrics, his voice, a homosexual falsetto, slyly welcoming Marlowe-Gould to his criminal eyrie. His ethnically balanced goon squad and lovely moll are also present, her shattered face protected by a mask of tape and metal splints ("You remember the night Joanne became ill?"). The mobster's voice modulates from gay teasing to coldly furious demands for his money. The long digression and shot setups suggest than the criminals' swank home base is, in design, symmetrical with the detective's "knight's castle" living arrangements, including the distant gleaming lights. The anti-genre implication is that romantic movie detective and crime boss are equally fantastical.

As if to test the limits of the genre's motifs' believability, mob boss Augustine-Rydell demands they all strip, this with-it Godfather going over to Primal Therapy: "We take off all our clothes — and the truth comes out!" One criminal comments dryly that: "George Raft never had to take off his clothes." The line seems a self-conscious reference to Hawks' implicit incest theme in **Scarface**, a sly comment on the repressed homosexuality many critics detect in Chandler's Marlowe (e.g., most of his male criminals are made sensuously attractive; see also 7.7).

Improbably, when they disrobe, they five a five-thousand dollar bill Marlowe-Gould was sent from Mexico as "thanks," whereupon Augustine-Rydell threatens him with confession or castration. Letting plot probabilities creak again as one more anti-genre comment, **The Long Goodbye** allows the detective to be himself saved at the last moment by the arrival of the missing $350,000.00. Marlowe-Gould leaves the mob untroubled, rich and "happy to have you drop by anytime," an anti-genre figure who has accomplished nothing against the crime lord.

Outside, several brief complications — Mrs. Wade Van Pallandt's departing car, a traffic accident, brief hospitalization, a journey to Mexico — allow the puzzling out of the plot, which itself is a genre comment, being logical but holding blanks and great improbabilities. Lennox-Bouton apparently stole the money, and, being involved with the privileged Mrs. Wade-Van Pallandt, had her hide it. Concerned over her husband, not trusting either love interest, Wade-Hayden's suicide occurs at just the right time, motivating her to solve Lennox-Bouton's trouble with the mob, incidentally saving Marlowe-Gould. The principal improbabilities are timing of the suicide, the criminals minimal effort to recover so much money, and why

Marlowe-Gould didn't recognize his friend's sinister character.

In the conclusion, Altman's film makes a complex comment on the genre in general and Chandler's work in particular. Using the five thousand as bribe (he trades the money for the truth), Marlowe-Gould learns that Lennox-Bouton is indeed still alive, being directed to a lush garden beside a stream, where the handsome sexual man sprawls charmingly arrogant in a hammock. The embittered detective learns that he did murder his wife, his explanation delivered in a boyish, slightly aggravated voice which lacks any hint of guilt:

> Lennox-Bouton: Well, I killed her but you can't call it murder. Wade told her about Eileen and me, she started screaming she was gonna tell the cops. She knew I was carrying money for Augustine, was gonna turn me in. I hit her, I didn't try to kill her, I hit her, I didn't mean it.
>
> Marlowe-Gould: I saw the photographs, man, you bashed her face in.
>
> Lennox-Bouton: She didn't give me any choice.
>
> Marlowe-Gould: Didn't have much choice, huh? So you used me.
>
> Lennox-Bouton: C'mon, that's what friends are for — I was in a jam. C'mon, have a drink. I had a dead wife, three hundred fifty thousand that didn't belong to me, I had to get out — it was as simple as that.

The exchange mocks Chandler's detective fiction, and the genre in general, in which the "double" motif often carries the works' significant comment.

In the Chandler novel *The Long Goodbye*, Marlowe at last recognizes his "double" Lennox as a moral defeatist, with whom he severs his friendship. In Chandler's *The Big Sleep,* the detective's search for the "double" represented maximally: "an investigation of his own identity, into his own soul's potential weaknesses and arrested tendencies . . . he begins to understand his corruptibility . . . . He is 'part of the nastiness now' . . . . "[7,8]

But in this anti-genre work, Lennox-Bouton comes across as a comically exaggerated movie murderer, enormously charming and sexual, but lacking *any* moral character or inner life. His dialogue, for example, can be rearranged into several mindless syllogisms, seemingly parodies of pop psychology books:

I killed her	I was in a jam.
But I didn't mean it	*That's what friends are for*
So you can't call it murder	So I used you

Altman's film's anti-genre criminal is neither vicious animal, nor gangland denizen, nor amoral psychopath, nor hired killer. Rather, he's a mindless reader of *I'm Okay, You're Okay* or other pop psychology, who sees his amoral, goal-oriented behavior as programmed and semi-endorsed by society:

> Marlowe-Gould: Simple as that, huh?
>
> Lennox-Bouton: Goddam simple. Cops have me legally dead; Augustine's got his money, he's not looking for me anymore; I got a girl that loves me — she's got more money than Sylvia and Augustine put together. What the hell — nobody cares!
>
> Marlowe-Gould: Yeah, nobody cares but me.
>
> Lennox-Bouton: Well, that's you, Marlowe. You'll never learn, you're a born loser!
>
> Marlowe-Gould: Yeah, I even lost my cat. (Draws gun and kills Lennox.)

The execution is the final anti-genre comment. Marlowe-Gould *has* followed the detective genre conventions, having "seen justice done."

One comment lies in the tone and feeling of the death; with no musical, visual, or narrative buildup to this retribution, the genre's moral rightness is stripped of viewer satisfaction, of emotional charge. Justice is reduced to Marlowe-Gould's half bitter, half embarrassed "Yeah — nobody cares but me." The genre supposedly works because the detective is a man of honor, but, by implication, our pleasure lies elsewhere. Likewise, the morbidly exciting death throes of the villain are reduced to a visual dissolving away of his figure in the water, a visual rendering of justice in a modern Godless, amoral, materialistic universe.

The conclusion also mocks the ending of **The Big Sleep**, and other crime-solved-and-romantic-fadeout genre films. In Hawks' **The Big Sleep**, the tough Bogart-Marlowe avoids the moral and legal guilt of killing the murder-commanding blackmailer by forcing his "opposite" out a door into a hail of his own mob's machinegun fire. In Altman's **The Long Goodbye**, the moral death is also cleverly arranged so no retribution will follow (as Lennox-Bouton puts it, nobody cares!). Marlowe-Gould does the job himself, affectlessly right out in plain sight, so the viewer feels the emptiness of the genre form.

The anti-**The Big Sleep** genre mockery is maintained to the end, for as Marlowe-Gould walks away from the execution he passes, on the road, Mrs. Wade-Van Pallandt, hurrying to meet her lover. Reversing the chemistry of Bogart-Marlowe and Bacall-Vivian, the woman does not spare more than a fearful glance for the detective. As with the genre devices of "double" and honor, Altman's film reverses the detective figure's romantic aura as moral truthseeker. The music shifts to the "Hooray for Hollywood" of the opening, signalling the terminal self-consciousness that has dominated the anti-genre work all the way through.

Finally, the critic Michael Mason argues that the last scene also comments on the repressed homosexuality some critics detect in Chandler's Marlowe:

> . . . Robert Altman expresses a deeper understanding of Marlowe's nature than most literary critics . . . . The closing shot is a careful imitation of the closing shot in **The Third Man**, a brilliantly cinematic allusion to indicate that Terry Lennox's depravity is like that of Harry Lime, and Marlowe's disillusion as profound as that of the sexually ambiguous Holly Martins.[7.9]

Mason's insight seems valid, but only as a neatly realized example of the genre's general mistrust of sexualized relationships, almost comically stylized throughout. In particular, Altman's **The Long Goodbye** argues that the honorable seeker of moral action in a corrupt world must be emotionally unfulfilled.

Thieves Like Us (1974)

Thieves Like Us is Robert Altman's anti-genre dissection of what might be called the "outlaw/outcast family" genre film. This category, best exemplified by **Bonnie and Clyde** and **The Grapes of Wrath**, includes such works as **Days of Heaven, They Live by Night, You Only Live Once**, and almost the entire "gangster genre." Major themes, suggested in part by Andrew Sarris,[8.1] include survival of the mutually supportive outsider family; tensions between accommodating and rebellious impulses; and, the possibility of a "counter society." As Robert Warshaw comments on gangster films, they express "that part of the American psyche which rejects the qualities and the demands of modern life . . . "[8.2]

Thieves Like Us commences with a two-and-one-half minute static view of the misty 1930s Mississippi countryside, a peaceful, lush, green pastoral. In the mid-distant lake, two fishermen can be heard: "Best time to go fish' is when it rains," "You can't paddle to save yourself." This low-key beginning suggests an underlying mood of the genre: the basic romantic belief in man's natural goodness, that people in the state of nature will behave well. This feeling dominates the first third of the **Grapes of Wrath**, the pastoral before the trek west begins. It also holds for the start of **Bonnie and Clyde** and other outlaw couple films; the romantic pairs seem to start off out-of-control due to simple sexual excitement, while being basically innocent and good-hearted.

Altman's **Thieves Like Us** makes fun of this idea almost at once: the "innocent" fishermen are revealed as escaped convicts; the gangling boy-man Bowie Bowers (Keith Carradine) and the hulking southerner Chicamaw (John Shuck). Immediately, mocking awareness of this mass-culture genre stick out: "Guard the boat!" Chicamaw-Shuck grunts like a radio serial smuggler. Down the road they spot the ancient jalopy that will be their getaway vehicle. Their dumb-witty dialogue ("I can tell [the driver] sells marijuana just by the way he drives . . . he just hit a pot hole!") further suggests Altman's film will be a self-conscious, strongly stylized work with an ironic attitude towards its "naive" outsiders.

The ancient escape car, a model-A Ford in the 1930s, holds the simple-minded driver/dealer Jasbo (John Roper) and the foolishly cheery old con T-Dub Masefield (Bert Remsen). The prison drug-dealer, a fool, only stops telling an idiotic story when Chicamaw-Shuck theatrically *clicks!* an immense 45-pistol beside his head, again growling like a radio gangster: "This is a stickup, Jasbo!" The ironic false note bugled here can be contrasted with the strong, sincere depiction of emotion that unite the outlaw outcasts in the other films: the sexuality and quest for excitement that fuses to-gether the couple in **Bonnie and Clyde**, and the tough beligerent individuality typified by Tom Joad (Henry Fonda's ex-con), telling the truckdriver from whom he promotes a ride that he "just wants to get along without pushin' nobody." The opposite of Altman's hollow criminals, Fonda's ex-con leaves the fascinated trucker, growling in amused contempt: "Well, I ain't a guy to keep you hangin' — it was homicide!"

Continuing his mockery of the outsider's "genuineness," the **Thieves Like Us** escapees next don comic "farmer disguises": im-mense, brand-new blue jeans ("What do you think we are — giants?") and tiny white shirts ("What do you think we are — midgets?"). As the car drives off, the title **Thieves Like Us**, to sinister thunder and a tinny radio organ playing "Home of the Brave," evokes a complex mood of mockery and grim foreboding. The ancient, comic getaway car moves off screen-right to screen-left, followed in a very long lateral traveling shot, the prolonged anti-normal screen motion visu-ally implying some grievous basic error, the camera's distance sug-gesting a modernist's attentive yet detached attitude. The high school doggerel the men sing — an unwanted bastard infant is left on the school steps — further implies their lack of community, in contrast to the theme of outsiders' mutual support running through much of the genre.

In the next sequence, the three escapees are shown awakening in a long-abandoned farmhouse, where their social confusion is further implied: there is quarreling and backbiting, T-Dub-Remsen chatters of how bankers are no better than they, hiding money so they can claim they've been robbed of great sums; and, at last, the tough criminals flee at a vaguely suspicious sound without helping their lame companion. This abandoned house sequence also mocks a genre convention: it is in a smashed sharecroppers' shack that Joad-Fonda learns how the farm families have been "tractored out," muttering bitterly: "Anyone ever tell me I'd be hidin' out on my own place . . . !" In **Bonnie and Clyde**, it's meeting the evicted farmer after a night in such dwelling that inspires Clyde (Warren Beatty) to exclaim in confused delight: "We're Clyde Barrow and Bonnie Parker — we rob banks!" In Altman's anti-genre work, the idea of the outlaw family justified by society's harshness is rejected; the escapees have no "cute meet" with the dispossessed, and by implication would probably have run away immediately if they had.

If there is any case made for the **Thieves Like Us** outlaws, it is implied in the next sequence. As night falls, Bowie-Carradine waits alone beside slightly elevated railroad tracks. Discovering a large dog, he crouches and speaks to the animal, the gangling youngster eventually huddling with the big mutt for warmth in one of the gaps between the supports for the right-of-way:

> Bowie-Carradine: (to dog) Lookee here — where'd you come from? Belong to someone — or just a thief like me . . . . Sure you don't belong to me . . . . Well, let's go back there . . . I don't got no more folks. You know, that's the first thing the law does — look up the places a man can write to and watch them places. Goodbye, mama. One thing about you, though — whatever I ever did was okay with you. And cousin Tom . . . .

Diane Jacobs has pointed out that "felony as such is mitigated . . . when Bowie asks the dog if he too is a 'thief,' we are meant to equate thief with tramp or homeless one."[8.3] In terms of the "outcast/outlaw family" genre, the implication is that such families are at best unnatural, and furthermore don't think in terms of moral or economical ideas ("whatever I ever did was okay with you. And cousin Tom . . . . "). The last line may be a sly jab at the contrasting attitudes of **The Grapes of Wrath**'s Ma Joad (Jane Darwell) and Tom Joad (Fonda). Altman's protagonist is the abandoned progeny of that ambivalent genre film.

In the morning, Bowie-Carradine reaches the dilapidated gas station of Chicamaw-Shuck's relative, Doc Mobley (Tom Skerritt), concluding the film's mocking of the genre's pastoral beginnings with the reunion of the outlaws and the addition of the love interest. Introduced to Keechie Mobley (Shelly Duvall), a large-eyed stick-figure beauty, we see Bowie-Carradine visually united at a table with the two escapees, even as his head continually turns to follow the girl. The conflict is emphasized by camera placement at the end of the railroad apartment, so the stressed youngster is multiply-framed, the sequence mocking the unlikely "spontaneous" Clyde-Beatty/Bonnie-Dunaway relationship, and indeed the variously-stylized "naturalness" of sex-love pairings in the genre.

The reading by the three cons of the newspaper accounts of their escape gives Altman's film a chance to reverse the basic theme of the mutually supportive outsider family. In **Grapes of Wrath**, Tom Joad-Fonda's reunion with his family is marked by two announcements: the order to vacate their farm, and the reading of the handbills promising work in California. Partly accommodating but mostly rebellious, the outcast family finally works together to deal with the inevitable as best they can. Similarly, in some ways, the first half of **Bonnie and Clyde** is elaborately designed to suggest supportiveness: Clyde-Beatty spends so much energy enchanting the girl, the small comic robberies seem to be almost love-dares, proving they both want the same exciting lifestyle, like "wild teenagers" before they settle down.

But in **Thieves Like Us**, this thematic idea is mocked and inverted. Instead, the news articles are occasions for each individual to demonstrate his lonely egomania and self-destructive impulses. T-Dub-Remsen, for instance, is annoyed by the vulnerability and imperfection suggested when the newspaper calls him "Three-toed" Masefield (later dialogue explains convicts cut off toes to escape work detail). Alternately, Chicamaw-Shuck is pleased to embarrassment at being referred to as Elmo "Tommy-Gun" Mobley:

> Chicamaw-Shuck: Only had a machine gun once in my life. Never even got to fire it — I just — held it.

All three laugh at their warden's lament that "if you can't trust a trusty, who can you trust?" Altman here slyly mocks both the mutually supportive outlaw family, and the possibility of "counter-society" suggested by the genre.

Finally, the sequence also reverses the convention of such genre works as **Bonnie and Clyde, Gun Crazy**, and **The Sugarland Express**, that women are even momentarily fascinated by outlaw behavior; for, as the men chortle over the newspaper accounts of themselves in the foreground, Keechie-Duvall can be seen on the porch outside listening to the radio. So, when Bowie-Carradine offers to buy her a coke, she responds matter-of-factly: "What with?" She points up the fact that despite their frontpage notoriety, the ex-cons are penniless. Moreover, as the strangely beautiful stick-figure young people sit on the porch, it is the boy-man who keeps joking, until the girl-woman reveals she's been listening, and must know at once why he was jailed as a murderer, allowing him to tell it his own way:

> Bowie-Carradine: Miss Keechie, you know what the Mississippi state animal is? You know, the state animal —
> Keechie-Duvall: I don't know — a deer maybe.
> Bowie-Carradine: No sir, it's a squashed dog in the road! You know what the state flower is?
> Keechie-Duvall: Did you shoot that man in Selpa?
> Bowie-Carradine: It was him or me. He come around the car after me with a gun . . . . It's a weed!
> Keechie-Duvall: That's dumb.

In passing, the hesitant shameful explanation is the very opposite of Tom Joad-Fonda's blunt: "Well, I ain't a guy to keep you hangin' —

it was homicide!"

Unlike the passionate desperate journeys of **The Grapes of Wrath's** Joads, or the self-assertive hysteria of the **Bonnie and Clyde** robberies (e.g., Buck-Barrow (Gene Hackman): "Get a good look at us — we're the Barrow Boys!"), the crimes of **Thieves Like Us** are suggested to be deliberately thoughtless undertakings, wretched reflexes and habits, the outlaw/outcast family gone mindlessly to seed. This particular stylistic choice fits the film's genre mockery: rather than a demonstration of rebellious impulses against society, the criminals live in a social fog. The camera pulls back from the modest southern town bank building to the three comically bickering over who does what, before finally drawing straws. The long-time criminal T-Dub Masefield sees no meaning at all in the robbery:

> T-Dub Masefield-Remsen: . . . C'mon, they'll just hold out the money for ya — it's all insured anyway.

Instead of showing the robbery, the camera stays on Bowie-Carradine waiting outside, apparently listening to a radio episode of "Gangbusters."

> Narrator: Gangbusters at war, marching against the underworld!
>
> SFX: Marching troops sound (created mechanically).

In one sense, this and later radio crime thrillers in the film are used to suggest totally debased romantic art (pity and terror as pathetic diversion), and as such are self-conscious comments on the audience's sensibility and expectations of the genre. Altman puts "Gangbusters" on the soundtrack to suggest why he *can't* in honesty give us a straight genre story, why he must mock it. By placing this self-reflexive material at what should be a work's "emotional payoff," the creator mocks artist, audience, *and* genre.

Again ironically, instead of a frantic getaway, Bowie-Carradine and Keechie-Duvall are shown "keeping company" on the porch over the garage. Their painful innocence — she's "never had a fella" and he's been in prison since sixteen — again contrasts with the easy-impulse sexual connections of the genre. Yet, simultaneously, Altman uses his dialogue to mock the phallic toying-with-his-gun sequence in **Bonnie and Clyde**:

> Keechie-Duvall: You know anything about cows, Bowie?
>
> Bowie-Carradine: Ever shoot a forty-five?

The second bank robbery is visually realized much like the first; Bowie-Carradine waiting in the car outside the Canton Exchange Bank to another radio serial: "Steve Gibson of the International Secret Police" (!). The juxtaposition of dull town, its exotic name, and ridiculous espionage thriller suggest a desperate human thirst for unreality, here shrouding dreariness in delusion to make a buck. Reinforcing this idea, a truck rolls by carrying an enormous mock

In the outcast/outlaw genre-commentary *Thieves Like Us*, the accomodation versus rebellion tension is rendered extremely bitterly. Here, the tough betrayer Mattie (Louise Fletcher), who set up the outlaw couple for police execution, impulsively saves the life of the innocent, perceptive Keechie (Shelly Duval).

In the outcast/outlaw genre film *The Grapes of Wrath*, the Joad Family idealizes the genre's tension between social accomodation and rebelliousness, via the love between patient Ma Joad (Jane Darwell) and her radicalized son Tom (Henry Fonda).

Coke bottle and a girl in Civil War flaired skirt praising the drink as healthy. The sequence also implies the genre outlaw/outcasts, with their weak counter-societies, have little hope against the elaborate mass-produced, sophisticated mother culture.

The long scene which follows, in some ways a comic-grotesque parody of the Joad family in action in **The Grapes of Wrath**, turns the major genre theme of the outlaws' accommodating versus rebellious impulses upside down. Inside a shabby-genteel period parlour, a homely pair of children don't look up as the radio reports on society's pitilessness. (Announcer: " . . . two Negroes, accused of murder, were taken from the sheriff, tortured, and lynched earlier today!") Moments later, when the little boy's firecrackers explode, the crooks rush out of their rooms in underwear with pistols drawn, the outlaw made to look ridiculous. Next, the lady of the house, Mattie Masefield (Louise Fletcher), like a cold bleak distrustful Ma Joad-Darwell, strides out to "disarm" the child and censure the shamefaced outlaws. Confirming their impotence, Mattie-Fletcher's plain sister Lula (Ann Latham) cheerfully rejects the silly advances of her old uncle (Lula-Latham: "He's like an octopus — eight hands going all at once!").

From the start, the sequence is a mocking stylization of the complementary worldviews of male and female genre protagonists, the impulses to rebel against versus those to accommodate society. As Andrew Sarris has noted of **The Grapes of Wrath**:

> [Fonda-Joad's] physical and spiritual stature is not that of the little man as victim, but as the tall man as troublemaker. His explosive anger has a short fuse, and we have only his word for it that he is tough without being mean . . . . His is ultimately the one man revolution of the ex-con with whom society can never to reconciled. By contrast, Jane Darwell's Ma Joad is the pacifier and unifer and high priestess of liberal reform at the altar of the sacred family.[8.4]

The same opposed tensions as a basic theme are present thoughout **Bonnie and Clyde**, suggested most clearly in an exchange of dialogue close to the end of the film:

Bonnie-Dunaway (longing voice): Clyde . . . what would you do if some miracle happened and we could walk out tomorrow morning and start all over again, clean, with no record, with nobody after us?

Clyde-Beatty (after thinking a moment): Well . . . I guess I'd do it all different. First off, I wouldn't live in the same state where we pull our jobs. We'd live in one state and stay clean there, and when we wanted to take a bank, we'd go to another state . . . and . . . .

In Altman's film, both points of view are even more grotesquely rendered.

The dinner sequence elaborates this tension, rendered in the bleakest terms: Mattie-Fletcher dominates the meal as a grim matriarch, treating children and criminals much the same. Her great arms and canny, darting eyes are in total control, dialogue establishing that her own husband is in jail. In fact, the pleasureless meal makes fun of the basic idea of the genre itself: outlaw/outcast life rendered as spiritless and unpleasant. As they eat the plain food, the family listens to T-Dub-Remsen's reading of the second robbery news story, grumbling at errors and all conversation halting as he foolishly enunciates a dead or alive reward in contrast to the newspaper sequence in **Bonnie and Clyde**, in which the outlaws slyly pull the paper from a mailbox as they drive past to scan it with delight. This "family life" aspect of the gangster genre is an unaccountably neglected feature, from the offscreen whipping scenes of **The Public Enemy**'s protagonist as a child, through the pathological "family" of **White Heat**, to the elaborated "counter societies" in films as diverse as **The Godfather** and **Gone With the Wind**. The after-dinner radio program sequence is interesting for debunking the theme of an outsider culture and society suggested by other genre films. In **The Grapes of Wrath**, for instance, the Okies are shown to have a rough honesty and decency towards each other, and beyond that a sort of folk culture, suggested by the square dance night at the Woodpatch Camp, harmonica renderings of the ballads "Red River Valley" and "I Ain't Gonna Be Treated This Way," Ma Joad's keepsakes, and so on. The outlaw family in **Bonnie and Clyde** have jokes (Buck-Hackman: "Boy, whatever you do, don't sell that cow!"), socialize with a couple they pick up, take each other's photographs, and even write poems. But the **Thieves Like Us** outcasts not only lack much mutual support or folkways, they often employ conventional escapist fantasies like radio programs (e.g., Narrator: *"The Shadow* . . . a man of wealth, a student of science, and master of other people's minds, devotes his life to righting wrongs . . . ") to isolate themselves. As L.J. Leff points out:

> In different rooms, Bubba plays with his fireworks, Chicamaw with his stolen money, Bowie with the watch he'll give Keechie, Noel Joy with her Rob-the-Bank costume, T-Dub with Lula's fingers and the thought of her granting him fantastic sexual favors. Radio, playing through the house [makes] these heterogenous characters . . . secure enough to liberate each one's private fantasy.[8.5]

The ironic point is that instead of *any* sort of *common* belief, each one marinates (and perhaps drowns) his lonely spirit in a mass-produced power fantasy. Like the joyless dinner, the radio sequence mocks the family feeling idea that is central to the Joads:

> Ma Joad-Darwell: . . . They was a time when we was on the lan' . . . . They was a boundary to us then. Ol' folks died off, an little fellas come. She was always one thing — we was the fambly — kinda whole and clear . . . .

The destructive effects of the mass-produced culture are shown allegorically when the drunken Chicamaw-Shuck is inspired to act out a robbery (one "The Shadow" character has spoken of as his "foolproof plan"). Chicamaw-Shuck uses the children as tellers and porter, straightback chairs atop the table as tellers' cages, but real guns for himself and T-Dub-Remsen. (The witty burnt-cork on the child's face for a Negro porter is Altman's mockery of period bigotry.) As one could expect, the foolish "perfect robbery" degenerates into a shouting bout, T-Dub-Remsen waving his pistol to extract favors from Lula-Latham, and Chicamaw-Shuck threatening Mattie-Fletcher, who again breaks up the childish routine. While Bowie-Carradine watches, amused, the other two withdraw into individual revelries: T-Dub-Remson acting passive to win Lula-Lathan; Chicamaw-Shuck drinking and brooding. But when the drunken Chicamaw-Shuck raises his voice in a final protest against their grim hostess, she "sobers him up" with a news article about the dead-or-alive reward which includes pictures of all three.

If this sequence mocks the theme of the counter-society — dominant social forces have just too many weapons — the next, starting with the morning departure of Mattie-Fletcher to visit her imprisoned husband, dissects it. On a rocker on the porch, T-Dub-Remsen and Bowie Carradine grow reflective:

> T-Dub-Remsen: Yeah, I made my mistake when I was a kid. Kids don't see things. I should have been a doctor or a lawyer or run for office — I should have robbed people with my *brain* instead of a gun.
>
> Bowie-Carradine: I don't suppose I could have done anything but played ball.
>
> Chicamaw-Shuck (drunk, dazed): What the hell time is it? Goddam, I feel awful!

Altman here slices to the core of the genre's themes: the sanctioning of the outlaw/outcasts socially-deviant behavior.

Characteristically, the theme is realized by contrasting a larger pitiless society (always) with either a mad entrapping passion (e.g., **Bonnie and Clyde**) or a sort of peasant's legitimacy (e.g., **The Grapes of Wrath**). As Sarris puts it: "Ford evoked nostalgia by humanizing Steinbeck's economic insects into heroic champions of an agrarian order of family and community."[8.6] Or in one "tractored out" farmer's words:

>   Muley Graves (John Qualen): (with great bitterness) We was
>   born on it, and we got killed on it, died on it. Even if it's
>   no good, it's still ours . . . .

In comparison, Altman's anti-genre outlaw/outcasts lack either passion or roots. Indeed, they extend legitimacy to no one (i.e., T-Dub-Remsen: "I should have robbed people with my *brain* . . . "). In a way, they are nomad-savages, as opposed to the genre's peasant-barbarian protagonists, believing in magic and aspiring to be a horde, rather than adhering to folk wisdom and aspiring to separate community. For example, T-Dub-Remsen's often-repeated remark that this will be his thirty-first, or thirty-second or thirty-third bank (he includes the play-robbery with the children) suggests an irrational nomad-warrior's superstitious mentality, half-bent on self-destruction.

At intervals, Altman's genre commentary work probes this darkest implication of the film themes, the aspect the other genre films work hard to artistically disguise: the outcast/outlaws awareness of and attraction to self-obliteration. Next, for example, Bowie-Carradine and Chicamaw-Shuck playfully drive cars along a double-lane road through the Mississippi countryside, each alternately speeding up to recklessly pass the other, a visual metaphor for their increasingly open, untragic courting of doom. Inevitably, Bowie-Carradine has a collision, the nighttime crossroads filmed in contrast black and white, Chicamaw-Shuck wrestling the bloody, dazed youth into his own car while the second smashed vehicle's woman driver sprawls grotesquely, shrieking, in the open road, the anti-genre's characters now indifferent to pain and mutilation even on a "just-folks" level. Stopped by two beefy lawmen, Chicamaw-Shuck ambushes them at pointblank range. The sequence is interesting in comparison with the first killing in **Bonnie and Clyde,** and the other outlaw couple films, which "trap" the viewer after he has identified with the high-spirited couple; this killing is much uglier and more calculated, just as the thieves' behavior up to now has been irritatingly childish rather than affectingly adolescent.

In the dark, Bowie-Carradine is returned to the gas station hideout, and put in a room wallpapered with World War I lovesong sheetmusic. Left to recover, the young outlaw is cared for by Keechie-Duvall, the two living out a short romantic idyll. The straightforward yet affecting love story calls attention to the stylizing of sex in the genre: the sexless Joad family or the psychopathology of such works as **Gun Crazy** and **Bonnie and Clyde**.

A dissolve leads to their love scene, anticipated by a tinny radio broadcast of "The most celebrated love story of all time — the tragedy of Romeo and Juliet." As he recovers, Bowie-Carradine seems to renew his innocence, taking childish pleasure in her acceptance of a watch he gives her. To the radio's thick Tchaikovsky violins and tinny: "Thus did Romeo and Juliet consummate their first interview — by falling madly in love with each other," the two are shown in soft warm color, and filmed in slow flowing tracking shots. After gentle kidding, the Shakespeare is repeated anti-realistically as the attractive pair make love a second time. Again, joking is succeeded by the staticky "thus did Romeo and Juliet consummate — " and more love-making. While the sound sequence is repeated, the three lovemakings are shot from left, right, and the bed's foot, so each repetition is yet somewhat new. The filming suggests a momentary anti-genre expression of healthy love, recalling de Rougemont's "happy love has no history."[8][7]

By morning, the mood shifts in a calculated anti-genre comment. The feeling is one of long domestication, Keechie-Duvall frying breakfast eggs as the boy-man reads the newspapers. Their talking echoes their sincere courting conversation, with Bowie-Carradine admitting the two new deaths, but now not regretting the murders but only his limited "take." Keechie-Duvall is affected ("I already am mixed up with you — "), leading to more lovemaking, treated comically via a final shot of the scorching eggs. What is missing here and later is the growth in affection and understanding seen between the other outlaw couples; instead, there is a hint of an increasing coarsening.

At night, conjugal good feeling is rekindled as Bowie-Carradine sweetly insists his lovely bathing lover no longer shave her armpits, the radio cheeping: "I Found a Million Dollar Baby." The mood is immediately broken when he insists on seeing the other thieves. They bicker and finally agree, but the mutual warmth is destroyed. The boy-man next meets the foolishly-grinning T-Dub-Remsen and his new wife Lula-Latham in a brightly lit parlour, the old man's white hair vainly dyed an unnatural dull black "as a disguise." Bowie-Carradine's boy-man is closed-mouthed and even sullen towards the couple after he learns they have put their own name on their marriage license, a sure aid to the police dragnet. Finally speaking of the distrusting Mattie-Fletcher, T-Dub-Remsen's affable idiot chortles: "She's real people — just like us, you know what I mean!" Unlike the limited, often amusing "family conflicts" in **Bonnie and Clyde** and **Grapes of Wrath**, Altman here mocks the genre's mutually supportive outlaw family theme, by showing his characters' dopeyness, touchiness, irrationality, and self delusion — irritating and endangering each other at every turn.

The anti-genre mockery grows still darker as Bowie-Carradine agrees to another robbery, breaking his promise to Keechie-Duvall, muttering coldly that: "Man never knows when he's going to need money and plenty of it in this business!" Smiling broadly, T-Dub-Remsen crows: "Hell, we'll never get *three boys like us* together again — that's for damn sure!" [my emphasis]. At once, the half-naked, growling, bullish figure of Chicamaw-Shuck leaps animal-like into the room. The title approximation and "hellish" touch in the dialogue, together with the shocking image of the three clearly disturbed, twistedly smiling grotesque criminals suggests a modernist's vision of the genre. The three figures seem to visually dissect the outlaw/outcast rebel archetype: basic animal frustration and self-rejection; hopelessly foolish and inadequate accommodation to society, and the ignorant, half-suicidal confusion in which they merge.

This momentary glimpse of the genre as hell is followed by the film's most superficial, "public" sequence, the third robbery. Anti-realistically, all three suited, expressionless men go inside, the action filmed from overhead. Instead of a radio crimeshow, the soundtrack is Roosevelt's "New Deal" speech calling for "all people's security and peace." The use of Roosevelt seems meant as a genre mockery: in **The Grapes of Wrath** the head of the nice government camp looked like F.D.R.; in **Bonnie and Clyde** a smiling F.D.R. poster appeared in the town the finally-at-peace couple visit, but here Roosevelt is identified with the banks and the pitiless society. (In fact, the film holds *no* attractive environments.) When a clerk tries to sound an alarm, they kill him, and the scene dissolves to the three silently bitterly drinking before making lonely accusing comments and separating again. The scene is notable as a deliberate intensification of Warshaw's basic evaluation of the genre:

> At bottom, the gangster is doomed because he is under the obligation to succeed, not because the means he employs are unlawful . . . This is our intolerable dilemma: that failure is a kind of death and success is evil and dangerous, is — ultimately — impossible. The effect of the gangster film is to embody this dilemma in the person of the gangster and resolve it with his death.[8·8]

As Bowie-Carradine drives home, the car radio announces T-Dub-Remsen's police shoot-out-death, Chicamaw-Shuck's capture, and the manhunt for "Bowie A. Bowers, Fast Trigger Killer." At the cabin, Keechie-Duvall has heard this news, and characteristically clearly sees his behavior as a romantic's adultery, one more shabby reverse of the genre theme of outlaw/outcast family mutual support:

Keechie-Duvall: You took them. It was me or them and you knew it and you took them.

As opposed to **Bonnie and Clyde**, romantic and realist are nakedly at war in both characters; he won't stop her going, then calls her a fool; she doesn't want to leave and wants him to make her stay. The dialogue catches the genre's love and hate of being an outcast, War-shaw's gangster: "what we want to be and what we are afraid we may become."[8][9]

Visually, the scene wittily reinforces the idea of anti-archetypes: a Bonnie and Clyde who don't grow in understanding, but in acri-mony. The couple's transformation into amoral, passionate animals is suggested by images suitable for a 1930s pulp mystery thriller cover: Keechie-Duvall's cheap, shiny rayon chemise and excited masochistic expression; Bowie-Carradine's narrow gangster's fedora, cruelly-suited slimness, and tight, closed facial expression.

The couple flee to a rundown period motel, the Grapes (of Wrath?) Motor Inn. T-Dub-Remsen bought it, proprietor Mattie-Fletcher admits, but he's dead, and she can't have them around while she's trying to get her husband paroled. Once more, outlaw family unity has broken down. Finally, the youth threatens to "make trouble" if they can't have refuge, the Ma Joad-Darwell/Tom Joad-Fonda tension stylized into desperate hatred.

To the morning-sick Keachie-Duvall, Bowie-Carradine can speak only of the imprisoned Chicamaw-Shuck and how he must be res-cued "to get them to Mexico." Incoherent, he mutters of giving her mother some money as he takes up his pistol, ending by asking her the Mississippi state tree (answer: telephone pole). Altman here directly strikes at the genre's "folksiness," stylizing used to seduce the viewer; the joke recalls the boy-man's first shamefaced admission of killing in self defense, contrasting with his icy new romantic acceptance of dealing out death. A Clyde Barrow-Beatty with his charm stripped away, Bowie-Carradine also hints at the perhaps fu-tile post-**Grapes of Wrath** life of Tom Joad-Fonda.

The freeing of Chicamaw-Shuck from the state prison is notable for its climax, the clearly-disturbed newly-liberated brute pointlessly killing their prison warden hostage, an elderly, frail, almost retired sheriff, the camera zooming in on the harmless old man's immense head wound. This particular image both recalls and inverts the **Bonnie and Clyde** sequence, showing the massive lethal head wounds suffered by Buck Barrow-Hackman, reversing the genre's use of the rural posse's overkill mentality to gain sympathy for the outcasts.

The pathetic murder is followed by a manic verbal attack from Chicamaw-Shuck on Bowie-Carradine's newspaper notoriety. Shock-ingly, newspaper coverage seems to be the loveless isolated thief's single measure of self worth. (Chicamaw-Shuck: "What the hell do the papers do but print about you all the goddam time — it rips my guts out!") The moment points up one more genre convention, the outlaw's perverse glamour-hunger, here stylized by a monster whose life is built around agonizing personal emptiness. A moment later, all control gone, he so insults his benefactor ("That damn pickaninny little Picuane girl!"), Bowie-Carradine draws his gun and abandons the man he's just freed on a country road. The unshaven, brutishfigure, alone in his broadstriped uniform, standing sweating on the road, roars like an agonized beast at his last disappearing friend, all reason gone: "Bowie, Bowie, Bowie!" This shocking image is outlaw/outcast genre archetype illuminated as unsocial, uncontractible animal, an "evil" Tom Joad-Fonda or Casey-Carradine. For, as Sarris suggests: "Fonda's Joad is no Job, and as much as his mouth spouts slogans of equality, his hands are always reaching for a club or a rock or a wrench as an equalizer against the social forces massed against him."[8.10]

The conclusion of **Bonnie and Clyde** is likewise reversed as, at the shabby motor inn in a heavy downpour, sickly, vulnerable Keechie-Duvall wakens and wanders to Mattie-Fletcher's office, pathetically appealing in her words of affection for her lover. The big older woman, eyes cold in a warm expression, suddenly grasps the girl in her powerful arms as the car rolls in and Bowie-Carradine enters their cabin. Abruptly dozens of shotgun-carrying uniformed rangers emerge from the overcast, buildings and brush, commencing a collosal barrage into the thin wooden cabin; in slow motion, we watch Mattie-Fletcher holding a wildly screaming Keechie-Duvall. Several critics have pointed out that in opposition to the end of **Bonnie and Clyde**, this slow-motion image is not used to obtain sympathy for the outnumbered outlaw/lovers, but rather to focus on the agony of **Thieves Like Us'** only vulnerable, sensitive individual.

This final ambush is the penultimate cruel inversion of the outlaw/outcast genre. Bowie-Carradine's pathetically thin body, wrapped in the girl's keepsake quilt, is dumped on the wet earth where his blood mingles with the rain and mud. By implication, Mattie-Fletcher has betrayed the "outlaw family" to obtain her husband's parole. The genre themes of mutual support, rebellion-versus-accommodation tensions, and a counter-society have all been resolved in the most negative fashion. The camera's lingering on the skinny, awkward, pathetic shape under the quilt gives the viewer time to realize Mattie-Fletcher not only set up the ambush, as originally planned, she was willing to see Keechie-Duvall die as well.

Thieves Like Us's concluding section is interesting in several ways: the sequence does not appear in the novel, but seems to have been added as a negative counterpart of **The Grapes of Wrath** conclusion, the "leavetaking" of the rebel Tom Joad-Fonda followed by the leavetaking of the accommodator, Ma Joad-Darwell. The concluding sequence takes place in a drab midwestern railroad station; dull, Depression-weary figures waiting on benches as Father Coughlin's radio voice scourges them.

(Coughlin: "There can be no coming out of the Depression until what you earn goes to sustain your loved ones — somebody must be blamed . . . . ")

Keechie-Duvall, visibly pregnant, in a black dress with tightly coiffed hair (suggesting an embryonic Mattie-Fletcher as well as Ma Joad-Darwell), lies to the woman beside her that her husband died of consumption, concluding by speaking of her pregnancy:

> Keechie-Duvall: If [he's a boy] he will surely not be named after his daddy, God rest his soul. He crossed me up once too often — he don't deserve to have no baby named after him . . . .

Her words are a razor-sharp anti-outlaw/outcast mockery of the famous concluding monologue in **The Grapes of Wrath**:

> Ma Joad-Darwell: Rich fellas come up an' they die, an' their kids ain't no good, an' they die out. But we keep a-comin'. We're the people that live. Can't nobody wipe us out. Can't nobody lick us. We'll go on forever . . . .

Perhaps the accommodating realists among the outlaw-outcasts can go on, Altman's film's conclusion implies, but their existence will be bleak, bitter, and guilt-ridden, founded on denial of both trust and possible community. As **The Grapes of Wrath** ends, with the trucks rolling down the highway like a line of prudent, armored turtles, so **Thieves Like Us** concludes with the train being called — Keechie-Duvall doesn't care where it is going — and the shabby isolated passengers ascending in slow motion the worn stairs to the tracks, the camera continuing to hold on the grim, empty passage, to Father Coughlin's righteous harangue.

California Split (1974)

Analyses of such genre works as **Treasure of Sierra Madre, Citizen Kane, The Last American Hero, They Shoot Horses Don't They,** together with Michael Wood's comments[9.1] on **The Hustler** and **The Cincinnati Kid,** suggest a definite "contest/success" film genre. Major themes and motifs include lovelorn self-destructive people; drift into the "underworld" (in several senses); tension between "gamesman," "manager" and "champion" archetypes; and, most of all, an exploration of the "too-great cost of success." Looked at in terms of these genre concerns, Altman's **California Split** is clearly an illuminating exploration of the contest/success film genre.

Reversing the genre motif of nightmarish or exotic locales, **California Split** commences in a bright but seedy L.A. gambling club, filled with cheerful bulldog-faced old ladies and blearly lower-middle-class types. Amusingly, there is a little A.V. presentation on poker's history, rules and etiquette, with a still from **McCabe and Mrs. Miller,** and shots of boorish modern players against the sententious narration ("Acquiring the knowledge to play card games such as poker is a social asset."). The tape/slide show notes that today's house is honest, and wants a fair game, explicitly excluding crime genre motifs.

When an argument over cheating breaks out between beefy sore loser Lew (Ed Walsh) and the irrepressibly glib Charlie (Elliot Gould), the former claims Charlie-Gould is working with tensed, hunched Bill Denny (George Segal), his punching-out causing Denny-Segal to scuttle under the tables in neurotic panic. Meanwhile, Charlie-Gould's comic character analysis ("The man goes broke, he can't handle it, the man is on tilt . . . the man is totally out of line.") identifies him as a childish reverse of a genre archetype, the power-hungry manager exemplified by **The Hustler**'s Bert-George C. Scott ("I make it my business to know what guys like you and Minnesota Fats are gonna do. I made enough off of you the other day to pay for [that big car] twice over.").

In the gambling club's bar, Charlie-Gould "picks up" the clenched

Denny-Segal, the two shown drunkenly betting on the seven dwarfs ("I got seven . . . Sleepy! Grumpy! Doc! uh, Dopey! Dumbo!"), this dissolving to their singing and capering "Roostus Rastus Johnson Brown," a comment on the genre's bar pickup convention. Staggering outside, the two are set upon by Lew-Walsh and others who brutally mug them, reversing the pickup convention's happy implications. In fact, **California Split** repeatedly comically mocks the "healthy outdoors versus claustrophobic gambling dens" genre visual motif; people in Altman's film go outside mostly to be mugged or robbed, to visit chiseling pawnshops or enervating jobs, to experience depression or loneliness.

Rescued by two young, goodlooking women-friends of Charlie (Ann Prentiss and Susan Peters), the two amateur gamblers and apparent amateur whores relax in the girls' shabby-comfortable bungalow. The four form an immature, warm, wacky community of lonely spirits: Barbara-Prentiss, a cheery Texas mom, serving a breakfast of beer and Fruit Loops; Charlie-Gould chattering of raising gambling stakes by running a Good Humor truck for a day (Charlie-Gould: "Well, you keep it all! You don't think I'm talking about working at this job legit, do you, man?"); Denny-Segal, tense and bleak; Susan-Welles childlike in pajamas. The sudden male friendship stylizes the genre motif of manipulator-manager seducing the gamesman, as in **The Hustler**:

> Eddie (Paul Newman): Now, when did you adopt me?
> Bert (George C. Scott): (with a friendly grin) I don't know when it was . . . .

The bungalow sequence concludes with Charlie-Gould cheering up the childlike Susan-Welles, who's tearfully fallen yet again for her latest patron.

Susan-Welles' childlike whore, and Barbara-Prentiss's businesslike one, are sly contrasts to Sarah (Piper Laurie), the agonized idealistic cripple in **The Hustler**, who, as Wood points out, represents "the woman as humanist, as the compassionate advocate of the honorable personal life."[9.2] Other genre women include **The Cincinnati Kid's** semi-intellectual Christian (Tuesday Weld) and promiscuous Melba (Ann-Margret). Altman's anti-genre view of its lovelorn females shows them as passive or active survivors, happy to be amused for a few hours, and so wacky or out of touch they're comic as thinkers.

Next day, Denny-Segal, shown barely hanging onto his job, is lured away to the track by Charlie-Gould's siren song. Charlie-Gould himself in a comic sequence, chats up a superstitious woman on the track bus, talking her out of a bet on the ridiculously named "Egyptian Femme." This brief sequence suggests the gambling world's paradoxical attraction, one filled with bored and boring homely types, yet evoking a crazy magic mirrored in the woman's irration-

116

ality and Charlie-Gould's wacky tout routine.

In the battleship-gray littered track interior, jammed with oddly garbed L.A. denizens and P.A. system echoes, the two men meet and bet on the same "Egyptian Femme." This and later gaming room sequences mock another genre visual convention. Instead of the optically distorted, oppressive gambling dens of **The Hustler, The Cincinnati Kid**, and other genre works, the concrete pens are filmed objectively: crowded, noisy, gritty kennels filled with sweaty, excited people rendered in bright light and deep focus.

What follows is perhaps the most successful attempt ever made to filmically render the special ecstatic delirium of the gambling personality. In a grandstand crowded with extras recalling Disney creatures (bearded bearlike men, ostrichy housewives in curlers), despite Denny-Segal's glumness, the mood soars towards hysteria as does Charlie-Gould's monologue, a standup comic's tour-de-force of masterful timing and pornographic groveling before the Fates. When the horses run, Charlie-Gould starts with simple screamed instructions to "Egyptian Femme," succeeded by offers to murder her, buy her a new dress, perform cunnilingus, take her to Tahiti, marry her, and slash his wrists in her oat bucket if she passes "Snips and Snails," "River Boat," "High Lo," "Langley" and the "Deacon." "Egyptian Femme" does, and they win, the triumph topped when the woman he touted *off* "Egyptian Femme" appears, and furiously pelts them with oranges as her escalator descends.

The screaming sequence in the grandstand is not only a comic triumph, it is significant for treating in comic terms the basic gambling genre psychopathology: engagement, excitement, aggression, then increasingly guilty assertion (often expiated as self-degradation). As Michael Wood schematizes the gamesman's behavior in both **The Hustler** and **The Cincinnati Kid**:

> The suggestion that you can't win without being a killer is followed by the perception that you can't be a killer without killing someone . . . [which is] almost annulled by the sheer fascination of the killing . . . . The result is a sense of adventure muddled by a faint sense of guilt.[9.3]

Simultaneously, the Charlie-Gould monologue is interesting as an anti-genre response to the idealistic credo of Eddie (Paul Newman) in **The Hustler**, Altman emphasizing the aggressive, acquisitive, competitive aspects of gambling. By contrast, the poetic monologue in **The Hustler** makes shooting pool against pros for big money into a mystical activity somewhere beyond Zen archery:

> Eddie-Newman: . . . It's a great feeling, boy, it's a great feeling when you're right, and you know you're right.

117

Like all of a sudden I get oil in my arm. Pool cue is a part of me. You know, pool cue has got nerves in it. It's a piece of wood but it's got nerves in it. You can feel the roll of these balls. You don't have to look. You just know. You make shots that nobody's ever made before. And you play that game the way nobody ever played it before.

Sarah-Laurie: I love you Eddie.

Altman's track sequence has also glorified Charlie-Gould's "manager" genre archetype over Denny-Segal's "gamesman" archetype.

The next sequence embroiders this anti-genre notion, as the two cheerful winners discover the semi-whores have a guest, "Helen Brown" (Bert Remsen as a beefy gushing/vulnerable female impersonator). Helen-Remsen plans for the three to have a night on the town to celebrate his newly acquired evening gown. (Helen-Remsen: "I never had the balls to wear anything like it!"). Inspired, Charlie-Gould stalks into the bungalow, impersonating a vice squad officer (Charlie-Gould: "Helen Brown? . . . Helen *Gurley* Brown?"), and intimidates Helen-Remsen until she flees.

The transvestite sequence in Altman's film is a comic comment on the "crafty, snakelike"[9.4] manager genre archetype, exemplified by a sequence in a depraved gambling club in **The Hustler**, in which the protagonist is warned:

Sarah-Piper-Laurie: . . . Doesn't any of this mean anything to you? That man, this place, the people. They wear masks, Eddie. And underneath they're perverted, twisted, crippled . . . . Don't wear a mask, Eddie. You don't have to. [She points] . . . . He'll break your heart, your guts. And for the same reason; 'cause he hates you, 'cause of what you are. 'Cause of what you have and he hasn't.

A comic contrast to **The Hustler, California Split** sends up the "masks" of the manager-archetype, making his manipulation funny by stylizing his victim as a silly, contemptible coward with a much more pathetic "mask."

The two protagonists and the girls attend a Mexican boxing match, a wild event in which fistfights break out in the audience, too, upon which Charlie-Gould and Denny-Segal promptly bet, an anti-genre mocking of the compulsion to track and tables. Even when the four are held up outside by a black, Charlie-Gould's manipulator wheedles the gunman into taking only *half* the money, more anti-genre kidding of the genre archetypes who must win everything or let their thumbs be broken, as well as of the genre's "healthy outdoors."

At this point, **California Split** seems to lose focus, the two men shown playing in another bright card palace filled with bleary

characters, apparently losing but still enraptured as hefty Phyllis
Shotwell belts out a ballad:

> This town is full of guys,
> Who think they're mighty wise,
> Just because they've learned a thing or two . . .

This too early conclusion recalls the ending of **The Cincinnati
Kid**, in which Robinson's The Man, after many bad omens, still
wins against McQueen's The Kid: "As long as I'm around, you're
second best, and you'd better learn to live with it." This unusual
ending is itself a major improvement on genre sports films. For, as
Andrew Sarris notes:

> Linked to the cliche of the underdog is the cliche of the Big
> Game or the Big Fight, the one event above all others that
> demonstrates the spiritual heights to which the most untal-
> ented underdog can rise by displaying "character." By con-
> trast, the greatness of real life athletes is measured by a great
> number of challenges they overcome in the course of a long
> career . . . [9.5]

Next, as if working from Wood's insight that "**The Cincinnati
Kid** . . . ends up just where **The Hustler** left us . . . not as a corrective
of the myth, but as another fine instance of it,"[9.6] Altman seems to
begin a second genre-commentary film that's a counterpart of his
first. The beginning this time is a non-comic argument between
Denny-Segal and his bookie over a loan while Charlie-Gould looks
on. Critics suggest that at this point, **California Split**'s point of view
shifts from Charlie-Gould to Denny-Segal.[9.7] This seems correct,
but more precisely, the second-half sequences roughly recapitulate
those of the first half. This organizing principle is in itself an interesting genre comment; instead of a single story, we get two different gamblers visions of similar events, linking it to **Citizen Kane**, the
most distinguished genre member, but in fact, Wood's conclusion
applies to all four films:

> If winning is made so marvelously appealing, it doesn't
> matter how many subtle and decent sermons against winning
> you sneak into the movie. For all the film's real energies
> come to it from the myth it sets out to criticize . . . . Being
> the best is such a domineering American dream that when
> properly expressed . . . it simply cancels every considera-
> tion.[9.8]

The mood and tone of this version of the myth are quite different, not spirited and relaxed, but compulsive and enervating. After the argument, Denny-Segal again slumps in a bar, but now insulted by a drunken abusive woman. Continuing the recapitulation, Denny-Segal goes to the two girls' bungalow, where he fails to sleep with the childlike Susan-Welles, a project frustrated when Barbara-Prentiss's practical "pross" interrupts, followed by both girls disappearing to Hawaii. As before, but more grimly, gambling preempts stability/sexuality.

In his stripped divorcee's apartment, Denny-Segal is upset when a muffled-voice figure outside insists his bookie sent him, eventually revealing himself as a teasing Charlie-Gould, wearing an enormous sombrero. A dream had sent him to the Tiajuana Dog Track ("Winner, winner, winner!"), but he only lost, not having invited Denny-Segal ("You weren't in the dream"). Meanwhile, Denny-Segal continues packing or piling up stuff to sell; he's heard of a highstakes cardgame in Reno and insists again and again that *he's gonna win*.

> Denny-Segal (exasperated): Look, I know how I feel. I don't wanna talk about it anymore because I know how I feel . . . .

The sequence is the edgy counterpart of the film's earlier bantering bus trip, Denny-Segal a comic/ironic mode version of **The Hustler**'s tormented poetic poolshark ("It's a really great feeling when you're right, and you know you're right —"), and its great tragic hero, Welles' Kane, who destroys his life chances for happiness with his bullying: "There's only one person who's going to decide what I'm going to do, and that's me!"

Mocking Denny-Segal's genre "gamesman" archetype, Charlie-Gould does his "Famous One-Armed Piccolo Player." Kazooing through his nose, he keeps one arm inside his jacket so it appears he's an amputee making music with the piccolo at his groin using his sexual organ! (it seems all that can support the wooden tube which sticks out the fly of his pants). Just so, he kids, the genre gamesman will win by sheer stamina.

Their search for a stake — Charlie-Gould shooting baskets against cocky teenagers, Denny-Segal selling car and typewriter — leads to a recapitulation of the track sequence, Charlie-Gould again invading the crowded littered concrete warrens, tailing mugger Lew-Walsh into the shabby men's room. Socked, the "manager" confuses his opponent by responding with a masochist's delight (Charlie-Gould: "Oh my God that was the greatest punch!"). The clumsy, vicious fight ends with Lew-Walsh collapsed in a toilet stall, Charlie-Gould stealing back his money and telling two entering bystanders: "You better call an ambulance — man lost the last race and tried to kill himself."

This gritty sequence, the grimmest in the film, can be seen as

Denny-Segal's counterpart "experience" to the hilarious "Egyptian Femme" race, a nightmare struggle against loss, degradation and guilt; delighted triumph for Charlie-Gould is sheer funk, fear and dumb luck for the gamesman character. In addition, the sequence is one more justification of the manager-archetype, who does the dirty work so his gamesman can operate.

In Reno, the two men make their way to the highstakes game in a casino's large private room, complete with attractive barmaid, buffet, and controlled-faced big-time players. The last suggests embodiments of Wood's schemata for the genre:

> "[The top players in **The Hustler** and **The Cincinnati Kid**] seem to be free of the moral constructions which tie up the heroes . . . [rather] they are the pure thrill and temptation of difficult success.[9.9]

At once, Charlie-Gould's whispered monologue to Denny-Segal proceeds to mock the genre convention, laughing at the archetypical champions:

> Charlie-Gould: . . . [He's a] doctor, engineer, he'd play this game forever — rather lose a patient than a hand . . . . [This one's] the best in the game, figure he learned to play in the Ku Klux Klan with a big sheet over his head . . . . Chinaman, looks like an Oriental prince, his father probably made a fortune selling frozen egg rolls . . . .

To further disintegrate this genre convention, a real leading U.S. gambler, Amarillo Slim, is at the table, an alert but opaque personality rather than the distinctive characterizations of Jackie Gleason's Minnesota Fats in **The Hustler**, or Edward G. Robinson's 'The Man' in **The Cincinnati Kid**.

But we see little of the climactic game. Denny-Segal makes Charlie-Gould leave because he's distracting, mocking the masterful manager vs. weak gamesman genre motif suggested in **The Hustler**:

> Eddie-Newman: How shall I play that one, Bert? Play it safe? That's the way you always told me to play it . . . safe, play the percentage. Well, here we go . . . fast and loose.

In comparison, we watch Charlie-Gould's comic-pathetic efforts to gamble with a tiny stake, the streetwise manager archetype weedling for change or mugging like a brainless tourist on his first casino visit. Instead of his archetype, we see the manager made vulnerable loner, a bewildered disciple without his lucky savior or tipoffs from Above.

The climax has Denny-Segal stagger up triumphant, Charlie-Gould gurgling about how long they could live at the tracks on his winnings. Denny-Segal plays blackjack, roulette, craps, winning and winning before the excited crowd, but sending Charlie-Gould away: *"You're gonna kill the streak!"* The clearly depressed Denny-Segal turns from the piled-up chips, which Charlie-Gould quickly counts and splits, blathering about the gambling life. Meanwhile, the winner sits drained, apart from the crowd. The second half of **California Split**, from the bookie troubles to rejection to cheery manager to obsession to dissatisfying triumph, thus stylizes **The Hustler**'s schema:

> Newman plays Gleason, [wins], then fails to show the staying power of a true champion .... A question about the cost of making it has turned into a diagnosis of failure (and therefore, into an apology for success) .... The movie smart turns, and makes [the manager] a smug archvillain, proof that you're not a nice guy if you even want to win .... Newman's not really wanting to win at all seems positively saintly and the movie ends in a blaze of righteousness.[9.10]

In a sense, Altman has put **The Hustler** protagonist ("not really wanting to win at all") and **The Cincinnati Kid** protagonist ("you're second best, and you'd better learn to live with it") into the same film. Together, the exhausted pair have a final edgy exchange:

Charlie-Gould (sarcastically): Do you always take a big win this hard?

Denny-Segal (bewildered/depressed): Charlie, there was no special feeling. Everybody said there was.

Charlie-Gould: Yeah, everybody knows that . . . (a joke). It doesn't mean a fucking thing, does it?

Denny-Segal: I want to go home.

Charlie-Gould: Oh, yeah — where do you live?

Denny-Segal: I'll se ya . . . (he leaves).

The last dialogue is a filmic realization of Wood's point:

> What is fascinating about **The Hustler** and **The Cincinnati Kid** is that they emphatically proclaim that the cost is too high, but can't propose with any conviction that we should stop trying to win. The contradiction at the heart of the myth of ruthless success is thus having a field day.[9.10]

Denny-Segal pauses a while with Charlie-Gould before the immense punch bowl they'd filled with chips, then leaves. Charlie-Gould joins the hefty Phyllis Shotwell again, here improvising to "Bye-Bye Blackbird" at the piano, mocking the Denny-Segal character's decision. The last scene is an elegantly balanced genre comment,

California Split assimilating **The Hustler** ("victory and banishment together add up to the perfect, complex, painful solution to the problem . . . of the anxiety of power")[9.11] as well as **The Cincinnati Kid** ("As long as I'm around, you're second best, and you'd better learn to live with it."). Neither viewpoint is shown to carry much moral freight; rather, each choice is a character's clarification of his own nature. In this, **California Split**, by showing alternatives, comments on **The Hustler** and **The Cincinnati Kid**, both caught in the paradox of the myth of ruthless success.

Nashville (1975)

Man is the performing animal with a seemingly deep rooted need to play a role, to adopt another identity, to pretend, to imitate. Long treated in the "show business" film genre, "performance" is seen by critic Richard Poirier as a particularly modern trait:

> By performance, I mean in part any self discovery, self watching, finally self pleasuring response to the pressures (of being an artist) . . . Only those who are both vulnerable and brave are in a position to know what is (cultural) waste and what is not.[10.0]

At the same time, the *experience* of the performing artist is far from pleasurable, but rather a very demanding spiritual predicament, as Wade Jennings notes:

> It is not Hollywood or the system that separates great stars from the usual reality, it is the very quality that makes them stars in the first place that also isolates and magnifies them . . . (while) the rewards of stardom are finally no more real than the fantasies, the illusions which the artist creates for others.[10.1]

It is this complex relationship between the performing artist and American life which is the heart of the genre — as artist, *craftsman*, symbol, model, tool, commodity — and the focus of **Nashville.**

The goal of dissecting the show business genre is suggested in the very first title sequence, a too-loud-too-fast commercial for the **Nashville** record album, built up of zooms into the major characters' faces, the braying of their names, and blaring bursts of song from their "hits." Notable for setting the mood and tone of the entire film, this beginning section is also significant as a mockery of the title overture to the classic movie musical, making fun of its teasing quality and commercial purposes. The noisy commercial also suggests the public relations and trailer element in many show business films, but instead of treating them as silliness, makes plain the money-hunger behind such efforts.

The next sequence shows a politician's soundtruck cruising the streets of Nashville, bearing signs marked "Hal Phillip Walker for President — Replacement Party." The loudspeaker voice, which all ignore, points out that we are all deeply involved in politics, then makes a vague, simplistic plea for change. This crude vote-getting is a comment on the preceding flashy commercial dealing with the film genre. It suggests that, like the TV commercial, this genre is better approached as complex campaigning or popularity contesting to "win the audience," rather than as art or socially motivated "communication."

We see a music recording studio, all darkness but the booth window holding a cold sinister face lit from below like a movie ghoul; music vet Haven Hamilton (Henry Gibson) is shown recording the righteously jingoistic ballad "We Must Be Doing Something Right (To Last 200 Years)." Breaking the spell he's cast, Hamilton-Gibson lashes out at the innocent piano player. At once, the power structure/sociology of the entertainment industry is suggested, an element of almost all genre films, here stylized as a hellish tyranny. As Molly Haskell puts it, this moment "establishes the whole power structure and pecking order of the film, the steely grip of this slimy, fascinating tyrant who presides over the folks here at home and the fans out yonder."[10.2] It also comically overturns the musical film genre convention of grand old show business seniors (e.g., the protagonists of **Yankee Doodle Dandy** and **The Al Jolson Story**). Finally, the song itself is a musical genre auto-critique: mocking the musical genre's tendency towards exaggerated patriotism, linking show songs to a TV commercial/big business "false innocence," and stressing through Hamilton-Gibson's cold professionalist the artificiality of the genre's mock-naivete messages. Consistently, Hamilton-Gibson also throws out kooky BBC documentarist Opal (Geraldine Chaplin) from the studio, a comment on the controlled reporting of show business.

In the next studio, contrasting with this coldblooded professional, gospel-singing housewife Linnea Reese (Lily Tomlin) happily leads a black chorus recording "Do You Believe in Jesus," lost in the song's affirming words and rhythm, which mock Hamilton-Gibson's plastic sentiments.

In a long airport scene, **Nashville** makes a modernist mockery of musical film genre history, allowing the following to show up to meet the city's current singing queen: a nineteen-sixtyish Peter-Paul-and-Mary folk-rock concert-film group called Tom, Bill, and Mary (Keith Carradine, Alan Nichols, Cristina Raines); a poster of a torchy, curvy, nineteen-fifties-type singer-siren, Connie White (Karen Black), who recalls such period stars as Jane Russell in **Gentlemen Prefer Blonds**; Hamilton-Gibson, with his show business "family" of mistress Lady Pearl and son Bud (Barbara Baxley, David Peel), suggesting twenties musicals like **Broadway Melody**; a drill team of performing children extracted from **Babes in Arms** or a similar forties musical. This "Sargasso sea of performers" mocks the genre cliche of "getting together and putting on a show", which involves and wins over viewers via its "spontaniety," using its double perspective to manipulate audience sympathies. The point is re-emphasized by the political campaigners — symbolizing the crude big business, technology and marketing engines which drive this "folk rite" genre.

The greeting sequence is capped by a final bitter genre comment: the lovely, sensitive, community favorite Barbara-Jean (Ronee Blakley), about to sing, collapses instead. In a grim commentary on the struggle and striving of genre protagonists, the overstrained and exploited woman collapses every single time she appears.

What follows can be taken as a parody of a stage show musical film's "production number" for the Age of Technology: the comic departures of various characters, as we watch from a static position, each in an appropriate vehicle for his status, to twanging banjo music. Stud Tom-Carradine travels in a VW van with some stewardesses, ambitious Bill-Nichols and bitchy Mary-Raines in a heavy chauffeured Cadillac; "music industry general" Hamilton-Gibson and family in a brightly painted jeep; and so on, the seventh or so car breaking off the bobbing wooden traffic gate with its energy. Moments later, as if to show that even mechanistic choreography cannot accommodate our hyperkinetic times, there's a minor throughway accident that causes a total traffic jam. Yet, almost at once, the chaotic tieup is converted to a chummy sort of picnic, with people wandering between the stalled cars and buying ices and sodas from a vendor. **Nashville** mocks the artificial camaraderie of the show business film by suggesting that in today's over-communicative age, such shifts into "performance" have become almost the norm. (What one commentator has called the "everyman into anchorman" effect.)

Besides furthering the story and developing some characters, the sequence, via BBC reporter Opal-Chaplin, mocks the music documentary. Speaking with earnest housewife Linnea-Tomlin, the reporter is depicted as distorting any event into pseudo-compassionate cliches; the traffic jam becomes "cars piled up" with "a leg sticking out." Similarly, told Linnea-Tomlin's children are deaf, she's so overwhelmed she won't continue the conversation. When she visits blacksinger Tommy Brown (Timothy Brown) and his charming friends in their plush van, she's giddily manipulated into believing the singer isn't even there. In her reporter, **Nashville** inverts the idea of the "objective" music documentary, showing such filmmakers' tendencies to be controlled by ignorance, preconceptions, and sheer unacknowledged star power, (viz. **Don't Look Back**).

The next sequence has Barbara Jean-Blakley in the hospital, likewise almost giddy at the overwhelming attentions focused on her. The show business film's comically frenetic Beverly Hills bedrooms (e.g., the sleeping quarters of **Bombshell, Hollywood Hotel**) are here taken to task, as even a healing environment is converted into a cocktail party suite hung with pictures, filled with bouquets, crowded with preening male admirers. Ironically, her doctor can barely squeeze in, manager-husband Barnett (Alan Garfield) is more crowd-harassed than caring, and cool self-serving lawyer John Triplette (Michael Murphy) can comment wittily but to the point: "She's fine. It's her husband I'm concerned about . . . . "

Following this, sequences at entertainers' clubs are intercut for greater tensions and ironies. The "outsiders club" The Demons Den action includes stud Tom-Carradine picking up a dizzy groupie, the hopeful Sueleen Gay (Gwen Welles) singing terribly, and her being asked to appear at a "smoker" by Triplette-Murphy. Intercut are moments at the Picking Parlor "insiders club," whose patrons include Hamilton-Gibson, the black Tommy-Brown, and folk-rocker Bill-Garfield and his cool wife Mary-Raines. Both sequences end in bitter comments: the naive Sueleen Gay-Welles is so bad yet so blind she's tricked into "agreeing" to strip; and an angry black attacks black star Tommy-Brown as an "Oreo" who has sold out, so the singer retreats in fear. The sequences thus invert show business genre conventions of deserved big break and ethnic star's gutsy pride.

Next, Linnea-Tomlin's mother character is shown in a moment of enormous feeling: patiently and delightedly drawing from her twelve-year-old deaf son, in words and sign language, the story of the swimming test he's just passed. This moving scene brings Linnea-Tomlin across as the most fully, warmly human character, while reminding us of the original magic of performance as ecstatic communication, the wonder of expression and mutual exchange of intimate feelings. These minutes resonate against later powerful adult performances of Blakley and Carradine, as well as invert the genre by showing how moving "show business" can be as a simple real achievement of ordinary people.

Linnea-Tomlin's idealized homelife is followed by two sad and grotesque show business counterparts: runaway hopeful Kenny (David Howard), face withdrawn and violin case sealed, renting a room from elderly Keenan Wynn, whose wife is hospitalized and son

128

dead. Also present is groupie L.A. Joan (Shelley Duvall), eerily tall, gaunt, hot-panted, blond-Afroed and platform-shoed. Immediately after, we watch Tom-Carradine waking up with Opal-Chaplin, both bleary and surly and hoping to get rid of each other as soon as possible. Unlike the cheery rooming houses and loyal older hopefuls of those "on the way up" show business genre films (**Going Hollywood, Stand In, A Star Is Born** (1937)), the mood in both scenes is bleak and empty. Whereas the genre treats ordinary life as shallow compared to the passionate show business, the contrast between these sequences and the Linnea-Tomlin family scene gives the reverse impression: a chilly Babel versus warm communion.

At the lovely wooded estate of Haven Hamilton-Gibson, a pleasant party is in progress around the big log cabin. Here Opal-Chaplin encounters subjugated son Buddy Hamilton (David Peel), who, in working for his father, suggests a reversal of the stage mother complex ("You know, dad's wanted me to do this all his life"). As he's charmed into singing his own sweet sincere music ("The Heart of a Gentle Woman"), Opal-Chaplin swivels away almost at once, drawn by the magnetic glamor of real visiting screen star Elliott Gould, sadly implying the incompatibility of sensitive sincere material and the entertainment business.

Meanwhile, the cool Murphy-Triplette character has revealed himself as an advance man for candidate Walker. In exchange for support and an appearance at a political rally/concert, Walker will back Hamilton-Gibson for governor. Shrewd and self-serving, Hamilton-Gibson studies the advance man; his milk-drinking, tough, successful star mocking the self-destructive big-star characters of the genre (e.g., **What Price Hollywood?, A Star Is Born**). Amusingly, hysterical fan/interviewer Opal Chaplin is dragged away from Hamilton-Gibson and Gould as the two stars cruelly kid the genre's motif of their affection for the public: "Well, that's the price of success, I guess." With delight: "It certainly is!"

At the Grand Old Opry, a radio program with a large live audience onstage, we have the first of **Nashville**'s serious music concerts, which are in fact treated as a recapitulation of recent film history. In particular, this concert is a stylized compendium of nineteen-fifties themes, totally false and comically hypocritical. Black Tommy Brown, for example, croons "The Bluebird of Happiness," whose cheery words and title both reflect the opposite of black experience. Instead, like some postwar "problems" films, (e.g., **Home of the Braves, Crossfire** — Jew for black, black for gay) they treat him as a different minority, a groveling-cheery homosexual ("I work the bars . . . New York to Frisco . . . lookin' for a special smile . . . one more dollar, one more day").

Haven Hamilton-Gibson's music both suggests and mocks the

personal tensions of nineteen-fifties togetherness and upward striving. As Molly Haskell points out: "The song 'For the Sake of the Children' is so artfully sincere in its hypocrisy that it serves as a primer for the Puritanism of the Bible Belt."[10.3] His "Keep a 'Goin' " is delivered with the paranoic eye-gleam and bared teeth of a 1950s conformist-executive who will do anything to win his next promotion (e.g., **Patterns, What Makes Sammy Run?**).

The final song, rendered by the cooly professional, clearly ambitious Connie White (Karen Black) in honey blond hair and lush, red, high school prom dress, is a skillful dissection of the nineteen-fifties Hollywood and Hit Parade submissive female. The lyrics take the nineteen-fifties believer in togetherness (**Lover Come Back, The Parent Trap**) and tip her over into psychosis:

> Well, I'd like to give you all I got
> But I don't know what that is
> And I'd like to take you with me
> But I don't know where that is
> And I know there must be somethin', some place
> And some way to live
> So just help me keep from slidin' down some more . . .
> Just help me keep from slidin' down some more . . .
> Some more . . . .

In her hospital room, the shy, scared Barbara Jean-Blakley, in some ways a cruel anti-genre version of this archetype, sits cross-legged in her bed, her unattractive husband Barnett-Garfield gobbling greasy Kentucky Fried Chicken beside her as they listen to the broadcast. Mocking the show business comradeship motif, even these two successes are busy, bleakly evaluating the competition. Penelope Gilliatt notes that: "[Barbara Jean-Blakley] implies that the character is [finger painting] not so much to blot out the sound on the radio of her replacement singer as to help her deal with the fact that her porcine manager-husband, who knows all too well how to manipulate her, is hurting her by listening so intently."[10.4]

Their subsequent exchange makes plain the fact of this horrible puppet-master relationship (Barnett: "Don't tell me how to run your life. I been doin' pretty good with it."). What's pertinent is that this is the inevitable underside of her genre persona as show business innocent, the way it's maintained to keep them both going (Barnett (desperately): "I help you, you help me, right?"). As a character, Barbara Jean-Blakley emobides a cruel inversion of the genre's "professionalism"; like a number of actual stage personalities, her real self is crippled and unstable, and its appeal rooted in these very inadequacies. The scene also mocks the central love relationship in

130

In *A Star Is Born* (1956), unemployed alcoholic Norman Maine (James Mason) accidentally strikes his Academy Award winning wife (Judy Garland), his face revealing both spite and shame. The shocking image suggests the genre's tension between successful performance and suppressed emotional compulsions.

In *Nashville* (1975), country-western star Barbara Jean (Ronee Blakley) is continually mesmerized/threatened, here by concert host Haven Hamilton (Henry Gibson). The commenting counterpart renders how "show business" both frightens and endears the artist, heightening the confusions of their own milieu of...

A Star Is Born.

At the "insiders club" King of the Road, Hamilton-Gibson, Connie-Black and their entourage relax, the genre inversion of stars as inadequate people rephrased in the unwillingness of the maniacally ambitious Connie-Black to acknowledge Barnett-Garfield's thanks for her substituting for his wife. The Connie-Black character cannot even speak politely of visiting movie star Julie Christie (Connie-Black: "Come on Haven, she can't even comb her hair!"). An anti-genre attitude toward stardom is suggested metaphorically in the bleak monologue of Lady Pearl (Barbara Baxley) describing her fears for presidential candidate Robert Kennedy even as she campaigned for him. **Nashville** often compares entertaining to campaigning, here again in a fresh sense: as a deliberate daring of the fates. Lady Opal-Baxley's semi-drunkenness enriches the metaphor, suggesting the alcoholism which comes from trying to blunt the strain in both trades.

Other plot threads are also advanced: Haven Hamilton-Gibson and Triplette-Murphy wheel and deal over his participation in the concert/rally, while folk-rocker Bill-Nichols wonders if his wife is unfaithful.

Nashville then cuts to Mary-Raines, who is indeed in bed with Tom-Carradine, the camera traveling up their bodies past her lovely face as she murmurs "I love you" to his handsome, bearded, sleeping one, then hilariously dissolving to a stained glass church window of the bearded Savior, a sly joke on star worship.

This shot commences a brief ironic survey of show business spirituality: carnal, Godless, young folks worshipping looks and style and star power; several churches with various entertainers taking part in services, including Barbara Jean-Blakley singing calmly in the small hospital chapel; finally, a preposterously comic Opal-Chaplin in an "auto graveyard," the "modern film artist" trying to find inspiration in the dead output of technological society (Chaplin: "These cars are trying to communicate! Oh cars, are you trying to tell me something?).

Next, we see Bill-Nichols and Mary-Raines in their hotel room, sullen over her suspected adultery. The room is a mess of unmade beds, dumped clothes, the remains of fast-food and room service meals. In its squalor and mistrust, the moment reverses the sub-genre "group success" story (e.g., **Three Little Words, The Best Things in Life Are Free**). Instead of a loyal, cheery, struggling team of entertainers, there is only mutual hostility and treachery and slovenliness. The inversion is embroidered in a conversation between Triplette-Murphy and Bill-Nichols, the most "mature" member quickly showing himself a hypocritical ignorant opportunist, the reverse of the genre's savvy, sincere young husband-hopefuls.

The honest aspiring novice subgenre (**Stand In, Going Holly-wood**) is mocked from another angle in a scene with the young disturbed-looking aspirant Kenny (David Howard). Instead of a good-if-unsympathetic parent, a phone conversation paints his mother as grinding away at the youth's spirit with warnings about southern fungus and a dirty rooming house. Meanwhile, he watches L.A. Joan-Duvall's eerily silent, tall, gaunt groupie, wide-eyed and bouncing softly in her underwear on his bed. Rather than the warm family versus the hotblooded-yet-decent show business folk of the genre stories, the scene suggests an ingrown deadening homelife pushing an unbalanced performer into an uncharted emotional No Man's Land.

On the open air "Opery Belle" riverboat stage, opposite grand-stands filling for **Nashville**'s second concert, harassed Barnett-Gar-field argues with Triplette-Murphy's smooth promoter, refusing to let Barbara Jean-Blakley take part in the concert/rally. The argu-ment commences a half-homage, half-mocking of the nineteen-sixties music-film style, with its new sexual and stylistic awareness, its neurotic naturalness in contest with social and personal limits (e.g., **A Hard Day's Night, Help, Alice's Restaurant, Woodstock**).

In a pink-and-white pinafore, willowy, regal, sweet and giving, Barbara Jean-Blakley's "Tapedeck in His Tractor" makes clear in a few moments the character's credibility as a great country music star. At the same time, the song is a fine-tuned comment on the western, from the title's deliberate consciousness of change to the lyrics equally unprecedented teasing sexuality ("Nothin' like the muscles of a hard drivin' cowboy man!"). "Dues," which follows, is emotionally the other side of the coin, a perceptive woman's despair at "careless disrespect."

> It hurts so bad, it gets me down down down
> I want to walk away from this battle ground
> This hurtin' match, it ain't no good
> I'd give a lot to love you the way I used to do
> Wish I could.

The lyrics also both suggest and play with another subgenre, the mistreated show business woman film (**What Price Hollywood?, I'll Cry Tomorrow**), showing the protagonist's torment but also calling attention to an unlikely self-awareness and sense of perspective.

Pausing, Barbara Jean-Blakley kids with the country music band, then talks teasingly to the crowd about a little boy on a radio call-in show, and finally her own childhood, the monologue drifting into confused, psychopathological rambling.

Her husband rushes in to take the exhausted, unstable woman offstage, the audience catcalling and booing his apologies. The sequence recalls accounts of the later unhappy appearances of Judy Garland, and in fact alludes to her in her monoloque — mocking the sly use by the genre of references to a character's real life to win over its audiences. The sequence also suggests the audience's resentment at being seduced into a sweet if hopeless infatuation. **Nashville** at heart is deeply bitter about both medium and genre, for as Jane Feur points out of this genre:

> . . . all Hollywood films manipulate audience response, but the musical could incorporate this response in the film itself . . . As Thomas Elsaesser says, "The world of the musical becomes a kind of ideal image of the (film) medium itself."[10.6]

In **Nashville**, all too revealingly.

Finally, Barnett-Garfield is manipulated by Murphy-Triplette into promising a free concert at the political rally the next day. The "getting together and putting on a show" genre convention here and elsewhere linked to the film's metaphor for the real harsh entertainment business.

We see the crowded, dark Exit Inn, another musician's club, holding clusters of edge characters: the rocky folk-rock couple Bill-Nichols and Mary-Raines with Opal-Chaplin; Tom-Carradine with eerie groupie L.A. Joan-Duvall; Linnea-Tomlin, whose attempts to reach Tom through the crush are half-comically frustrated (a reverse of the Hollywood "cute meet"). Called onstage, Tom-Carradine asks the rest of "Tom, Bill and Mary" to join him in "Since You're Gone," Mary-Raines playing intensely to the handsome adulterer. The music focuses attention on the hot young star as an object of desire, preparation for the inversions and comments on this genre theme in the next few sequences.

The Exit Inn is now cut against Triplette-Murphy's fund-raising smoker, in which the sweet but totally untalented Sueleen-Gay (Gwen Welles) starts vamping to the all-male crowd, foolish in a shiny green dress, cape and eye-mask on a stick. She then begins her own song "I Never Get Enough," a screeching tone-and-a-half off pitch. The Sueleen-Welles character is a reversal of an early genre archetype, the girl hopeful who succeeds in Hollywood in spite of herself (**Mary of the Movies, Polly of the Movies, Ella Cinders, Show People** (all 1920s)). The original films, Patrick Anderson points out[10.6] "may be viewed as satire directed at the numerous Hollywood personalities and films which enjoy fame and fortune despite the fact that they exhibit a total dearth of talent." **Nashville** inverts the genre convention: Suellen-Welles, singer, is only defused by her grotesqueness. The smoker guests mostly look at each other, in embarrassment.

At the Exit Inn, the handsome, sexy Tome-Carradine begins a modernist bittersweet love song, "I'm Easy," by saying: "I'm going to dedicate this to someone kind of special who just might be here tonight." The audience includes lovers Chaplin, Duvall, and Raines, as well as Linnea-Tomlin, whom he has been after, and significantly the words apply to them all. For Tom-Carradine, too, is a carefully drawn genre inversion, a self-aware male version of the beautiful, idolized, female Hollywood star who wants only to be loved by the "right man"[10.7] (e.g., **The Barefoot Contessa, The Goddess, Harlowe, Inside Daisy Clover, Valley of the Dolls, Legend of Lilah Clare**). As he idealistically portrays himself:

> It's not my way to love you
> Just when no one's looking
> It's not my way to take your hand
> If I'm not sure
> It's not my way to let you see
> What's going on inside of me
> When it's a love you won't be needing
> If you're not free.

The words suggest the unfulfilled female sex symbols of the 1950s films. But **Nashville**'s genre inversion is not just the idea of using a male. More important, he is clearly aware of his partners' motivations: they either show no need for love (Duvall, Chaplin), or are not free (Raines, Tomlin). The sequence comments on the 1950s sex symbol archetype in another way: the camera frames Mary-Raines, then goes to deep focus so Opal-Chaplin's face is clear beside hers. Again, the screen shows the head of groupie L.A. Joan-Duvall, then deep focuses to place Linnea-Tomlin's head next to it. The shots thus deliberately aestheticize the erotic mood, drawing attention to it as a construct, even as the women's own vague, edgy awareness of each other implies the ridiculousness of the long-used genre theme. Tom-Carradine comments bitterly, bringing home the point:

> Please stop pullin' at my sleeve
> If you're just playing
> If you won't take the things
> You make me want to give
> I never cared too much for games
> And this one is driving me insane

136

You're not half as free
To wander as you claim.

He concludes by confirming an ironic awareness of his nature
and plight, and his determination to endure:

Because I'm easy, yeah I'm easy
Give the word and I'll play the game
As though that's how it ought to be
Because I'm easy.

At the fund-raiser, Sueleen Gay-Welles is booed and lets Triplette-Murphy talk her into stripping. Her graceless, agonized act
again mocks the subgenre of "inadvertent success" films, but also the
1950s "tragic sex symbol" movies; the sequence implies there is
never a Mr. Right, but Sueleen Gay-Welles is too empty even to
want one, and she seems to think any humiliation is worth possible
"success" (Sueleen Gay-Welles: "Someday I'm gonna be a bigger
star than Barbara Jean" i.e., bigger psychotic). Parallel editing
stresses these two anti-genre archetypes: Tom-Carradine as enter-
tainer-stoic-survivor, and Sueleen Gay-Welles as entertainer-self-
numbed careerist, both twisting on the hooks of their sexual natures,
ironic extreme alternate visions of the "dream of success" subgenre.

In Tom-Carradine's room and bed, he nuzzles with Linnea-Tomlin, smiling for the first time as she teaches him "I love you" in sign
language. He seems to be really drawn to the woman, but she must
go. Almost too readily, the singer calls another girlfriend as Linnea-
Tomlin dresses, kissing her, watching her go, then getting rid of the
girl on the line. The sequence locks up his anti-genre, tough, self-
aware sex object character, if still one human enough to hurt a Ms.
Right he wants but can't get.

Similarly, his counterpart Sueleen Gay-Welles is last seen being
accosted by Linnea-Tomlin's creepy fat husband (Ned Beatty), who
helped set up the degrading smoker, before he's scared off by a
friend. Told she can't sing, she smiles as to half admit it, but says she
will keep on. To the end, she remains an anti-genre archetype: aspiring entertainer as untalented, stubborn, self-deluded dope.

Nashville's final sequence, the big concert/rally, continues its
analytic approach. It begins with newsman Howard K. Smith's
uneasy analysis of candidate Walker's bizarre campaign: " . . . whatever he may be doing [the candidate] is not going away . . . for
there is genuine appeal, and it may be related to the raw courage of
this man running . . . . " Nashville repeatedly compares campaigning
and performing; this comment points out the analytic focus of
the film's conclusion: How can performance, itself an act of courage,

be criticized?

The concert/rally takes place in an enormous copy of the Parthenon, suggesting and mocking the political metaphor (running a society by voting parallels choosing art and culture by applause). While the candidate waits unseen (and sinister) in an entourage of Cadillacs until called onstage, husband-manager Barnett-Garfield and self-serving advance-man Triplette-Murphy argue over the enormous political banners which had not been part of their deal. Barbara Jean-Blakley's husband gives in when the organizer threatens not to let her sing (Barnett-Garfield): "You'd put a knife in my wife's back like that!"). The moment like others suggests the sub-genre dealing with stars manipulated by the corrupt system (e.g., **Inside Daisy Clover, The Big Knife, The Bad and the Beautiful**). The analytic point here is that the stars tend to bring on such abuses with their own one-track personalities, hunger for adulation and career pre-eminence.

The third and concluding concert sequence in **Nashville**, including haggling promoters, painfully analytic and autobiographical songs, and gratuitous violence, completes a knowing mock-history of the recent "ecstatic" music film style (**Woodstock, Let It Be, Altamont**), up to 1975.

The concert begins as Barbara Jean-Blakley, willowy and radiant in white organdy pinafore, and Haven Hamilton-Gibson in rhinestoned white-on-white cowboy suit, sing the lovely "One, I Love You." The treatment communicates both the artists' great vulnerability, and the mysterious double-edged nature of the performance ritual itself. Images and lyrics define art as a prop for an incomplete personality, yet simultaneously the loving creation of a joyful idyll:

> When I feel my life vanishing
> Like waves upon the sand
> With nothing to replace it
> But invention.
> So I make my rhymes and sing my songs
> An' still they don't understand
> To make 'em laugh was never your intention.

The beautiful song sequence of paired canny man and unstable woman is anti-genre in the basic sense of suggesting the *inadequacy* of genre film to depict the multiplex nature of actual performance: self-serving, self-knowing, heart-wrenching and psychopathological all at once. The sequence powerfully undercuts and "corrupt system" subgenre conventions by implying the true performer is too caught up in his special fate to be "corrupted," an illuminating comment on, for instance, the muddled, morally equivocating

138

suicides (weak performer or rotten business?) in the various versions of **A Star Is Born**.

Barbara Jean-Blakley's last song carries this idea to an agonizing extreme. Her intensely felt autobiographical lyrics are so painfully sweet one feels she is giving us the bright pure shards and fragments of her real joyful childhood, of her life itself. These ecstatic great silvery swings of a disintegrating personality again suggest the genre's *inadequacy* with their overwhelming effect — performance as deliverance:

> When I think of the children
> Alone and afraid
> Abandoned and wild
> Like a fatherless child
> I think of my momma
> And how she could sing
> Harmony with my daddy
> Our laughter would ring
> Down the highways
> On the beaches
> Just as far as memory reaches.

Finished, making a wide sweeping bow, shots crack out and the lovely tall figure drops. Of all critical "explanations," the murder works best as sheer anti-genre bravado. Suicide and attempted suicide are major show business film genre motifs (e.g., **A Star Is Born, What Price Hollywood?, Sunset Boulevard, Inside Daisy Clover**), and Carolyn See's observations about suicide in the Hollywood novel apply equally well to the Hollywood films:

> The conventional way out in these novels, when things get to sad or boring or heartbreaking is suicide. And it is so conventional that all attitudes towards it are possible; it is *de rigeur* for almost every occasion. It can be a gesture, a protest, an escape or even a comeback.[10.8]

Nashville restores the power of death motif by inverting its genre treatment; despite her archetypical vulnerability, it takes an outside bullet to stop this artist's striving for perfection. And that makes the death tragic.

The rallying of the performers to help the woman and forestall panic is another anti-genre comment. The "corrupt system" subgenre films all say that the center of show business is political manipulation. But here, the most extreme political act, assassination, is negated by a communal artistic rite: the calming of the crowd through song. Wounded and angry, Haven Hamilton-Gibson cries: "This isn't Dallas, this is Nashville . . . . You show 'em what we're made of!"

In the lull after Barbara Jean-Blakley is carried off bleeding, another hopeful, the crude blond ragdoll Albuquerque (Barbara Harris) leads the crowd into "It Won't Bother Me," a song Tom-Carradine has played to his various bedmates, suggesting indifference. Ironically, this "break" is achieved without struggle, and her rendering is one of nervous, ignorant enthusiasm:

> They say this train don't give out rides
> But it don't worry me
> All the world is takin' sides
> But it don't worry me
> Cause in my empire life is sweet
> Just ask any bum you meet
> The fact may be, the world ain't free
> But it don't worry me.

Nashville ends not in triumph or heartbreak, as most musicals or show business films, but with a "new beginning," a natural talent come out of nowhere, inverting another motif. Finally, in two genres filled with personalities, Molly Haskell has pointed out what may be **Nashville**'s most interesting genre reversal:[10.9]

> . . . . While some characters are more "major" than others, they are all subordinated to the music itself. It's like a river, running through the film, running through their life. They contribute to it, are united for a time, lose out, die out, but the music, as the last scene suggests, continues.

Conclusions

Robert Altman's ten "genre commentary" films in many ways constitute a complete, definable stage of his filmmaking career. As I suggested in the Introduction, with **Buffalo Bill** (1976), he moves on into more general, abstract concerns, a series of films which might be described as analyses of "entertainment" itself as elaborate illusions created by various forms of performance.

Meanwhile, what can be said of the genre commentary films? One reason I chose to discuss all ten was to classify and clarify the various genre commentary strategies Altman devises, and chart their refinement through several works until **Nashville**, where most of them appear. Briefly listed, these devices include:

> *familiar genre themes in new social context*: A commentary technique in **M*A*S*H**, in which classic war film themes are treated as their sexual counterparts in the war zone. More subtly, in **Nashville**, the familiar genre themes and motifs of the show business film/musical are treated in the country music context, quite often with the archetypes' level of awareness altered (either self-conscious of their condition, or self-deluded where they were once vaguely self-aware).

> *several genre classics synthesized into one auto-critical work*: Such "cannibalized" works include **Brewster McCloud** (integrating elements of **The Wizard of Oz, The Bluebird**, and **Eight-and-a-Half**), **McCabe and Mrs. Miller** (integrating elements of **My Darling Clementine** and **The Man Who Shot Liberty Valance**), and **Images** (integrating elements of **Psycho, Repulsion**, and **Persona**). **California Split** varies in being a counterpart of **The Cincinnati Kid** followed by a counterpart of **The Hustler**. **Nashville** integrates elements of **A Star Is Born, Harlow**, and **What Price Hollywood?**, as well as having its music structured around film and music history as a whole.

commentary film structured from classic films and source novel: This seems to be the case in **The Long Goodbye**, in which the elements of both Chandler's *The Big Sleep* and Hawkes' **The Big Sleep** appear.

"de-romanticizing" and "deep moral focus": There is a tendency in many of the films to bare characters' moral and psychological failures from the first. In **Thieves Like Us**, for instance, unlike **The Grapes of Wrath** or **Bonnie and Clyde**, outlaw/outcast family life is immediately shown to be bleak and ruthless at best, and hopelessly self-destructive at worst, with only a few momentary pleasant interludes. Similarly, in **Nashville**, the untalented, insensitive characters are not redeemed (e.g., Sueleen Gay-Welles, Barnett-Alan Garfield); rather their limitations and self-delusion continue to cause pain for themselves and others (as opposed to the eventual redemption of the show business genre's apparently untalented starlet or hard-driving producer in say, Busby Berkeley musicals).

direct inverstion of genre themes' "psychological strategies": One way of looking at genres is that each handles an irreconcilable human conflict; the "gambling film," for instance, deals with the too-great cost of success, and so on. One of Altman's genre commentary approaches is to expose these conflicts directly. **Countdown**, for example, uses the basic science fiction theme of technological society being in increasing complicity with the abhorrent, often treated in terms of alien invasions which make science necessary. In **Countdown**, by contrast, our conflicts about abhorrent technology are faced head on: the protagonist must triumph over the tendency to be "taken over" by technology. Similarly, in **That Cold Day in the Park** and **Images**, the consequences of a destructive obsessional love and madness as a way of life are confronted rather than "romanticized." In **California Split** itself, we are shown alternatives to the too-great cost of competition for success: withdrawal, and involvement in the game for its own sake.

outsider protagonist: Another genre commentary device is the use of outsiders as leading story characters, people who never learn or understand genre conventions. Examples include the "nonbeliever" astronaut in **Countdown**, the tribe of M*A*S*H surgeons with their non-western nicknames, the first-time entrepreneur-towntamer in **McCabe and Mrs. Miller**, and many of the naive or ignorant aspiring stars in **Nashville**.

fool-narrator: One more commentary device is the use of a commenting character who makes explicit traditional genre attitudes, but who is also somewhat contemptible, encouraging the viewer to look at the genre anew. These include Ted Knight's pompous space program newscaster in **Countdown**, Michael Burns' naive hippie in **That Cold Day in the Park**, Rene Auberjonois' bizarre bird lecturer in **Brewster McCloud**, and Geraldine Chaplin's documentary filmmaker in **Nashville**.

abbreviated genre histories: Mostly a *tour de force*, but also a device which creates perspective and detachment. Examples include the moon trip as a flight film history reprise in **Countdown**, the football game which is a counterpart of war film genre history in **M*A*S*H**, and the airport welcome that sums up pre-World War II film musical history, along with the three concerts (one per decade) in **Nashville**.

direct genre theme attacks: In several films, the key theme of that genre is directly questioned by the protagonist. For instance, the insecure towntaming "Westerner" in **McCabe and Mrs. Miller**, facing death, mutters to his lover: "I don't know what it is . . . I guess I never been this close to a person before." (What Warshaw and other critics see as his archetypic blind spot.) The detective in **The Long Goodbye**, at the scene of the death, self-consciously cries out: "Yeah, everybody's having a party now!" (Mirroring Chandler's own expressed self-consciousness over his "man of honor" on the "mean streets" as entertainment.) In the same way, the last song sequence in **Nashville** suggests the *inadequacy* of the show business genre ("dream of success" and "corrupt system") in dealing with the subtle, enormously complex "entertainment illusion," the apparent subject of Altman's next group of films.

These are notable artistic analytic strategies in Robert Altman's genre commentary films. Besides their success as artistry, of what interest are they to the film scholar?

I see three major values of Altman's work on genre-commentary for film scholarship as a whole:

First, as a guide to understanding genre-commentary in much filmmaking today. As a table on the following page suggests, there is

Genre	Martin Scorsese	Woody Allen	F.F. Coppola	B. DePalma	P. Mazursky
sci fi/horror		Sleeper		The Fury Carrie	
love/romance	Taxi Driver Who's That Knocking at My Door	Manhattan			Blume in Love Unmarried Woman
war		Bananas	Apocalypse Now	Greetings!	
fantasy		Stardust Memories Love and Death	You're a Big Boy Now	Get to Know Your Rabbit	Bob and Carol Alex in Wonderland
western			Brigadoon		
madness		Interiors		Sisters Dressed to Kill	
detective			The Conversation		
outcast/outlaw/ *gangster*	Mean Streets Boxcar Bertha	Play It Again Sam Take the Money and Run	Rain People Godfather I & II	Hi Mom!	Harry and Tonto Willie and Phil
contest/success	Raging Bull				
show business	New York, New York Alice Doesn't Live Here Anymore The Last Concert	Annie Hall		Phantom of the Paradise	Next Stop, Greenwich Village

now a strong tendency for notable filmmakers to experience their careers in terms of working in many genres, making a special commentary on each. Professor Jack Shadoian supports this tendency to see much current filmmaking as commentary, viewing it as an aspect of genre history:

> By the late sixties, the genre enters, along with the rest of cinema, an age of uncertainty. It is forced inward, towards its own procedures, which become increasingly sophisticated . . . . Now the audience must be seduced into accepting new aesthetic resources and complex (and sometimes schizophrenic) attitudes . . . . Our removal from the story, our detachment and our importance and our not caring, is a sustained happening in us during the film.[11.1]

Professor Shadoian proposes that the purpose of today's genre works *is* precisely to "*address* our boredom, passivity, and ineffectuality . . . the methods of analysis seem within reach . . . [but] no film can afford to become a treatise."[11.2]

In fact, Altman has sought to do this, shaping his artistic forms so they act as illuminating genre essays as much as successful genre art. In doing this, he encourages us to look at contemporary films *as* self-conscious genre comments quite as much as original creations.

Second, systematic reorganization of film study on a genre-theoretic basis. Altman's tendency to comment on several works, and "classics" at that, by different filmmakers from different periods, via one film, contains the idea that the heart of film study is genre study, quite as much as it is a chronicle of development (historical view) or evaluation and ranking of individual talents (*auteur* policy). Altman's work implies that films must be aesthetically judged by the extent to which they explore and illuminate the tensions and contradictions of a particular genre and its themes.

The endsheets of this book offer a representation of this evaluative system. Very briefly, films are categorized by genres Altman has treated, then placed in one of three modes: major heroic/tragic works which tend to illuminate the themes; moralizing/melodramatic works which tend to resolve or otherwise find "easy answers" to the problems they pose; and comic/ironic works which, like the Altman films they include, are commentary-counterparts of the first mode.

While the chart is of course extremely schematic, it does suggest some of the interesting implications of such re-ordering of film study. Note, for example, the tendency of genres to "fade into" each other: science fiction to often be almost war films or fantasy. Likewise, the madness film shades off into fantasy or the success/contest genre. A genre's antimony (western as tension of wilderness/past vs. garden/future) suggests the antimony of adjacent genres, here war film (battlefield, chaos, moral anarchy) vs. detective film (society, law morality). "Push" the western towards chaos and moral anarchy, and the result is a war film — a cavalry picture! This Unified Theory of Genres recasts the medium's history — not linear progress nor auteur self refinement, but talents cultivating complementary or unsympathetic genre contexts.

The tendency to see filmmaking primarily in terms of genre is a recurrent idea in scholarship, not limited to myself, Professor Shadoian, and William Everson. For example, Professor Robert Philip Kolker has recently pointed out that John Ford's **Fort Apache** and Stanley Kubrick's **Paths of Glory** can be seen as complementary views of the war film genre:

> [In **Fort Apache**] Ford is secure in the belief that the American democracy he celebrates is the best of all social political orders, and his characters act out narratives that confirm the fitness and security of that order. For Kubrick [in **Paths of Glory**], fitness and security become traps to destroy his characters, traps from which they cannot extricate themselves. In Kubrick's fictions, Fordian stability becomes a prison house and his characters are both — and often simultaneously — inmates and jailers.[11.3]

In investigating the concept of filmmaking as primarily genre commentary, Altman's works have a special value in providing completely thought out, integrated examples of this process. One might say they are the genre-study counterparts of such key *mise-en-scene* works as **Birth of a Nation** and **Citizen Kane**, complex compendiums of styles and structural devices which allow the re-ordering of film study.

Third, Altman's genre-commentary works challenge the filmmaker/film scholar to exceed himself, to transcend the genre even more intelligently. Altman clearly opposes the temptation to misuse genres, not only via spoofs (e.g., **Blazing Saddles**) or pilfering (e.g., **Judge Roy Bean**) but in the simplistic way suggested by Michael Pyne and Lynda Myles discussing **Star Wars**:

> "I researched kids' movies" [George Lucas said] "and how myths work; and I looked very carefully at the elements of films in that fairy tale genre which made them successful . . ."[11.4]

146

For many educated and perceptive individuals, however, manufactured genre works lead to the same responses as Dr. Frankenstein's manufactured people. Altman, by comparison, has sought to engage, through his genre commentaries, every aspect of our sensibilities and affections. For the intelligent and critical viewer, it may be said of Altman, as of James Joyce:

> Besides the attractiveness of surface — the wit, the verbal felicity, the rhythm and texture . . . I get the pleasure of exploration and puzzle solving. Each time I enter the maze I find new corridors. Each time, I come closer to an apprehension of the great design and its working out, an apprehension of what Joyce called "lovingly moulded" form . . . . For me the significance of the form Joyce made and I all but apprehend is a humane and charitable understanding of mankind that makes me glad to be alive and part of it.[11.5]

References

Introduction

0.0   Sarris, Andrew, "Bottom Line Buffaloes Altman" (New York: *The Village Voice* July 5, 1976) p. 108.

0.1   Kaminsky, Stuart M., *American Film Genres* (New York: Dell Publishing Co., 1974).

0.2   Feineman, Neil, *Persistence of Vision: The Films of Robert Altman* (New York: Arno Press Cinema Program, 1978).

0.3   Kaminsky, op. cit., p. 10.

0.4   Billman, C.W., "Illusions of Grandeur: Altman, Kopit, and the Legends of the West," (Salisbury State College, Salisbury, Maryland: *Literature/Film Quarterly*, Summer, 1978) p. 253.

0.5   Combs, R., "Playing the Game, or Robert Altman and the Indians" (London: *Sight and Sound*, Summer, 1979), p. 1137.

0.6   Kael, Pauline, *Reeling* (New York, Warner Books Edition), p. 144.

0.7   Kael, Pauline, ibid., p. 380.

Chapter One

1.1   Sarris, Andrews, "Bottom Line Buffaloes Altman" (New York: *The Village Voice*, July 5, 1976) p. 107.

1.2   Sontag, Susan, "The Imagination of Disaster" (Dayton, Ohio: *Hal in the Classroom: Science Fiction Films*, Pflaum Publishing) p. 36.

1.3   Sontag, Susan, ibid., p. 36.

1.4   Sontag, Susan, ibid., p. 36.

1.5   Shirley, John, "Paranoid-Critical Statements" (*Thrust: Science Fiction in Review*. Reston, VA: Thrust Publications) Summer, 1979, p. 39.

1.6   Sontag, Susan, "The Imagination of Disaster" (Dayton, OH, *Hal in the Classroom: Science Fiction Films*, Pflaum Publishing, Inc.) p. 36.

1.7   Sontag, Susan, ibid., p. 30.

1.8   Sontag, Susan, ibid., p. 34.

1.9   Sontag, Susan, ibid., p. 32.

1.10   Sontag, Susan, ibid., p. 25.

Chapter Two

2.1   Stoller, R.J. *Sexual Excitement — Dynamics of Erotic Life* (New York: Touchstone Books, 1979), p. 31.

2.2   de Rougemont, Denis, *Love in the Western World* (New York: Harper & Row, 1940), p. 39.

2.3   Wood, Robin, *Hitchcock's Films* (New York: A.S. Barnes & Co., Inc., 1965), p. 96.

2.4   Haskell, Molly, op. cit., p. 185.

2.7   Wood, Robin, op. cit., p. 83.

2.8   Crawford, JoAnn, "Truffaut's 'Adele H.' and Absolute Devotion" in (New York: *Thousand Eyes Magazine*, February 1977) p. 6, 7.

2.9   Luhr, William & Peter Lehman, *Authorship and Narrative in the Cinema* (New York: G.P. Putnam's Sons, 1977), p. 134.

2.10   Kael, Pauline, "The Current Cinema, All for Love" (New York: *The New Yorker*, October 27, 1975), p. 130.

2.12   de Rougemont, Denis, *ibid*, pgs. 52, 51.

Chapter Three

3.1   Though comparatively little recent critical-analytic work on
      the war film exists (perhaps due to Vietnam?), a recent com-
      prehensive study of the post World War II war novel (Jones,
      Peter, *War and the Novelist*, (Columbia & London: Univer-
      sity of Missouri Press, 1976) commences by dissecting out
      the same themes I find in **M*A*S*H**: the war novel as
      "Bildungsroman"; attitudes towards the military command
      structure; and the relationships of sexuality and the violence
      of war (together with impressions and exploration of the
      psychology of combat).

3.2   Durgnat, Raymond, "King Vidor" (New York: *Film Com-
      ment*, July, 1973), p. 11.

3.3   Kagan, Norman, *The War Film* (New York: Harcourt Brace
      Jovanovich-Jove Books, 1977), p. 112--127.

3.4   Kagan, Norman, ibid., p. 140--145.

3.5   Kagan, Norman, ibid., p. 112.

3.6   Kagan, Norman, ibid., p. 10, 14, 16, 56.

Chapter Four

4.1   Kaminsky, Stuart M., in *American Film Genres* (New York:
      Dell Publishing Co., 1977), p. 147.

4.2   Galleger, Tag, "Three Blue Birds" (New York: *Film Com-
      ment*, July-August, 1976), p. 22.

4.3   MacDonald, Dwight, "8½; Fellini's Obvious Masterpiece"
      (New York: Berkeley Medallion: *On Movies*, 1969), p. 39--
      56.

4.4   Greenberg, Harvey R., *The Movies on Your Mind* (New
      York: Saturday Review Press, E.P. Dutton, 1975), p. 17--18.

4.5   Greenberg, Harvey R., ibid., p. 14.

4.6   Galleger, Tag, op. cit., p. 23.

4.7   Rabkin, Eric S., *The Fantastic in Literature* (Princeton, NJ: Princeton University Press, 1976), p. 114.

4.8   Rubinstein, Roberta, "Brewster McCloud" (Berkeley, CA: University of California, *Film Quarterly*, Winter, 1971), p. 20.

4.9   Rabkin, Eric S. Op. cit., p. 114.

4.10   Greenberg, Harvey R., *The Movies on Your Mind* (New York: Saturday Review Press–E.P. Dutton, 1975), p. 22.

4.11   Greenberg, Harvey R., ibid., p. 28.

4.12   Rubey, Dan, "Star Wars -- Not So Far Away" (Berkeley, CA: *Jumpcut* n18, 1978), p. 12.

4.13   Kaminsky, Stuart M., in *American Film Genres* (New York: Dell Publishing Co., 1977), p. 147.

4.14   Budgen, Suzanne, *Fellini* (London, England: British Film Institute Education Department, 1966), p. 64.

4.15   Greenberg, Harvey R., op. cit., p. 23, 25.

4.16   Rabkin, Eric S., op. cit., p. 114.

4.17   Budgen Suzanne, op. cit.

4.18   McDonald, Dwight, "8½; Fellini's Obvious Masterpiece" (New York: Berkeley-Medallion: *On Movies*, 1969), p. 43.

4.19   Greenberg, Harvey R., op. cit., p. 26.

4.20   McDonald, Dwight, op. cit., p. 41, 42.

4.21   Galleger, Tag, "Three Blue Birds" (New York: *Film Comment*, July-August, 1976), p. 23.

4.22   Greenberg, Harvey R., op. cit., p. 29.

4.23   Budgen, Suzanne, op. cit., p. 53.

4.24   Budgen, Suzanne, op. cit., p. 65.

5.1   Wollen, Peter, *Signs and Meaning in the Cinema* (Indiana: Indiana University Press, 1972 (3d ed.), p. 96.

5.2   McBride, Joseph and Michael Wilmington, *John Ford* (New York: Plenum Publishing Co., 1975), p. 55.

5.3   McBride, Joseph and Michael Wilmington, ibid., p. 93.

5.4   Place, J.A., *The Western Films of John Ford* (New Jersey: The Citadel Press, 1974), p. 70.

5.5   Lovell, Alan, "The Western" (Berkeley, University of California Press: *Movies and Methods*, 1976), p. 169.

5.6   McBride, Joseph and Michael Wilmington, op. cit., p. 89.

5.7   French, Philip, *Westerns* (New York: Oxford University Press, 1977), p. 124.

5.8   Warshow, Robert, "The Westerner" (Berkeley, CA: The University of California Press, *Film: An Anthology*, ed. by Daniel Talbot, 1967), p. 161.

5.9   McBride, Joseph and Michael Wilmington, op. cit., p. 88.

5.10   Place, J.A., op. cit., p. 65.

5.11   Warshow, Robert, op. cit., p. 152.

5.12   Place, J.A., op. cit., p. 68.

5.13   Warshow, Robert, op. cit., p. 152.

5.14   Place, J.A., op. cit., p. 70.

5.15   McBride, Joseph and Michael Wilmington, op. cit., p. 187.

5.16   Place, J.A., op. cit., p. 63.

5.17   McBride, Joseph and Michael Wilmington, op. cit., p. 96

Chapter Six

6.1 Sarris, Andrew, *Confessions of a Cultist* (New York: Simon & Schuster, 1971), p. 291.

6.2 Butler, Ivan, *The Cinema of Roman Polanski* (New York: A.S. Barnes and Co., 1970), p. 63–65.

6.3 viz., Andrew Sarris' remark: "Take it as it comes, and don't worry about the puzzle. When pieces to a puzzle are lost forever, the puzzle ceases to be a mystery, and becomes a permanent incompleteness." in "Personna" (New York: Simon & Schuster, *Confessions of a Cultist*, 1971), p. 291.

6.4 Feineman, Neil, *Persistence of Vision: The Films of Robert Altman* (New York: Arno Press Cinema Program, 1978), p. 87.

6.5 Butler, Ivan, op. cit., p. 73.

6.6 Wood, Robin, *Ingmar Bergman* (New York: Praeger, Inc., 1969), p. 150.

6.7 Durgnat, Raymond, *Films and Feelings* (Cambridge, MA: The M.I.T. Press, 1967), p. 217–218.

6.8 Wood, Robin, op. cit., p. 156–158.

6.9 Butler, Ivan, op. cit., p. 71–72.

6.10 Feineman, Neil, op. cit., p. 87–90.

6.11 Falonga, Mike, "Images" (Berkeley, CA: *Film Quarterly*, University of California Press, Summer, 1973), p. 46–48.

Chapter Seven

7.1 Chandler, Raymond, *The Simple Art of Murder* (Curtis Publishing Co., New York, 1939), p. 1.

7.2 Shatzkin, Roger, "Who Cares Who Killed Owen Taylor?" (Gerald Pearly and Roger Shatzkin, eds., *The Modern American Novel and the Movies*, New York: Frederick Unger Publishing, 1978), p. 90.

7.3   Lipnick, Edward, "Creative Post-Flashing Technique for 'The Long Goodbye' " in (New York: *American Cinematographer*, March, 1973), p. 278–279.

7.4   Farber, Manny, *Negative Space* (New York: Stonehill Communications, 1971), p. 12.

7.5   Tarantino, Michael, "Movement as Metaphor: The Long Goodbye" (London: *Sight and Sound*, Spring, 1975), p. 98–102.

7.6   Sarris, Andrew, "The World of Howard Hawks" (Joseph McBride, ed., *Focus on Howard Hawks*, New Jersey: Prentice Hall, 1972), p. 51.

7.7   The repressed homosexual view of Chandler's Marlowe is discussed in Michael Mason's "Marlowe, Men and Women" in Miriam Gross's *The World of Raymond Chandler* (New York: A.W. Publishers, Inc., 1977). **The Long Goodbye** seems to mock the idea, notably in Augustine-Rydell's: "We'd take off all our clothes — and the truth comes out!" (truth comes out = sexual erection = homosexuality revealed). In fact, Gould-Marlowe's world view is that of a repressed homosexual in many ways: contemptuous Hemingwayesque males; ascendent and/or bewilderingly attractive young males; and either indifference to beautiful women or vague implication in their brutalization.

7.8   Shatzkin, Roger, op. cit., p. 90–91.

7.9   Mason, Michael, op. cit., p. 101.

Chapter Eight

8.1   Sarris, Andrew, "The Raisins of Wrath?" (New York: *The Village Voice*, October 18, 1973), p. 77–78.

8.2   Warshaw, Robert, *The Immediate Experience* (New York: Atheneum, 1974), p. 130.

8.3   Jacobs, Diana, *Hollywood Renaissance* (South Brunswick, NJ: A.S. Barnes & Co., 1977), p. 84.

8.4   Sarris, Andrew, op. cit., p. 78.

8.5   Leff, L.J., "Quilts, Radios, and Baseball Gloves: The Accessible World of Thieves Like Us" (Dayton, OH: *Film Heritage*, v12 n2), p. 31.

8.6   Sarris, Andrew, op. cit., p. 78.

8.7   de Rougemont, Denis, *Love in the Western World* (New York: Harper Torchbooks, rev., 1954), p. 15.

8.8   Warshaw, Robert., *The Immediate Experience* (New York: Atheneum, 1974), p. 133.

8.9   Warshaw, op. cit., p131.

8.10   Sarris, Andrew, op. cit., p. 78.

Chapter Nine

9.1   Wood, Michael, *America in the Movies* (New York: Basic Books, Inc., 1975), p. 66, 88, 93–95.

9.2   Wood, Michael, ibid., p. 66.

9.3   Wood, Michael., ibid., p. 93.

9.4   Kerbel, Michael, *Paul Newman* (New York: Pyramid Communications, 1974), p. 61.

9.5   Sarris, Andrew, "Why Sports Movies Don't Work" (*Film Comment*, Nov/Dec, 1980), p. 50.

9.6   Wood, Michael, ibid., p. 95.

9.7   Feineman, Neil, *Persistence of Vision: The Films of Robert Altman* (New York: Arno Press, 1978), p. 55.

9.8   Wood, Michael, op. cit., p. 96.

9.9   Wood, Michael, op. cit., p. 93.

9.10   Wood, Michael, op. cit., p. 91–92.

9.11   Wood, Michael, op. cit., p. 91–92.

9.12   Wood, Michael, op. cit., p. 92.

Chapter Ten

10.0   Poirer, Richard, *The Performing Self* (New York: Oxford University Press, 1971), p. xiii.

10.1   Jennings, Wade, "Nova: Garland in 'A Star Is Born' " (Pleasantville, NY: *Quarterly Review of Film Studies*, Summer 1979), p. 320.

10.2   Haskell, Molly, "Nashville," (New York: *The Village Voice*, June 11, 1975), p. 60.

10.3   Haskell, Molly, ibid., p. 60.

10.4   Gilliatt, Penelope, "Nashville" (New York: *The New Yorker*, June 10, 1975), p. 54.

10.6   Feur, Jan, "The Self Reflective Musical and the Myth of Entertainment" in Altman, Rick, ed., *Genre: The Musical* (London: Routledge & Kegan Paul, 1981), p172.

10.6   Anderson, P.A., *In Its Own Image: The Cinematic Vision of Hollywood* (New York: Arno Press Cinema Program, 1978), p. 96.

10.7   *Time*, August 23, 1948, p. 42, describes Betty Grable as "a hot looking number who is really just a good kid waiting for Mr. Right."

10.8   See, Carolyn, *The Hollywood Novel* (Ann Arbor, MI: University Microfilms, 1963), p. 90.

10.9   Haskell, Molly, op. cit., p. 61.

Chapter Eleven

11.1   Shadoian, Jack, *Dreams and Dead Ends: The American Gangster/Crime Film* (Cambridge, MA: M.I.T. Press, 1977), p. 287--288.

11.2   Shadoian, Jack, ibid.

11.3   Kolker, Robert Philip, *A Cinema of Loneliness* (New York: Oxford University Press, 1980), p. 87.

11.4   Pyne, Michael and Lynda Myles, *The Movie Brats* (New York: Holt, Rinehart & Winston, 1979), p. 133, 131.

11.5   Tindall, W.Y., *A Reader's Guide to James Joyce* (New York: Farrar, Straus, and Giroux, 1959), p. 133–134.

Filmography

COUNTDOWN. Script: Loring Mandel, from the novel by Hank Searls. Direction: R.A. Photography (Technicolor, Panavision): William W. Spencer. Editing: Gene Milford. Music: Leonard Rosenman. Art direction: Jack Poplin. Set decoration: Ralph S. Hurst. Players: James Caan (Lee), Robert Duvall (Chiz), Joanna Moore (Mickey), Barbara Baxley (Jean), Charles Aidman (Gus), Steve Ihnat (Ross), Michael Murphy (Rick), Ted Knight (Larson), Stephen Coit (Ehrman), John Rayner (Dunc), Charles Irving (Seidel), Bobby Riha, Jr. (Stevie). Produced by William Conrad (Productions) for Warner Bros. 101 min. (G.B. 73 min.).

1969

THAT COLD DAY IN THE PARK. Script: Gillian Freeman, from the novel by Richard Miles. Direction: R.A. Photography (Eastmancolor): Laszlo Kovacs. Editing: Danford Greene. Music: Johnny Mandel. Art direction: Leon Erickson. Players: Sandy Dennis (Frances Austen), Michael Burns (The Boy), Susanne Benton (Nina), Luana Anders (Sylvie), John Garfield, Jr. (Nick). Produced by Donald Factor and Leon Mirell for (Factor-Altman-Mirell Films). 115 min. (G.B.: 105 min.).

1970

M*A*S*H. Script: Ring Lardner, Jr., from the novel by Richard Hooker. Direction: R.A. Photography (DeLuxe Color, Panavision): Harold E. Stine. Editing: Danford B. Greene. Music: Johnny Mandel. Song: Johnny Mandel and Mike Altman ("Suicide Is Painless"). Art direction: Jack Martin Smith, Arthur Lonergan. Set decoration: Walter M. Scott, Stuart A. Reiss. Players: Donald Sutherland (Hawkeye Pierce), Elliott Gould (Trapper John McIntyre), Tom Skerritt (Duke Forrest), Sally Kellerman (Major Hot Lips), Robert Duvall (Major Frank Burns), Jo An Pflug (Lt. Dish), Rene Auberjonois (Dago Red), Roger Bower (Col. Henry Blake), Gary Burghoff (Radar O'Reilly), David Arkin (Sgt. Major Vollmer), Fred Williamson

(Spearchucker), Michael Murphy (Me Lay), Kim Atwood (Ho-Jon), Tim Brown (Corporal Judson), Indus Arthur (Lt. Leslie), John Schuck (Painless Pole), Ken Prymus (Pfc. Seidman), Dawne Damon (Capt. Scorch), Carl Gottlieb (Ugly John), Tamara Horrocks (Capt. Knocko), G. Wood (General Hammond), Bobby Troup (Sgt. Gorman), Bud Cort (Private Boone), Danny Goldman (Capt. Murrhardt), Corey Fischer (Capt. Bandini), J.B. Douglas, Yoko Young. Produced by Ingo Preminger for Aspen/20th Century-Fox. 116 min.

1970

BREWSTER McCLOUD. Script: Brian McKay (uncredited), Doran William Cannon. Direction: R.A. Photography (Metrocolor, Panavision): Lamar Boren, Jordan Cronenweth. Editing: Lou Lombardo. Music: Gene Page. Songs: Francis Scott Key, Rosamund Johnson and James Weldon Johnson, John Phillips, sung by Merry Clayton, John Phillips. Art direction: Preston Ames, George W. Davis. Players: Bud Cort (Brewster McCloud), Sally Kellerman (Louise), Michael Murphy (Frank Shaft), William Windom (Haskel Weeks), Shelley Duvall (Suzanne Davis), Rene Auberjonois (Lecturer), Stacy Keach (Abraham Wright), John Schuck (Lt. Alvin Johnson), Margaret Hamilton (Daphne Heap), Jennifer Salt (Hope), Corey Fischer (Lt. Hines), G. Wood (Capt. Crandall), Bert Remsen (Douglas Breen), Angelin Johnson (Mrs. Breen), William Baldwin (Bernard), William Henry Bennet (Band Conductor), Gary Wayne Chason (Camera Shop Clerk), Ellis Gilbert (Butler), Verdie Henshaw (Feathered Nest Sanatarium Manager), Robert Warner (Camera Shop Assistant Manager), Dean Goss (Eugene Ledbetter), Keith V. Erickson (Prof. Aggnout), Thomas Danko (Color Lab Man), W.E. Terry, Jr. (Police Chaplain), Ronnie Cammack (Wendell), Dixie M. Taylor (Nursing Home Manager), Pearl Coffee Chason (Nursing Home Attendant), Amelia Parker (Nursing Home Manageress), David Welch (Breen's Son). Produced by Lou Adler (Adler-Phillips/Lion's Gate) for M.G.M. 105 min.

1971

McCABE AND MRS. MILLER. Script: R.A. and Brian McKay, from the novel "McCabe" by Edmund Naughton. Direction: R.A. Photography (Technicolor, Panavision): Vilmos Zsigmond. Editing: Lou Lombardo. Music: Songs by Leonard Cohen. Production design: Leon Ericksen. Art direction: Phillip Thomas. Players: Warren Beatty (John McCabe), Julie Christie (Constance Miller), Rene Auberjonois (Sheehan), Hugh Millais (Dog Butler), Shelley Duvall (Ida Coyle),

Michael Murphy (Sears), John Schuck (Smalley), Corey Fischer (Mr. Elliott). Produced by David Foster, Mitchell Brower for Warner Bros. 121 min. On 16mm: Warner (U.S.).

1972

IMAGES. Script and direction: R.A. (with passages from "In Search of Unicorns" by Susannah York). Photography (Technicolor, Panavision): Vilmos Zsigmond. Editing: Graeme Clifford. Music: John Williams (with sounds by Stomu Yamash'ta). Art direction: Leon Ericksen. Players: Susannah York (Cathryn), Rene Auberjonois (Hugh), Marcell Bozzuffi (Rene), Hugh Millais (Marcel), Cathryn Harrison (Susannah), John Morley (Old Man). Produced by Tommy Thompson for Lion's Gate Film/The Hemdale Group. 101 min.

1973

THE LONG GOODBYE. Script: Leigh Brackett from the novel by Raymond Chandler. Direction: R.A. Photography (Technicolor, Panavision): Vilmos Zsigmond. Editing: Lou Lombardo. Music: John Williams. Art direction: none. Players: Elliott Gould (Philip Marlowe), Nina van Pallandt (Eileen Wade), Sterling Hayden (Roger Wade), Mark Rydell (Marty Augustine), Henry Gibson (Dr. Verringer), David Arkin (Harry), Jim Bouton (Terry Lennox), Warren Berlinger (Morgan), Jo Ann Brody (Jo Ann Eggenweiler), Steve Coit (Detective Farmer), Jack Knight (Mabel), Pepe Callahan (Pepe), Vince Palmieri (Vince), Pancho Cordoba (Doctor), Enrique Lucero (Jefe), Rutanya Alda (Rutanya Sweet), Tammy Shaw (Dancer), Jack Riley (Piano Player), Ken Sansom (Colony Guard), Jerry Jones (Detective Green), John Davies (Detective Dayton), Rodney Moss (Supermarket Clerk), Sybil Scotford (Real Estate Lady), Herb Kerns (Herbie). Produced by Jerry Bick (Lion's Gate Films) for United Artists. 111 min.

1974

THIEVES LIKE US. Script: Calder Willingham, Joan Tewkesbury and R.A., from the novel by Edward Anderson. Direction: R.A. Photography (color): Jean Boffety. Editing: Lou Lombardo. Visual consultant: Jack DeGovia. Radio research: John Dunning. Players: Keith Carradine (Bowie), Shelley Duvall (Keechie), John Schuck (Chicamaw), Bert Remsen (T-Dub), Louise Fletcher (Mattie), Ann

Latham (Lula), Tom Skerritt (Doc Mobley), Al Scott (Capt. Stammers), John Roper (Jasbo), Mary Waits (Noel), Rodney Lee, Jr. (James Mattingly), William Watters (Alvin), Joan Tewkesbury (Lady in Train Station), Eleanor Matthews (Mrs. Stammers), Pam Warner (Woman in Accident), Suzanne Majure (Coca-Cola Girl), Walter Cooper and Lloyd Jones (Sheriffs). Produced by Jerry Bick and George Litto for United Artists. 123 min.

CALIFORNIA SPLIT. Script: Joseph Walsh. Direction: R.A. Photography (Metrocolor, Panavision): Paul Lohmann. Editing: Lou Lombardo. Production design: Leon Ericksen. Players: Elliott Gould (Charlie Waters), George Segal (Bill Denny), Ann Prentiss (Barbara Miller), Gwen Welles (Susan Peters), Edward Walsh (Lew), Joseph Walsh (Sparkie), Bert Remsen ("Helen Brown"), Barbara London (Lady on the Bus), Barbara Ruick (Reno Barmaid), Jay Fletcher (Robber), Jeff Goldblum (Lloyd Harris), Barbara Colby (Receptionist), Vince Palmieri (First Bartender), Alyce Passman (Go-Go Girl), Joanne Strauss (Mother), Jack Riley (Second Bartender), Sierra Bandit (Woman at Bar), John Considine (Man at Bar), Eugene Troobnick (Harvey), Richard Kennedy (Used Car Salesman), John Winston (Tenor), Bill Duffy (Kenny), Mike Greene (Reno Dealer), Tom Signorelli (Nugie), Sharon Compton (Nugie's Wife), Arnold Herzstein, Marc Cavell, Alvin Weissman, Mickey Fox and Carolyn Lohmann (California Club Poker Players), "Amarillo Slim" Preston, Winston Lee, Harry Drackett, Thomas Hall Phillips, Ted Say, A.J. Hood (Reno Poker Players). Produced by R.A. and Joseph Walsh (Won World/Persky Bright/Reno — executive producers: Aaron Spelling, Leonard Goldberg) for Columbia. 109 min.

1975

NASHVILLE. Script: Joan Tewkesbury. Direction: R.A. Photography (Colour, Panavision): Paul Lohmann. Editing: Sidney Levin, Dennis Hill. Political Campaign: Thomas Hal Phillips. Songs: "200 Years" (lyrics by Henry Gibson, music by Richard Baskin), "Yes, I Do" (lyrics and music by Richard Baskin and Lily Tomlin), "Down to the River" (lyrics and music by Ronee Blakley), "Let Me Be the One" (lyrics and music by Richard Baskin), "Sing a Song" (lyrics and music by Joe Raposo), "The Heart of a Gentle Woman" (lyrics and music by Dave Peel), "Bluebird" (lyrics and music by Ronee Blakley), "The Day I Looked Jesus in the Eye" (lyrics and music by Richard Baskin and Robert Altman), "Memphis" (lyrics and music by Karen Black), "I Don't Know If I Found It in You" (lyrics and music by Karen Black), "For the Sake of the Children" (lyrics and music by Richard Baskin and Richard Reicheg), "Keep a Goin'" (lyrics by Henry Gibson, music by Richard Baskin and Henry Gibson), "Swing Low Sweet Chariot" (arrangements by Millie Clements), "Rolling Stone" (lyrics and music by Karen Black), "Honey" (lyrics and music by Keith Carradine), "Tapedeck in His Tractor (The Cowboy Song)" (lyrics and music by Ronee Blakley), "Dues" (lyrics and music by Ronee Blakley), "I Never Get Enough" (lyrics and music by Richard Baskin and Ben Raleigh), "Rose's Cafe" (lyrics and music by Allan Nicholls), "Old Man Mississippi" (lyrics and music by Jonnie Barnett), "One, I Love You" (lyrics and music by Richard Baskin), "I'm Easy" (lyrics and music by Keith Carradine), "It Don't Worry Me" (lyrics and music by Keith Carradine), "Since You've Gone" (lyrics and music by Gary Busey), "Trouble in the U.S.A." (lyrics and music by Arlene Barnett), "My Idaho Home" (lyrics and music by Ronee Blakley). Players: David Arkin (Norman), Barbara Baxley (Lady Pearl), Ned Beatty (Delbert Reese), Karen Black (Connie White), Ronee Blakley (Barbara Jean), Timothy Brown (Tommy Brown), Keith Carradine (Tom Frank), Geraldine Chaplin (Opal), Robert Doqui (Wade), Shelley Duvall (L.A. Joan), Allen Garfield (Barnett), Henry Gibson (Haven Hamilton), Scott Glenn (Pfc. Glenn Kelly), Jeff Goldblum (Tricycle Man), Barbara Harris (Albuquerque), David Hayward (Kenny Fraiser), Michael Murphy (John Triplette), Allan Nicholls (Bill), Dave Peel (Bud Hamilton), Cristina Raines (Mary), Bert Remsen (Star), Lily Tomlin (Linnea Reese), Gwen Welles (Sueleen Gary), Keenan Wynn (Mr. Green), James Dan Calvert (Jimmy Reese), Donna Denton (Donna Reese), Merle Kilgore (Trout), Carol McGinnia (Jewel), Sheila Bailey and Patti Bryant (Smokey Mountain Laurel), Richard Baskin (Frog), Jonnie Barnett, Vassar Clements, Misty Mountain Boys, Sue Barton, Elliott Gould and Julie Christie (Themselves). Produced by R.A. (associate producers: Robert Eggenweiler, Scott Bushnell) (executive producers: Martin Starger, Jerry Weintraub) (ABC Entertainment) for Paramount. 161 min.

Addendum

After Nashville
(Buffalo Bill through Health)

> "To say, then, that *Finnegan's Wake* is about itself is to say that, including our reality, *Finnegan's Wake* is about our ideas about it and they are *Finnegan's Wake*."
> —William York Tindall, *A Reader's Guide to James Joyce*, p. 237 (N.Y.: Farrar, Straux and Giroux, 1959)

Given this book's thesis, it seems natural to ask if any new pattern may be seen in Robert Altman's latest group of films — **Buffalo Bill and the Indians, Three Women, A Wedding, Quintet, A Perfect Couple,** and **Popeye.** The following is intended as a tentative response to the question.

It appears that rather than genre-commentary, the new films have a broader concern. They each deal, in different ways, with how experiencing a film is less a "new experience" than an evocation of personal ideas and states in such a way that they provide a new experience. Each in a different way, the films emphasize how through his self-conscious responses, the viewer acts as both puppet and puppet-master of himself in the course of the entertainment experience.

Buffalo Bill and the Indians. In his treatment of the first "Wild West Show," Altman emphasizes the personal and social effects of maintaining *its* illusions — evoking the viewer's support of the western genre and show business in general (the show is often called Codyland — viz. Disneyland). Like the film viewer before the screen, Buffalo Bill is at heart aware that his show is a fabrication and fraud, and a personally degrading one — but simultaneously the foundation of both his *persona* and way of life. Bill's toadies and sycophants are the counterparts of the cliches and myths about the past which sustain the viewer's own suspense of disbelief in an ordinary movie, or any film.

Three Women. The introductory sequence, a geriatric hydrotherapy session suggesting nothing so much as weary souls entering the River Lethe, contains the film's central idea. It starts with Shelly Duval as a gallant social isolate maintaining civilized behavior in a friendless vacuum — a metaphor for a decent ordinary individual's fragile lonely self-image. Soon she is seduced into opening her life to the childish adulating empty Sissy Spacek character, who in time usurps her name, home and role, while evolving into an unpleasant, socially successful slut. The film can be seen as a nightmare metaphor for the loss of control and submission to impulses implicit in ordinary film viewers' temporary identification with the protagonist.

A Wedding. The ceremony which is the film's heart prominently includes the statement that weddings are a unique intersection of the most social and most personal forces. Much the same can be said of filmmaking. The idea is suggested in various ways by the forty-eight characters — like many professionals, emotionally disinterested in the central ritual, their lively "real" antics emphasizing the numbingly controlled central ritual. By emphasizing their lively love matches, like on-set romances, the viewer becomes conscious, by metaphor, of the orthodox medium's ponderous limitations in terms of story sense, character development and so on. The fights between the couples' inlaws are like bitter story conferences . . .

Quintet. The freezing, doomed futuristic city/society in which "quintet" — an elaborate game of ritual murder — is played out has suggested to more than one critic a grim metaphor for the world of big money filmmaking. Counterparts can be found for artist, actor, producer and critic — each extremely stylized, professional attitudes and behaviors elaborated into sterile philosophies — all but one permanently locked into the doomy, self-destructive contest of wills. **Quintet** realizes and foregrounds the bitter, self-deluding forces that shape many films, while "story" and "characters" become brutal, shadowy and unreal.

A Perfect Couple. A romance between a young woman rock commune member and a musical, patriarchal old-world family's businessman-son, the film seems concerned with the film experience as pure orchestration as opposed to drama or behavior. A multitude of unstressed counterpoints — incidents, characters, story structures, visual motifs — abstract the narrative forces. Thus, each lover is associated with their family's music — rock versus classical — while the two families are much alike in discipline, rituals, conflicts, types. **A Perfect Couple** seems more concerned with the abstract romantic plot idea than its own which is self-consciously resolved in a final mixed rock and classical music performance . . .

166

Popeye. Altman's comic-strip musical explores the limitations of character realization through behavior. The focus: as a character becomes more and more a blob of light, when do our feelings for him stop? Robin Williams "Popeye" is progressively dehumanized by making him inarticulate and obsessed ("I yam what I yam"); emphasizing gestures (wink, swagger, pipe smoking) and features (giant forearms, sailor suit); providing near-duplicates (Pappy, Sweetpea). **Popeye** is very cool entertainment — not involved, the viewer senses the extent to which all films must maintain their hold on our imagination and curiosity. Through contrivances . . .

Health. Its storyline the election of a health products and practices society's new president, its subject a surrealistic treatment of politics as pure performance. Lauren Bacall's frontrunner is a literally dreamy Eisenhower, raising her arm in a proto-fascist salute, but immediately falling into a narcoleptic trance; Glenda Jackson's leftwing candidate is a Stevensonian complete to hole in her shoe, hooded white robes, and abstract midnight speeches from the rooftops which no one understands. The voters are frequently costumed as vegetables.

The above addendum is a very tentative effort to find unifying concerns in Robert Altman's newest films. It ignores the fact that, like those discussed earlier, these are also to some extent designed as entertainment, and likewise idiosyncratic concerns. The efforts in this addendum and earlier were made in part because Robert Altman seems to always work on the frontiers of his artform — and those achievements as a "filmmakers filmmaker" are the most fascinating aspect of his creations.

Bibliography

1. Robert Altman

Auwerter, Russell. Altman interview in *Directors in Action*, Bob Thomas, ed. New York: Bobbs Merrill, 1973.

Dempsey, Michael. "The Empty Staircase and the Chinese Princess." *Film Comment*, Sept./Oct., 1974.

Feineman, Neil. *Persistence of Vision: The Films of Robert Altman*. New York: Arno Press Cinema Program, 1978.

Karp, Alan. *The Films of Robert Altman*. Metuchen, NJ: Scarecrow Press, 1981.

Kass, Judith. *Robert Altman: American Innovator*. New York: Popular Library, 1978.

Rosenbaumm, Jonathan. "Improvisation and Interaction in Altmanville." *Sight and Sound*, Spring, 1975.

Rosenthal, Stuart. "Robert Altman" in *International Film Guide*, Peter Cowie, ed. London: Tantivy Press, 1975.

Wood, Robin. "Smart Ass & Cutie Pie: Notes Towards an Evaluation of Altman." *Movie 21*, Autumn, 1975.

2. Film Genre

Frye, Northrop. *Anatomy of Criticism*. Princeton, NJ: Princeton University Press, 1957.

Grant, Barry K. *Film Genre: Theory and Criticism*. Metuchen, NJ: Scarecrow Press, 1977.

Hernandi, Paul. *Beyond Genre*. Ithaca: Cornell University Press, 1972.

Kaminsky, Stuart M. *American Film Genre: Approaches to a Critical*

Theory of Popular Film. Dayton, OH: Pflaum, 1974.

Neale, Stephen. *Genre*. London: British Film Institute, 1980.

Schatz, Thomas. *Hollywood Genres: Formulas, Filmmaking and the Studio System*. Philadelphia: Temple University Press, 1912.

Soloman, Stanley. *Beyond Formula: American Film Genres*. New York: Harcourt, Brace, Jovanovich, 1976.

3. Science Fiction

Baxter, John. *Science Fiction and the Cinema*. New York: A.S. Barnes, 1970.

Johnson, William, ed. *Focus on the Science Fiction Film*. Englewood Cliffs, NJ: Prentice Hall, 1972.

Parrinder, Patrick. *Science Fiction: Its Criticism and Teaching*. London & New York: Methuen, 1980.

Sobchack, Vivian. *The Limits of Infinity: The American Science Fiction Film*. New York: A.S. Barnes & Co., 1980.

Sontag, Susan. "The Imagination of Disaster" in *Against Interpretation*. New York: Delta, 1966.

4. Love/Romance

Charney, Maurice, *Sexual Fiction*. London and New York: Methuen & Co., Ltd., 1981.

de Rougemont, Denis. *Love in the Western World*. New York: Harper & Row, 1940.

Durgnat, Raymond. *Eros in the Cinema*. London: Calder & Boyars, 1966.

Giddis, Diane. "The Divided woman: Bree Daniels in **Klute**" in *Movies and Methods*, Bill Nichols, ed. Berkeley, CA: University of California, 1976.

Haskell, Molly. *From Reverence to Rape*. New York: Penguin Books,

1974.

Kael, Pauline. "The Current Cinema: All for Love." *The New Yorker*. October 27, 1975, p130.

Spoto, Don. "Love and Pain" in *Camerado*. New York: New America Library, 1978.

Tennov, Dorothy. *Love and Limerence: The Experience of Being in Love*. New York: Stein and Day, 1979.

5. *War*

Jacobs, Lewis. "World War II and the American Films." *Cinema Journal*, VII, Winter, 1967/68, p1–21.

Jones, K.D. & Arthur F. McClure. *Hollywood at War: The American Motion Picture and World War II*. New York: A.S. Barnes, 1973.

Jones, Peter. *War and the Novelist*. Columbia, MS & London: University of Missouri Press, 1976.

Kagan, Norman. *The War Film*. New York: Harcourt, Brace, Jovanovich, 1977.

Manville, Roger. *Films and the Second World War*. New York: Delta, 1976.

McInerney, Peter. "Apocalypse Then: Hollywood Looks at Vietnam." *Film Quarterly*, Winter, 1979/80, p21.

6. *Fantasy*

Attebery, Brian. *The Fantasy Tradition in American Literature*. Bloomington: Indiana University Press, 1980.

Evans, Walter. "Monster Movies: A Sexual Theory" in *Journal of Popular Culture*, Winter, 1974, p31–38.

Evans, Walter. "Monster Movies and the Rites of Initiation." *Journal of Popular Film*, Winter, 1975, p124–142.

Galleger, Tag. "Three Blue Birds." *Film Comment*, July/August,

1976, p22.

Gordon, Andrew. "**Star Wars**: A Myth for Our Time" in *Literature/ Film Quarterly*, 6(1978), p314--325.

MacDonald, Dwight. "**Eight and a Half** — Fellini's Obvious Masterpiece" in *On Movies*, New York: Berkeley Medallion, 1969, p39--56.

Rabkin, Eric C. *The Fantastic in Literature*. Princeton, NJ: Princeton University Press, 1976.

Rubinstein, Roberta. "**Brewster McCloud**." *Film Quarterly*, Winter 1971, p20.

Todorev, Tsvetan. *The Fantastic: A Structural Approach to a Literary Genre*. Ithaca: Cornell University Press, 1970.

Valenti, Peter L. "The Cultural Hero in the World War II Fantasy Film." *Journal of Popular Film*, 7:310--321.

7. Western

Armes, Roy. "The Western as a Film Genre" in *Films and Reality*. Baltimore: Penguin, 1975.

Everson, W.K. *A Pictorial History of the Western Film*. New York: Citadel Press, 1967.

Fenin, George N. *The Western: From Silents to the Seventies*. New York: Bonanza Books, 1973.

French, Philip. *Westerns: Aspects of a Movie Genre*. New York: Viking, 1974.

Kitses, Jim. *Horizons West*. Bloomington: Indiana University Press, 1970.

McBride, Joseph and Michael Wilmington. *John Ford*. New York: Plenum Publishing, 1975.

Place, J.A. *The Western Films of John Ford*. Secaucus, NJ: Citadel Press, 1974.

Smith, Henry Nash. *Virgin Land: The American West as Symbol & Myth*. New York: Vintage, 1950.

Warshow, Robert. "The Westerner" in *The Immediate Experience*. New York: Atheneum, 1976.

8. Madness

Butler, Ivan. *The Cinema of Roman Polanski*. New York: A.S. Barnes & Co., 1970.

Elsaesser, Thomas. "**Shock Corridor** by Sam Fuller" in *Movies and Methods*, Bill Nichols, ed. Berkeley, CA: University of California Press, 1976.

Falonga, Mark. "**Images**." *Film Quarterly*, Summer, 1973, p43--46.

Greenberg, Harvey. "**Psycho** — The Apes at the Window" in *The Movies on My Mind*. New York: E.P. Dutton, 1976.

Naremore, James. *Filmguide to* **Psycho**. Bloomington/London: Indiana University Press, 1973.

Simon, John. *Ingmar Bergman Directs*. New York: Harcourt, Brace and Jovanovich, 1972.

Wood, Robin. *Ingmar Bergman*. New York: Praeger, 1976.

Wood, Robin. "**Psycho**" in *Hitchcock's Films*. New York: A.S. Barnes & Co., 1965.

9. Detective

Cawelti, John G. *Adventure, Mystery and Romance: Formula Stories as Art and Popular Culture*. Chicago: University of Chicago Press, 1976.

Chandler, Raymond. *The Simple Art of Murder*. New York: Curtis, 1939.

Gregory, Charles. "Knight Without Meaning? Marlowe on the Screen." *Sight and Sound*, Summer, 1972.

Oliver, Bill. "**The Long Goodbye** and **Chinatown**: Debunking the Private Eye Tradition." *Literature/Film Quarterly*, Summer, 1975.

Shaheen, Jack. "The Detective Film in Transition." *Journal of the University Film Association*, 28(1975), p36.

Soloman, S.J. "The Private Eye Genre: Houston's **The Maltese Falcon**" in *The Film Idea*. New York: Harcourt, Brace, Jovanovich, 1972.

10. Outlaw/Outcast/Gangster

Baxter, John. *The Gangster Film*. New York: A.S. Barnes, 1970.

Farber, Manny. "The Outlaws." *Sight and Sound*, Autumn, 1968.

Grace, Harry A. "A Taxonomy of American Crime Film Themes." *Journal of Social Psychology*, August, 1955, p129--130.

Karpf, Steven. *The Gangster Film: Emergence, Variation and Decay of a Genre, 1930–1940*. New York: Arno Press, 1973.

Kinder, Marsha. "The Return of the Outlaw Couple." *Film Quarterly*, Summer, 1974.

Leff, L.J. "Quilts, Radios and Baseball Gloves: The Accessible World of **Thieves Like Us**." *Film Heritage*, XII:2, p31.

Sarris, Andrew. "The Raisins of Wrath?" *The Village Voice*, October 3, 1973, p77, 78.

Shadoian, Jack. *Dreams and Dead Ends: The American Gangster/Crime Film*. Cambridge, MA: M.I.T. Press, 1977.

Simmons, Garner. "The Generic Origins of the Bandit Gangster Subgenre in the American Film." *Film Reader*, 3(1978).

Warshow, Robert. "The Gangster as Tragic Hero" in *The Immediate Experience*. New York: Atheneum, 1970.

11. Contest/Success

Farber, Manny. "The Fight Films" in *Negative Space*. London: Studio Vista, 1971.

Greenberg, Harvey R. **"The Treasure of the Sierra Madre** — There's Success Phobia in Them Thar Hills!" in *The Movies on Your Mind*. New York: E.P. Dutton, 1975.

Richards, Jeffrey. "Frank Capra and the Cinema of Populism" in *Movies and Methods*, Bill Nichols, ed. Berkeley, CA: University of California, 1976.

Sarris, Andrew. "Why Sports Movies Don't Work." *Film Comment*, Nov./Dec., 1980, p49.

Sayre, Nora. "Win This One for the Gipper! and Other Reasons Why Sports Movies Miss the Point." *Village Voice*, Dec. 1, 1975, p30, 32, 35, 37.

Wood, Michele. "Gambling Films" in *America at the Movies*. New York: Delta, 1976.

12. Show Business/Musical

Anderson, P.A. *In Its Own Image: The Cinematic Vision of Hollywood*. New York: Arno Press Cinema Program, 1970.

Altman, Rick. *Genre: The Musical.* London, Routledge & Kegan Paul and the British Film Institute, 1981.

Film Heritage. Fall, 1975 (entire issue devoted to **Nashville**).

Jennings, Wade. "Nova: Garland in **A Star Is Born**." *Quarterly Review of Film Studies*, Summer, 1979.

McVay, Douglas. *The Musical Film*. New York: A.S. Barnes, 1967.

Movie, musical issue, no. 24.

See, Carolyn. *The Hollywood Novel*. Ann Arbor, MI: University Microfilms, 1963.

Shaffer, Lawrence. "Night for Day, Film for Life." *Film Quarterly*,

Fall, 1974, p2.

Taylor, John Russell and Arthur Jackson. *The Hollywood Musical.* New York: McGraw-Hill, 1971.

Weis, Elisabeth (ed.). *The Movie Star.* London and New York: Penguin Books, 1981.

Norman Kagan, M.F.A., Ph.D. candidate (Columbia University, New York City) is writer-producer of informational films, including four years of *U.S.I.A. Science Report,* seen in 110 countries worldwide. His books include *The Cinema of Stanley Kubrick, The War Film, Greenhorns: Foreign Filmmakers Interpret America,* and *American Skeptic: Robert Altman's Genre Commentary Films.* He is a member of the Association of Independent Video and Filmmakers, the American Science Film Association (secretary trustee), the Informational Film Producers Association, the National Science Writers Association, and the University Film Association.